Glimpses
of the Soul

Glimpses
of the Soul

A Collection of Real Life Experiences

David Warrior

WARRIOR BOOKS * INDONESIA

Cover Concept, the Author
Cover Illustration, Milan Yudiro
Book Design, Creative Concepts, England

Typeset in Palatino Linotype,

Produced through www.lulu.com

ISBN: 978-1-4478-0975-3

Contents

Preface
page 7

Introduction: An Arbitrary Starting Point
page 14

Part 1: The Opening
page 39

Photographs
page 181

Part 2: All the World's a Stage
page 183

Photographs
page 323

An Arbitrary Ending
page 331

Acknowledgements
page 335

Other Books About Subud
page 336

*This book is dedicated to my mother, Olive J Warrior,
my wife Elektra, who has supported me in all my endeavors,
and our children, Hassan and his wife Nikki, Halley and Jonathan,
who are my motivation to keep learning.*

Preface

Where Bapak Walks

Throughout this book I have kept my references to Bapak Muhammad Subuh Sumohadiwidjojo, the founder of Susila Budhi Dharma (Subud), to the minimum. In no way should that be taken as a sign that I am unaware of the greatness of this man and the enormous importance of the mission I believe he was given by Almighty God.

I have experienced for myself how my body would spontaneously tremble the closer I physically came to Bapak. I would say that Bapak's inner was vastly bigger than his physical body and his life force was tangible. The only other person I have ever felt anything like that is with Bapak's daughter, Ibu Rahayu.

I certainly hope that this story of my experiences, and whatever understanding I have gained from fifty years of doing the spiritual latihan of Subud, will prompt every reader to acquire the books that Bapak wrote himself about his experiences, from the night of his first receiving in Semarang, Central Java, to his advice, knowledge and wisdom, about the life of mankind, both in this material world and in the spiritual realm.

For new Subud members, I would strongly recommend reading Bapak's talks on a regular basis. There are hundreds of talks that have been translated into English and can be downloaded from the Subud Library Website for members.

Through Bapak's own words you will quickly see how pedestrian and unimpressive my own experiences that I have described in this book are. There is no comparison and I would not attempt to make any.

If I could give this book to Bapak to read, it would be like a three-year-old boy taking his first attempt at drawing a picture of a house, in crayons, to his famous architect grandfather, hoping his grandfather would admire it and stick it on the fridge.

The only consolation for me is that over all these years, I have been able to refer to Bapak's talks and books and see that my few experiences fit with a few of Bapak's explanations about the latihan and the workings of the inner.

Of course, when you start to read Bapak's talks and books it quickly becomes obvious just how vast Bapak's experience and knowledge was. Experiences that go beyond this world and are not restricted to time in terms of the past and future. So many things that I still have no direct experience or knowledge of. Not even a glimpse yet. But one lives in hope.

Yet through the latihan, most Subud members have at least had a small taste of the 'sugar'. We have experienced, in some small way, proof of the essence of what Bapak talks about.

To repeat my analogy, before we did latihan we had only heard descriptions of sugar from our various religious teachings, but we never knew what sweetness tasted like. Through doing the latihan that Bapak passed on to us, we begin to experience and know the taste of sweetness and, over time, that knowledge completes and compliments what we are taught in our respective religions.

What I believe, and hope this book may serve to do, is give examples of how any average person, like myself, really can receive a measure of knowledge and benefits from the latihan, as Bapak has explained, in accordance with our individual capacity and needs.

Because Subud is a receiving, not a religion, no-one can promise what any member will receive. Not even Bapak, because, as Bapak said, that decision is God's alone. What I can say is that once we are opened, anything is possible and I do not know any Subud member, who has diligently been doing latihan, complain that they have never received anything.

Another piece of advice, or request from Bapak that I follow is that we should not take Bapak as our idol. If we do, we may soon end up worshipping or depending on Bapak instead of God. This is a pitfall of religion because it is so much easier for the heart to trust a physical, charismatic person, or even a tangible relic, than to trust an invisible, 'intangible' God.

Bapak always said he was an ordinary human being. But, I have to say an exceptional human being, by any measure, and we Subud members both love and respect him as we would a wise and benevolent grandfather. But at the same time Bapak repeatedly reminded us that we must stand on our own two feet to walk our own unique path.

That I believe is what will make a grandfather happy and certainly Bapak's stated hope for us. That we all arrive at a common destination at the end of our varied journeys through life as complete, individual human beings.

The very nature of the wonderful gift God gave to Bapak, and the mission to pass the latihan on to as many people as wish to receive it, is that the latihan opens the connection between each individual person directly to their inner and where they experience the life force of Almighty God beyond the influence of either their heart or mind.

Once we have received that gift, we experience the presence of a life, a force, within us that will work to purify and guide us towards becoming a complete, unique human being, living our life in this world in accordance with our true nature.

Once opened we become responsible for our own progress as we grapple with the desires and temptations of our lower forces, but now with an amazing inner guide to help us, through the grace of Almighty God.

Proof of The Pudding

As Bapak often said about our experiences in the latihan "There has to be a result" and "We have to put our receiving from the latihan into practice." So, aside from describing many of the experiences I have had since coming into Subud, I also, somewhat reluctantly, share some of my understanding about those experiences.

Beyond that, I offer a few of my thoughts on a variety of things in our daily life which I treat as my personal insights, gained as a result of the working of the latihan in me.

My reluctance to share my personal understanding is from a nagging concern of my heart that I will sound like a kind of guru, or some may think I am trying to put myself on a kind of spiritual pedestal, because, if I do create that impression, it would be completely counter-productive, and negate the very purpose of this book entirely.

So why do I take that risk you might ask. I do it because I feel called to write this book in response to Bapak's own words. It is not enough just to say we are in Subud, we need to be able to show what the benefit and result of our Subud experience is. Something which most Subud members are very reluctant to do for fear of appearing arrogant or, as I mentioned in my case, being seen as thinking I am special.

But, if I do not share a few examples of my thoughts and understanding about 'life' that I gained from my experiences through the latihan, then I cannot demonstrate any proof to you, the reader, of any result or benefit from joining Subud and doing latihan.

In fact, that nagging concern I have had, kept me from writing this book for over three years. But the feeling that writing this book is what I am supposed to do has persisted. So, I must have the courage to over-rule my doubting heart and simply let my fingers type and accept whatever response may come my way from you, the readers.

A Book for Every Life

One thing I have learned over the past 65 plus years is that every person has an amazing life, but few ever share their stories. The kind of stories grandfathers tell their grandchildren, but rarely tell anyone else. I too have felt a great reluctance, almost embarrassment about sharing some of my stories because I assume, and I am probably very wrong, that a person who writes about their own experiences must feel they are pretty special, and I certainly do not feel special at all.

What my hope and intention is here, is to write a book that presents some of the key experiences in my life, both inner and outer, that relate directly to the latihan and what those experiences have taught me.

So if you decide to continue reading, please remember that 'I' am not the subject of this story. I am not what is important. It is the story, experiences and learnings, not the author, that may hold some value for you.

Having said that, I have felt it necessary to provide some context and background so you will know these are the experiences of a real person, not a work of fiction or imagination. Rather than call this book an autobiography I would describe this story as simply identifying the stepping stones of one ordinary person's journey through life. I write as a witness to my own life.

For my brothers and sisters who have been in Subud for many years I doubt that there is anything particularly unusual or strange in this book, because I have heard so many unique stories of remarkable experiences from Subud members of my generation and older. Stories of their experiences to tell their grandchildren, that are real, but just as magical as any Fairy Tale or myth.

However, I do hope that for third and fourth generation Subud members who live in this frenetic time of digital technology and social media, who face a whole new set of challenges, the experiences I describe here will be of benefit to you to increase your faith in God, the amazing gift of the latihan and the invaluable advice that Bapak has provided for us in his books and talks. May God always guide and protect you as you proceed down your own unique spiritual path to reach, God willing, your most noble self.

Lastly, I ask your forgiveness and I offer my sincerest apologies if anything I have written here either offends or disturbs anyone. Nothing could be further from my purpose.

For Some Clarity

The word 'Bapak' in Indonesian means 'Father' and is the common and respectful way to address any elder man in society. It is a small window into Indonesian culture that expresses a close and warm relationship between younger members of society towards all elder men. Elder women are addressed as 'Ibu', which means 'Mother'. In Indonesia everyone should be considered as family. In English we use the words Mister and Misses, which I find are quite cold and detached in comparison.

When I mention 'Bapak,' I am referring to Bapak Muhammad Subuh Sumohadiwidjojo, the founder of Subud.

The name 'SUBUD' is an abbreviation of three words. Susila, Budhi, Dharma. There are already a lot of fine explanations of the meaning of these three words available. You can even Google it, so I will not attempt to add to those and will only summarise the meaning as "the qualities of a complete, noble human being." Something that all Subud members aspire to achieve before they leave this world.

Jiwa is the Indonesian word for 'soul', the inner being that will continue after our life in this world. It is the source of the life force. When it leaves our body permanently, we say we have died.

Nafsu is the Indonesian word all Subud members are familiar with. It is the name for the various forces that work within us. These are forces essential for our life in this world as they drive our desires, however, they can be a double edged sword because their influence can literally dominate our thoughts, feelings and actions to the point we lose contact with our Jiwa.

Material forces are everything that exists physically in this world, all of which influence our worldly life. There are different 'levels' of forces with the mineral, or earth, being the lowest, then the Flora or vegetable force that feeds on the mineral. Above the vegetable level is the Fauna or animal level which feeds on the vegetable. After the animal level comes the Human force.

Just through the consumption of food we can see that everything that exists in this world also exists within human beings, so all these forces are connected and influence our being.

Bapak went into great detail about these forces and how they influence human beings in his book *Susila Budhi Dharma*. When I tried to read this in my early years in Subud these things went right over my head. I didn't have a clue what it all meant. That is proof, if any is needed, that I am really not that smart. So much for my pedestal!

I also see that my one-page prologue has now finally ended on the thirteenth page.

*

Introduction

An Arbitrary Starting Point

It was on Sundays that I would wake up at around 6am, spend ten minutes in the bathroom, get dressed and make my way downstairs to the kitchen. I would cut two slices of bread, spread on a thin layer of rationed butter followed by my grandmother's home made strawberry jam to make my sandwich. I would then pick up the threepenny piece my mother would leave for me on the kitchen table, wrap my sandwich in brown paper, place it in my little shoulder bag and set off for my regular Sunday morning walk through Hainault Forest.

I was seven years old and had been doing this every Sunday during the spring and summer months since I was five, provided the weather was good. It was the mid nineteen fifties, a time when children could go for walks and play outside freely without parents having to fear for their safety. There were very few cars and the idea that some stranger would abduct or harm a young child was virtually unthinkable.

It would take me some twenty minutes to walk from my house on Manford Way to the edge of Hainault forest that ran along the Romford Road, where I would enter the forest. Almost as soon as I was in the forest I would be filled with a complete sense of peace, safety and happiness. I seemed to absorb the feelings of the old, sturdy trees, the smells and multiple colours of the forest with ferns, grasses and especially the vibrant greens of the various mosses attached to the trunks of the trees. But that was not my real purpose to be in the forest or what drew me there. This was my time to 'speak with God'.

And I spoke as though to a benevolent, patient Being who

truly loved and cared for me. I spoke to Him about the many things I saw going on in my small world. I had many questions. But this week, I recall, I spoke about my parents, whose marriage had become full of pain and hurt. Indeed, it would fall apart when I was eight years old.

I talked to Him often about my brother, who was five years older than me and faced many problems like being bullied at school and having to deal with his dyslexia at a time when schools did not recognise this as a real condition, and teachers mostly considered it simply as laziness or a form of 'retardation'.

I was asking for God to help them. I was asking for advice about how I should be because there was nothing I could do except to be a witness. I would not call it praying, I was just telling my story to God, firmly believing He would do something to help.

I would also ask questions about life, questions any young child might ask a grandfather, about the nature of the forest, about the cruel things I had seen people do, about the kind and loving people I had met.

Of course I never heard a voice respond to my stories and questions, but instead I felt the 'answers' entering my being like pure water being poured into me through my feelings. That was enough to convince me that He was listening and all would be well.

After walking for about two hours I would reach the opposite edge of the forest, near Lambourne End, where there was a Pub called the Bee Hive, that had some tables and chairs outside. It was here that I would buy a glass of orange juice for threepence and eat my jam sandwich.

After finishing my snack, I would start my journey home, taking the shorter route along Lambourne End Road. I would now be thinking about my mother who would be preparing Sunday lunch, and equally important, looking forward to our dysfunctional family's weekly dose of British lunacy emanating from the radio. That ground breaking piece of programming known as The Goon Show.

I know now that at that time in my life I knew very clearly who 'I' was. On those Sunday walks I was still able to feel my 'inner-self' and separate it from my worldly heart and mind. I could think simply, but objectively about how my heart was responding and dealing with my everyday life.

Like watching a film, I could review my experiences of love, pain, happiness, sadness, fun and excitement that we all experience at that age and see them from the 'inner' me. My inner was the audience and my outer was the actor in the film and everyone else was either a star or an extra acting their parts.

It was the 'inner' me that could discuss all these outer 'worldly experiences' with God in a very calm, peaceful and empathetic way. This was not a childhood fantasy, that is really how it was at that time. Of course I assumed that this was in no way different to everyone else, so I never felt a need to ask or talk about this. I only mention it now because, in the context of this book, it seems it could be relevant.

The Colour of Hell

I was about six years old visiting my grandfather's house. In the kitchen cabinet there were six new, transparent plastic dessert bowls. Back then this new material was considered very novel. Each bowl was a different colour and I used to enjoy covering my eyes with the different bowls to see how the world looked in mono colour.

One day my uncle came into the kitchen as I was checking out the plastic bowls and he asked me what I was doing. I said I was wondering if, when a person dies they have to go to hell and the punishment was they could only see in one colour, which colour I would choose.

Even at that age my love for painting and for nature meant I would consider that a world of only one colour would be hell.

My mother came into the kitchen and I remember my uncle saying "You'd better watch this boy, he's weird!" I don't know why this particular memory popped up for this book, but it did. "Mine is not to reason why…"

A Change of Circumstances

After my grandmother passed away we moved to my grandfather's house, about two hours walk from our house on Manford Way. I often walked to their house on Alborough Road on Saturdays. I did a lot of walking in my youth.

It was a few weeks after we had moved that, one night, my mother came to my bedroom and, instead of tucking me in, she sat next to me. I was now eight years old.

My mother put her arm around me and said she wanted to ask my advice. Needless to say I was a little taken aback that my mother was asking me for 'advice'.

She proceeded to tell me how she felt about my father, who she loved, but found it too hard to live with him. She had suffered a lot of physical and emotional abuse from him for too long, something that I and my brother were very aware of. So I was not surprised that she wanted to talk about leaving my father.

She explained that she had come to the point where she wanted a divorce, but she was concerned about what the consequences would be for my brother and me. She then asked me what I thought she should do, what I thought would be best.

This may have just been a smart, psychologically softer way for her to raise the subject of divorce with me, rather than just telling me bluntly that she was getting divorced and my brother and I were going to have to deal with it. But her question struck me as sincere. This was not a game.

I sat quietly for a moment, not really knowing what to say, but slowly I began to experience that same feeling as when I was walking in the forest, only now, instead of answers pouring into me I heard words slowly start to flow out, like cool water from within. I can clearly recall how I just listened to myself speaking and wondering where these words came from.

The words explained the condition of my father, his childhood experiences through the war, including losing his mother and the damage that had done to him. It was his deep insecurities that made him so dependent on my mother and his fear of losing her that could make him so angry and abusive.

With a quiet, calm feeling inside, I told my mother that it was alright for her to divorce him because they were both suffering too much. That God loved them both and would take care of my father, and my mother would be able to grow and become the person she really was inside. I remember seeing my mother's tears falling as I spoke and she gave me a long hug.

Looking back now these did not seem like the words of an eight-year-old, but at the time, I just accepted that those were the words that came from, or through me.

It was a few weeks later that my parents separated and my father moved out. Their divorce was finalized a few months later. She never married again.

Spiritual Paths

One night, not too long after my father moved out, I was having dinner with my mother and she began to tell me that she had been attending a 'Spiritualist' church where they did spiritual healing. She explained how she had also asked a clairvoyant at the church about her future, now that she would be a single mother. She was most concerned about the future for my brother and me.

She told me that the clairvoyant had said that she need not worry about me at all. That I had my own path and that by the time I was twenty-one I would be in the Far East. I had no idea what that meant any more than my mother did. He also said he could hear voices singing the 23rd Psalm around me. It was all a bit mystifying for me, and my mother too.

My mother did not mention anything the clairvoyant had said about my brother or herself.

A few days later my mother asked me to accompany her the next day to the Spiritualist Church, where she was going for another session of healing. I had no idea what to expect and my mind started to try and imagine what a Spiritualist Church might be like. Would it be filled with ghosts and angels or spirits I wondered. So it was with some feeling of trepidation that the following evening I entered the small church building with my mother.

As we came through the heavy wooden doors, as best I remember, there were three steps down to the floor and as I descended the steps I began to feel a cold tingling sensation in my feet, like a mild electric current. I immediately said to my mother that I felt electricity coming up my feet and legs and she looked a little perplexed.

In the main hall there was a large circle of six or seven healers each with a person sitting on a chair next to them receiving healing. Other patients sat waiting around the perimeter of the hall.

When my mother was called I sat on another chair next to her while the healer placed his hands on her shoulders. I was very curious as to what, if anything was actually happening.

At some point I recall the healer looked at me, smiled and

invited me to put my hands on top of his. Immediately I felt that same tingling electrical current pass through my hands, which in truth I found a little bit scary.

Later that night, once we were home, my mother mentioned that after her session the healer had asked her if she would allow me to be trained as a healer. At barely nine years old I did not feel at all comfortable about this weird spiritual stuff and we never discussed it again.

That was the one and only experience I had with a Spiritualist Church. There were times though, over the years, when my mother felt unwell, that she would ask me to place my hands on her shoulders and head and I would feel that 'electricity' passing through my hands. It seemed to work for her.

Change and Change Again

When I was eleven my mother bought a large house in Kingston-on-Thames and it was there that we moved in 1962. My grandfather did not want to move from his area, north of London, so he sold his house and bought a small apartment in Gants Hill, close to his circle of friends.

In 1963 we moved again to a rather expensive flat, close by, in the area of Norbiton. I was now twelve and it was here that I met our neighbour Michael Sutton, a very charismatic man ten years my senior who belonged to a rather exclusive group that studied the teachings of Gurdjieff at a centre run by a Mr John Bennett, who had himself been a pupil of Gurdjieff.

Michael seemed to take to me, or perhaps he enjoyed my inquisitive mind, and for the next five years he virtually adopted me as his younger brother, or perhaps protégé is a better word. Apparently this gave me some kind of social status which allowed me access to his circle of friends, who frequently gathered at his flat at weekends.

Michael was a very well-known figure on the 'Kingston scene', or as it was more commonly called back then, 'The In-crowd.' He was a very charismatic figure, very intelligent and full of creative energy, all of which made him a natural leader.

Michael would have parties for his select group of friends virtually every weekend, that would start on a Friday night and end on the Sunday afternoon. These would not be the usual kind of parties with loud music, wild dancing and endless beer, that were all too common in the sixties.

This group were among the most avant-garde assembly of people I have ever met. They would more likely be listening to Greek and Moroccan music while experimenting with odd concoctions of drinks and yes, this was the beginning of the drug culture entering the UK.

It was all pretty elitist. But then it was the sixties and these were people at the forefront of what much of the sixties were about.

Among this group there were those who, having taken the ferry across to France, had hitchhiked to Nepal and Tibet, including Michael himself. Several of them would regularly spend a month or two in Paris, Spain or Greece where they would find any kind of work just to survive. There were painters and poets, designers and musicians and of course young, budding philosophers.

There were even some who seemed like ordinary, 'everyday' people you might meet in any pub, until you started talking to them. Then you would discover that their interests were always wide ranging and generally outside of the mainstream. Their conversations mostly concerned subjects like 'what is the meaning of life', comparative religions, anti-matter, seeking a spiritual path, Sufism and other such esoteric subjects. The subjects of money, politics, and fashion were very rarely discussed. They certainly did not shop in Carnaby Street.

You had to be considered a 'somebody' to be allowed into this group. Not famous, but someone who Michael would describe as intellectually and spiritually 'awake,' well read, or at least uniquely eccentric.

Now here I was, a 13-year-old 'nobody' who was allowed to sit amongst these people, free to observe, witness and learn so many things about life, philosophy and the wider world. Knowledge that no school could ever teach you. I felt privileged but, being so young, I knew my place and stayed pretty quiet as an observer and a student of life.

Life Gets Stranger

By the time I was 14 my life began to split in two. On the one hand I was like any normal boy at that age, in that I lived a fairly narrow life during the week. I did a paper round, went to school, came home, did my homework, had dinner and watched TV. But on the other hand, at the weekends I was transported away to this expansive, mentally stimulating, kaleidoscopic world in the flat next door. A world that few of the good people of Kingston even knew existed back in 1965.

Even Normal Can Be Strange

I recall early one Sunday morning I was picking up my load of newspapers when the news agent asked me if I could also do another boy's paper round because he had called in sick. Happy to earn an extra few shillings, I immediately agreed. Shortly afterwards I set off on my bike with two heavy loads.

First I did my round on Kingston Hill and then cut across Warren Road to the crest of Coombe Hill to deliver the second load of papers to the huge houses and mansions that lined this wide road.

As I came speeding down Coombe Hill on my bike with my

last delivery, I gauged how far ahead the last driveway would be. I made a right turn, cutting across the empty road, toward the open entrance, when I was surprised by a very tall man leading a donkey with a small boy on its back coming out of the driveway. I almost crashed into the donkey and my heart was pounding as I continued up the driveway to the main house.

In the early morning autumn mist it was like a scene out of a Federico Fellini film. Very surreal, and yet, ordinary at the same time. Almost to be expected in England during the sixties. Donkey rides on Coombe Hill at 7am, why not?

I arrived at a glass conservatory and saw five or six people inside milling around in total silence. I took out the thick wad of Sunday papers and colour supplements and handed them to a lady who smiled and nodded without saying a word. I was beginning to feel this huge mansion was pretty creepy.

As it turned out, that brief, 'near disaster' with the donkey was my first introduction to John Bennett, the owner of Coombe Springs, and his youngest son Ben. I don't know if the donkey had a name, but if you have met one donkey, you've met them all.

A few months after this incident my neighbour Michael invited me to attend one of Bennett's regular 'Work Sundays'. These started early in the morning and were attended by approximately 50 people, men and women who would be given tasks to be completed in total silence before evening. Most of the women prepared and cooked lunch and dinner while others cleaned the enormous house.

Almost all of the men, including myself, were given tasks outdoors in the vast grounds that surrounded the main house. I can recall attending three of these silent 'Work Sundays' without the least idea what the purpose was.

Oriental Semaphore

It was at the last Work Sunday I attended where, after dinner when we were allowed to talk again, I was invited to participate in an actual training session called 'movements', run by Bennett, that I was told were based on some ancient form of Tibetan dance movements.

This training was held in a very large and impressive nine sided wooden building called the Djameechoonatra or Djami for short. It had been designed by Frank Lloyd Wright who, for a while, was also a follower of Gurdjieff's teachings, I have been told.

The entrance into the main hall of the Djami was by way of stairs leading from the ground floor room, where shoes were removed and coats were hung, and through a trap door in the centre of the hall floor above. Once everyone had climbed the stairs into the main hall the trap door was closed and that was it, there was no way out. With the carpeting it was almost impossible to even see the trap door any more.

With today's health and safety rules the Djami would never be given a building permit. There were no fire exit stairs, not even an emergency exit door to jump out of. But it did have some nice stained glass windows, but way too high to leap through in case of fire.

Once gathered in the hall, everyone started to organize themselves and I found myself standing in the second row of about seven rows of seven people. I stood there not having any idea what to expect.

Bennett started the session by calling one of his assembled pupils to come and stand up in front. Then on Bennett's command a nice lady started playing some music on the piano. The music had an almost military beat to it.

The person who had been called to the front then struck a

pose, somewhat like an Egyptian hieroglyph, and held this position for three beats of the music. These positions were spontaneous, not taught.

It had been explained to me that after three beats the front row had to copy his pose as he then struck a new pose for three more beats. After those three beats the second row, where I was, had to copy the first pose while the front row had to copy the man's second pose as the man himself struck a third pose and so on all the way back through the seven rows.

If it sounds complicated imagine trying to describe it in writing.

After about ten different poses the man at the front was changed for another person and we went through a dozen more poses. Bennett then called stop and, standing next to the piano, he surveyed the fifty odd people for his next victim.

Probably, in revenge for the near disaster with the donkey, he decided to point at me, the 14-year-old 'nobody' who knew nothing about Gurdjieff's teachings or Tibetan movements. In fact, only two people in the hall even knew my name. Why me? I thought to myself.

I proceeded to nervously make my way to the front and I could feel a form of stage fright welling up in my stomach. It was at that precise moment I understood why there were no exit doors in this building.

So I stood at the front to lead the next session of spontaneous movements for all these adults to follow. The piano drummed out another improvised tune and I started a kind of stop-motion mime trying to follow some sort of story about the earth, the sky and the sun that I was desperately making up in my head.

This ordeal felt like it went on forever, but finally Bennett said "stop" and I quickly walked back to my place in the second row trying to hide my embarrassment.

To my surprise Bennett commented to the assembly that

"often it is the young people that can show the older ones the way". Immediately my embarrassment increased tenfold. But later, as we left Coombe Springs, Michael was beaming all the way back to his flat like a proud older brother.

However, from this experience I knew that the way of Gurdjieff was definitely not the way for me. Even then I could not see how anyone could find their inner spiritual path by training their will and strengthening their worldly faculties. Trying to train the mind with the will of the ego to discover spiritual knowledge that is beyond the capability of the mind to understand just seemed like a fool's errand to me.

But I was only 14, what did I know, and I really didn't think too deeply about these things or that strange house with a strange wooden hall where people did strange movements, and I soon forgot all about Coombe Springs. After all, in the sixties there were plenty of other strange spiritual groups and teachings to explore.

Two Roads, Two Lives

It was in the middle of my fourteenth year that I found my double life was becoming very difficult to maintain. The gap was getting too big between my schoolboy life during week days and the weekend world of 'grown ups' who were living extraordinary lives of learning, creating, growing and exploring. It was getting too hard for me to bridge these two worlds.

As September came round and the new school year was about to start, I was feeling very conflicted. Michael had just gone to spend a couple of months in Paris and I was left mostly to myself with no more weekend gatherings happening next door.

I found the thought of returning to school quite incongruous. My exposure to the much more exciting, creative and stimulating world of my neighbour and his circle of friends had simply taken me too far from the life of a schoolboy.

I attended the Hollyfield Road Secondary School in Surbiton, at that time one of only two, very liberal, Secondary High schools in the UK that had a special stream that focussed on the arts. This meant that those of us who were in that stream did not attend classes in Algebra, Trigonometry, Chemistry, Religious Knowledge and Sports with the rest of our classmates. Instead we had classes in life drawing, painting, ceramics, printing, design, music, drama and theatre.

I probably should mention here that this was the school that Top Topham, one of the founding members of the Yardbirds, and Eric Clapton also attended. Their last year was my first year.

But even with such a wonderful, creative educational environment I still found the idea of returning to school felt like going to jail.

Looking back, it is clear that the many weekend experiences and events I had witnessed over the previous two years had so fascinated my curious mind that my inner and outer balance had been overwhelmed and drowned out. Somehow at 14, school life for me had lost its relevance, so I simply stopped going.

At that time I just knew that I really needed to have that inner conversation again, to know again who I was and where I was going in life. I needed to walk in the forest again to find my inner compass. Unfortunately, there were no forests in Kingston.

Getting Lost to Find My Self

It was September 1965 and the school term had started. At that time my mother, who was an executive secretary at a very large construction company in London, would wake me up at seven each morning and leave me my bus fare to school and money for a snack on the kitchen table before she went off to work. I would get dressed and make myself breakfast before she left.

At 8am I would grab my sketch book, pick up the money and leave the flat, but instead of taking the bus to school I would walk down to the River Thames in Kingston and then continue walking along the tow path to Teddington Lock. From there I would follow the tow path on to Richmond. Then I would leave the river and go to a tea shop in Richmond and buy a crispy cheese roll to take away. Carrying my roll in a paper bag I would set off again down the road to Kew.

My Substitute Forest

The first time I entered Kew Gardens I knew I had found my new forest. It was early September and the gardens were devoid of visitors during week days. The gardeners were rarely seen, now that autumn had descended on their world.

I would sit by the manmade lake and just absorb the peace and beauty surrounded by so many amazing trees, brought from all around the world, which had been planted more than a hundred years earlier.

I soon felt that calm feeling of my childhood walks return and I would begin to have those inner conversations. But the conversations now were quite different to when I was seven years old in Hainault forest.

There were more issues involved now. There were more unknowns and far more questions. During the last seven years I had experienced and observed so many things that my thoughts were far more complex.

I was now a more complicated person. My heart and mind were no longer half empty like a seven-year-old. They were overflowing with so many thoughts, ideas, knowledge and influences that had become part of my life, part of me.

For six weeks I walked to Kew Gardens virtually every school day unless it was really pouring down with rain which, surprisingly, was not very often. It was at Kew that I found myself again and I discovered the many new aspects of 'myself' that had grown and developed within me. I was and remain very grateful for the gift of Kew gardens.

Unfortunately, my absence from school for six weeks had not gone unnoticed at the local Board of Education. Eventually a letter was sent to my home which was opened by my mother and for the first time she became aware of my secret life.

This was understandably a very difficult issue for my mother to grasp, let alone accept, and I felt very sad and guilty, because I knew how much she worried about my future. However, I also knew that she too had left home at fifteen and lied about her age so she could join the WAAF (Women's Auxiliary Air Force) in the Second World War. A year later at sixteen she was driving crash tenders at RAF airfields. So perhaps I did not feel quite as guilty as I otherwise might have done.

To comply with the Board of Education instructions, a parent had to accompany me to meet with the headmaster and explain why I had missed six weeks of school, so that he could decide a suitable punishment and plot a course for me to catch up with my studies.

My mother could not attend this meeting because my grandfather had just gone into hospital, so I actually ended up having my rarely seen father come all the way from North London just to accompany me to meet Mr Humphries, the Headmaster.

To my surprise, when I finished explaining to the headmaster how my life was, and why I had been absent for six weeks, he looked rather stunned and seemed lost for words.

He then tried to collect himself before proceeding, in a very formal voice, to inform me and my father that by law I could not leave school until I was fifteen. However, in my case he saw no point in forcing me to complete the last term, and without any hesitation he then gave me a signed Bible that every pupil was given when they finished school, shook my hand and wished me good luck. That was it. My school days were over.

I was now on my own and I felt both elated and scared at the same time as my father and I walked down Hollyfield Road to the bus stop. My father seemed to find the whole experience very amusing. We had a cup of tea in a café in Kingston before he caught his train back to North London. I am sure he offered me a few words of wisdom, but all I can remember was him saying, "Things will work out, don't worry," as he disappeared into Kingston Station.

Like a Kite Without a String

At fourteen I was too young to legally work and so I spent most of my time at home writing, painting and teaching myself to play guitar. It was the sixties after all. (I bought my first guitar from Top Topham for five pounds.)

This lifestyle of mine was a great source of worry for my mother. She was from a different generation and it was very difficult for her to understand how I was going to make my way in life. I think she felt she had somehow failed as a mother.

I, on the other hand, felt that my mother had, against all odds, done a great job. She had given far more than anyone could have asked to raise me and my brother all these years and I both loved and admired her very much.

Dealing With Life

Now that my mother was aware that I was not going to school I increasingly felt I must take responsibility for myself and my decision to drop out of school. And so in January 1966, once I had turned 15, I left home.

I took on a series of menial jobs so I could at least feed

myself and be halfway independent. At that age I could not earn enough to rent even a single room, however, I considered myself very fortunate because I never felt like I was homeless. I was always able to stay at various friends' flats.

It was through my neighbour Michael that I had made so many friends over the previous three years; friends who were in their twenties and thirties and were already established financially. More importantly they accepted me as a kind of 'novelty' younger brother. They seemed quite happy to let me sleep on their sofa or a mattress on the floor for two or three nights at a time, after which I would go and stay at another friend's place.

I was always happy to help out with cleaning and washing-up wherever I stayed, and it was definitely an advantage that I could put all my possessions into one small duffle bag, which made my presence quite unobtrusive.

I owe much to many people who made it possible for me to survive that winter and spring of 1966.

Expanding My Horizons, Slightly

In early June of 1966 I left Kingston and hitch-hiked down to the picturesque seaside town of Swanage in Dorset where my brother and many other young people from Kingston went to work each summer.

My brother was a professional chef working in one of the best hotels in Swanage. I can't say that he was exactly overjoyed to see his little brother turn up unannounced. Our lives had been quite separate since I was twelve, when he left home and started full time work.

It was the beginning of the holiday season so I soon got a job in the kitchens of another very good hotel and discovered that this was an excellent solution for someone in my situation as the hotel provided staff with accommodation, three meals a day and some money at the end of the week.

I should note that the manager of the hotel insisted on calling my mother to check that I was not a runaway and that I really was 15 and old enough to be employed. I know my mother was very relieved that I was close to my brother, working and being fed. In her typical style she told him he had her full permission to work me to the bone and knock some sense into me.

Two more years passed with summers working in Swanage and winters surviving in Kingston. I am very grateful for those three seasons in Swanage and very grateful to the many people who made it possible for me to survive in Kingston for those two winters.

This is the period I refer to as my youth. It was a life of hard work, beach parties, Saturday night dances, glasses of scrumpy, and a lot of adventures. I had so many valuable experiences and still carry a large collection of very happy and funny memories from those times, and it was then that I made some friends for life.

Swanage, and the friends I made, were like sunshine for my heart in the summer and a perfect, normal, healthy balance for the more esoteric side of my life during the winters in Kingston.

Like Three Musketeers

It was the winter of 1967-68, across the river from Hampton Court Palace, on a large piece of wasteland behind the railway station I was brought to a ramshackle dwelling among half a dozen other ramshackle dwellings. This one had a name; 'Watersmeet'.

This is where I spent most of that winter, living with a small band of hopefuls that included Ramzi Addison and Maurice Baker. As usual, I was the youngest person in the group by about four or five years.

Maurice recently (2022) wrote his autobiography entitled *Angel on My Sofa*. A very engaging and honest account of the journey through life of a very talented musician and songwriter who possessed a unique perspective on life. His book also contains the lyrics to many of his songs that are an expression of his being. Maurice has also written several books and produced CDs of his songs, many aimed at children.

In his autobiography, he has a chapter on that winter spent at Watersmeet. He describes me and my artistic activities in surprisingly upbeat tones. I am sure I was much more of a pain to have around than he lets on.

What we three did not know at that time was that in little over two years we would all find ourselves in Subud doing latihan. Each finding our own way to Subud, too shy to mention to each other that we all secretly wanted to be good, normal people, get married and settle down. And we certainly didn't want to admit that we ever thought about God in our lives. But somehow, during that very cold winter, a bond had formed between us that brought each of us to the Subud Latihan, and that bond still exists to this day.

For me, there are two events that stand out from that time at Watersmeet. Firstly, picture if you will, the three of us, fully dressed in winter clothes, sitting on the sofa in front of a 'one-bar' electric fire, in the octagonal living room, late at night, because the bedrooms were far too cold and damp to sleep in.

We were listening to 'Another Side of Bob Dylan' way into the night, as we usually would do. On one particular night we were half dozing when we spotted a tiny dormouse appear from a small hole in the raised wooden floor. The mouse came to get warm in front of the fire and climbed up on our shoes where it amused itself playing with our shoelaces. None of us moved and at some point I just fell asleep, exhausted by all the excitement.

I also recall one Sunday morning we were milling around in the tiny kitchen, taking stock of the fact that all the cupboards were bare. We were all really hungry, and money was scarce. The decision was taken, I believe by Ramzi, who made the announcement that "duck hunting season had just opened".

Ramzi armed himself with an antique pellet gun that looked like a Luger pistol, and stealthily crept between the bushes to the riverbank. There followed soon after, several attempts to shoot one of the ducks that lived on the River Mole which ran right behind our hovel before flowing into the Thames. He managed to hit a duck and it was very annoyed. It flew up and did a lot of squawking before returning to the calm waters.

I think we discovered that day that we were all far more suited to be gatherers than hunters, because I don't think anyone was successful with the pistol. I'm pretty sure that all the ducks survived. I say that now because I know that no one had made any orange sauce that day.

Ramzi retired as a big game hunter and later went on to get his PhD in Business Management. He was then forced to spend many years as a senior lecturer at Lincoln University in Christchurch, New Zealand. We are now awaiting the completion of his book, which he assures us will be far superior to either Maurice's book or this one.

Real Men!

Work was hard to come by during the winter, but as we came into spring there was one company that started hiring, and the pay was excellent. This was Nielsons, where people recently released from incarceration were quickly hired. Their job would be to load up open trucks at 6.30am, with neatly folded, heavy canvas panels, wooden telegraph poles, guy ropes and pulleys, and a lot of heavy wooden stacking chairs. Finally, there would be the one-meter-long iron pins and a number of two kilo sledgehammers.

Once loaded, the trucks would speed off to the local café where everyone would eat an enormous English breakfast. Less than an hour later the trucks would be making their way to whatever wedding, flower show, dog show or event within 3 hours driving distance, had rented the huge marquee tents.

The work was hard and heavy duty. Swinging a two-kilo sledgehammer to knock in one-meter-long iron stakes to hold the guy ropes, raising the poles, unfolding and raising the canvas panels, not to mention unloading up to five hundred folding chairs, three at a time, was just the kind of job designed for burly ex-cons and ex-marines.

So, it should be no surprise that Ramzi, Maurice and myself all worked at Neilson's at various times. We showed them what real men were like!

Transitions and Turning Points

At the end of the holiday season of 1968, I returned to Kingston and visited my mother. She felt that I should move back into my room in Norbiton Hall and try to find a decent job. I could see she was still anxious about my future and I was beginning to feel the same too, so I agreed to give it a try. It wasn't long after that she pulled a few strings and arranged an interview for me at the Construction Company she worked for.

Having done their due diligence of asking me a few questions I received a letter a week later offering me the position of 'Trainee Quantity Surveyor'. This meant I was assigned to a senior QS and spent a lot of days out at various large construction sites taking endless measurements and making detailed hand written notes in a small black book as part of my on-job-training. In 1968 iPads and smart phones were still pure science fiction, so everything was hand written in pencil.

I also attended the Hammersmith College of Building and Art one day a week, where I learned the basics of construction. I literally had to learn to lay bricks and mix concrete in addition to learning the theoretical side of the job. So this now became my routine life during week days.

But come Friday night I would return to my preferred life as the adopted young mascot in a group of very remarkable people and follow them down to one of three local pubs in the town center. These pubs were the only community centers available in Kingston. After closing time, we would all walk back to my neighbour's flat and the weekend would really begin.

During this time, I was fascinated to observe the nature of the Social and Cultural Revolution that was unfolding in the UK throughout the sixties. Whilst the majority continued to live very sensible, well planned-out lives for a secure and comfortable future, there was a growing generation who had abandoned that approach. This was a decade of changes that saw a magnificent burst of creative freedom and increasing spiritual awareness.

The direction of these changes, whilst being distinctly anti-establishment, were a social revolution rooted in the ideals of peace and tolerance and the search for new knowledge, new experiences and a new society.

Unfortunately, with this freedom there came excesses and within a period of three years I had to say goodbye to four of those remarkable people who I had come to know so well. All four had succumbed to drug addiction and overdosed. Heroin was the dark predator that stalked the clubs, pubs and parties of this generation.

Fortunately, I never had any interest in drugs or the other high risk activities that became common amongst young adults in London at that time. As the young 'mascot' in the group I was also protected from these excesses by my neighbour Michael who, as de facto leader of the group, made it very clear to everyone that I was 'off limits' to any such activities.

This put me in a unique position to observe and learn about so many aspects of life, good and bad, without suffering the potential consequences that those who engaged in, and survived those activities, would face in later life.

Here I would like to apologize that this background introduction is both far longer than I expected and more focused on me than I intended.

It is a glimpse of my early life, before I joined Subud, which I share simply to give some context to what comes later. So let me close this introduction with the last story that explains how I joined Subud.

It's Time to Settle Down

It was a Sunday afternoon, towards the end of November 1968, and I was sitting in my neighbour's flat when he asked me when my eighteenth birthday was. I answered that it would be in the coming January and he said "Right, perfect! Tomorrow night you are coming with me."

The following evening, Michael and I walked into Kingston and round to the back of Bentalls department store, where a narrow alleyway lead to a one-story, prefabricated building that looked like an army barracks, sandwiched between much taller buildings. This, apparently, was where the Kingston Subud group met on Mondays and Thursdays.

I had heard the name Subud mentioned several times over the previous two years but it seemed to be something shrouded in mystery and I really did not know anything about it other than the founder came from somewhere in the Far East.

We entered the building and I was introduced to two very

nice older men in their mid-forties who, I was told, were appointed as official 'helpers'. We all sat down and I was served tea while they explained the basic purpose of Subud and that it was not a religion nor was it a replacement for religion. Subud had no rule book, no teachers and no membership fees. So far so good I thought.

The helpers went on to explain that the focus of Subud was on the relationship of each member with God as an individual and was simply the opening of each person's contact with the power of Almighty God within them, which was received spontaneously during what they called the 'latihan'. This did not really mean much to me but it sounded easy enough, a lot easier than Tibetan dancing for sure, so I signed up.

I was told there is a three month probation period for candidate members to allow them to meet the helpers, ask questions and get a better sense of what they could expect from Subud and the latihan before they decide whether they wanted to join Subud and receive this 'latihan' or not.

Now it just so happened that I had for some time begun to have concerns about my freewheeling lifestyle. After meeting these Subud members, who all seemed perfectly nice, normal, successful and good people, I thought perhaps this really was the time for me to settle down and start living a normal, sensible life. Subud felt like it would be my path back to a traditional, secure, albeit perhaps a bit boring, but comfortable life. It felt right.

I didn't actually go back to the hall again until the three months were up in January 1969. Again Michael was the one to remind me that the three months wait was over and it was time for me to get 'opened' and said he would accompany me.

And so off I went to be 'opened' in Subud one day after my eighteenth birthday.

✳

PART 1

The Opening

The Opening

It was 7.30 on a Monday evening that I sat in the small ante-room where about twenty Subud members, all men, were gathered, drinking tea and catching up with news and stories of their weekend. I sat there feeling like a fish out of water even though several members came over and introduced themselves and wanted to know something about me. Then the door to the main latihan room opened and about fifteen women came out, which prompted the men to stand up and start moving into the main room.

The main room for 'latihan' was about the size of an average junior school classroom. After all the men had entered they spread out and stood in no particular pattern. Two helpers came over to me and asked me if it was my sincere intention to worship Almighty God and that my desire to be 'opened' was truly from my own free will and not because I had been persuaded or forced by anyone else. I answered both questions in the affirmative.

I was told to close my eyes, empty myself of thoughts as much as possible and not be distracted by what other members may be receiving.

I moved to the edge of the room with my back close to the wall and closed my eyes. One of the helpers then said "Begin" and almost immediately the room came alive with various voices and sounds and I was aware that many people were moving around. One member was even running around the hall.

I realized that I was not doing too well with the 'empty your thoughts' and 'don't be distracted' part of the instructions.

In fact, various thoughts kept bubbling up like "Why am I here?" and "What are they all doing?" The latihan, as far as I could observe, did not seem to conform to any kind of religious or spiritual worship I was familiar with, but I resigned myself to wait out the half hour, and then all the thoughts and questions drifted off into the distance. Even the loud sounds and singing seemed to be coming from far off. I actually felt peaceful.

It must have been about twenty minutes into the latihan that, as I stood quietly, almost like in a day dream, I suddenly got a rude awakening. I felt myself thrust forward two steps and almost tripped over. I recovered my balance and looked back to where I had stood. I was sure that a member had tried to run between me and the wall and had knocked or pushed me out of the way. But it was clear that the space between me and the wall was too narrow for anyone to even squeeze past me. Somewhat confused I returned to my spot and actually moved close enough to the wall that it touched my shoulders.

A few minutes later I was back in my peaceful state when I was thrust forward again and this time I found myself on the floor, basically in the position of worship. I could smell the carpet and my mind was really having a hard time trying to figure out how that had happened again. There was no answer, so I gave up worrying about it. Soon after that the helper called "Finish" and the room quickly fell silent.

The following Thursday I returned for my second latihan. It still felt pretty odd for the first ten minutes until I stopped thinking about it and found that deep, peaceful feeling inside. The only thing different was that this time I noticed a kind of vibration in my legs and arms. It wasn't just a feeling. My arms and legs were physically shaking, but I still felt peaceful so I didn't think too much about that either.

So that was my opening and follow-up latihan experience. A bit weird, but nothing sensational I thought at the time.

Back to Normal

The next night was Friday night which meant off to the pub with Michael and the usual gang. Ever since I was fourteen I had been going regularly each Friday and Saturday night to the local pub with all these older friends. Although I was not really that keen on alcohol I would feel obliged to have one or two 'half-pints' of beer that would last me through the evening and give me the appearance of being kind of grown up.

But this Friday was special because this Friday I was already 18 now, and finally I was actually legally old enough to drink in a pub, much to the relief of the landlord who had been very patient for four years. So I ordered my usual half pint of mild beer and brought the glass to my lips when, suddenly, I felt the urge to be sick. I lowered the glass for a moment and then tried again. And again I felt like gagging.

My mind whirled around to find some explanation. The best it could come up with was my sense of smell must be off, perhaps some allergy to hops. So I put the glass down and ordered a vodka and lime. I got the same gag response. Next a rum and coke, but it too could not pass my lips. By now I was really wondering what was going on and, equally important, I was running out of money.

I finally concluded that I must be coming down with some heavy 'flu and, in desperation, I ordered a black current cordial, which I had no problem consuming.

The following night was Saturday night. The high point of every weekend but, unfortunately, my Friday night experience with alcohol was repeated. This time, after I gagged on the beer, I went straight to ordering a black current cordial and saved myself a lot of money.

I was now convinced that I must have some very strange illness that prevented me from consuming my beer. I really didn't think about it much beyond that.

The next day I was with my mother. She had invited me to join her for Sunday lunch and had very kindly bought a large pork chop for me, which was soon in the pan. We chatted as she cooked until finally she presented me with an excellent lunch.

I cut into the perfectly cooked, tender pork chop and brought my fork to my lips, but immediately started to gag. I tried the potatoes, the sweet corn and Brussel sprouts and had no problem. So once again I lifted the piece of pork to my lips and once again started to gag. I simply could not eat the pork chop and I began to apologise profusely to my mother, who I thought would be really hurt after all the trouble she had gone to. What made it worse was I had no rational explanation for her. I had no explanation even for myself! To my surprise and relief, she was perfectly fine about it and immediately offered to make me something else.

I was left pondering what kind of illness would stop me drinking alcohol and eating pork chops with no other symptoms. Whatever it was, I just hoped it would pass soon. Fifty years later and it still hasn't passed.

While today I can manage a sip or two of wine or champagne at a celebration without gagging, I have no desire to drink and certainly no desire to eat pork.

At that time, in 1969, I was aware that the Jewish and Islamic religions forbade the eating of pork and Islam warns of the negative effects of consuming alcohol, but for several weeks after this experience I did not make the connection between religious teachings and what I experienced.

For me this was the first small 'proof' that I really did have an inner and it really could guide me in my life in a spontaneous way with no thinking or will power involved. It was not my decision to stop drinking alcohol or stop eating pork. It was not something I had wished for or even thought about.

I should say that my mind spent quite a lot of time trying to rationalize this experience in worldly terms like "I must be getting sick". I find it quite astounding now how completely unaware my ego was that I had an inner. It never occurred to me that there could be a higher authority within me that could actually over-ride my ego, remove my desires and manifest itself in my daily physical life.

The desire of the ego to be in total control and to make all my own decisions was still there, but fortunately it seems my heart and mind were willing to give up that control without much of an argument when the inner stepped in to make changes. At least when it came to alcohol and pork.

Many months later I realized 'giving up' what the ego desires is what 'surrender' is all about, and much later I understood that surrender was the first step towards learning obedience. But more on that later.

Peeling the Outer Onion

This first simple experience I have come to realize, actually embodied many of the elements of life when you start to follow the spiritual path. It took me several years to gain an understanding of what was actually happening to me in that first week in Subud and what its value was going to be for my future.

I was fortunate to have come to Subud with no preconceived ideas or expectations, simply because I knew virtually nothing about Subud. I just accepted whatever experience I was given. I now recognize that 'acceptance' is a major element of trust and faith in God. At the time however, I really didn't think very much about it.

As time went by I began to gain the understanding from these experiences that, as we grow up, our heart and mind create a sense of 'I', an image and character that we come to believe is who we are in this world, and that we become totally familiar with. This persona we create is like the software that drives the hardware (physical body) as the vehicle we use to live our lives in this world.

The most fundamental desire of this persona we may call the ego, is to have full control of what we do, what we think, what we feel and the decisions we make. It also chooses what we believe and don't believe, including in spiritual matters. Ironically, our worldly heart and mind, filled by our desires and thinking, can know nothing about the spiritual world beyond what they have heard or read while growing up.

Imaginary Values Defended to the Death
My Religious Beliefs Revisited

Over the years since being opened I have frequently pondered the role of religion in the life of man in this world, which, according to history and Cable News, seems to cause as much harm as it has done good. The question that arose for me was "Is it the religion that is wrong, or the followers?"

I share my thoughts on this in Part ll of this book, 'All The World's a Stage'.

Beyond the Limitations of the Mind

Because we possess the gift of human intellect, the mind can easily manipulate the written word, as in a religion. It is quite different when a person has a true spiritual experience from the inner.

When we have spiritual experiences they are, by their nature, beyond the understanding, and therefore, beyond the control of our heart and mind.

It is when we try to explain an inner experience that we become aware of the inadequacies of language and, therefore, the potential weakness or limitations of religious and spiritual teachings. A challenge I am facing now in writing this book.

Borrowing an Analogy from Bapak

We can demonstrate the impossibility of words to describe or communicate spiritual experiences with a common material substance like sugar. Certainly we can describe with words exactly what sugar is, the different types of sugar, how they are processed, what the benefits and dangers of sugar are. All that we can do very well with words.

We can have workshops on sugar and listen to experts describing the history and future of sugar. We can explain the uses of sugar and even make diagrams of the molecular structure of sugar.

We can read and study everything about sugar for a lifetime and become famous as a world expert on sugar. We can easily get great throngs of followers who also want to become experts in sugar and may see their teacher as the greatest sugar guru ever, and yet, we still cannot not know or explain what 'sweetness' is if we have never experienced tasting sugar. Words cannot do that.

It may be that our guru has tasted it, and those who wrote books have tasted it, but they cannot guarantee that any of their followers will ever get to taste sugar.

So it is that we may study religious teachings our whole life but, at the moment we face death, we still may not know anything about the life of our own human soul or our inner condition resulting from all our actions in life.

Even if we have studied with people who have tasted sugar they cannot explain what sweetness tastes like. We cannot learn the true nature of sugar through thinking or studying. We can only understand the nature of sugar and its sweetness through experience, that is by tasting sugar.

What we need is to be given some sugar to taste from the one who creates and has the authority to distribute sugar. In the realm of the human soul and the life force that is only God, who created us and has full authority over all things.

Validating Beliefs
Receiving a Taste of Sugar

This I soon understood after being opened, was the enormous difference between the Subud Latihan and every other spiritual path or method I had heard about. The latihan had connected me with my own personal spiritual guru within. This guru had shown how it could change my life by simply stopping me drinking alcohol and eating pork. Like all Subud members, through this inner guru I got a tiny taste of sugar, so I now know what sweetness is, but I cannot explain it.

In this way I came to realize that my inner had shown me that what is taught in religion, regarding the consumption of alcohol and pork, really was based on some inner truth, because at that time my heart and mind had no desire or interest in any traditional religion, nor did I have an opinion on the subject of alcohol or pork, and certainly had no desire to stop consuming either one of them. It was my inner guiding me.

I was not following any doctrine or cultural rules. It was a silent command from my inner and fortunately my heart and mind just obeyed without much questioning of 'why?' Apparently my ego did not feel threatened by the sudden and inexplicable loss of alcohol and pork in my life, even though it was not my ego's decision.

Over time, through the latihan, like so many Subud members, I have had many experiences that both confirm a lot of the explanations given by Bapak and also the truth behind what we are taught in religion.

Companions for Life

It transpired that three of my good friends from my Swanage days, who were not part of my neighbour Michael's esoteric group, had also joined Subud at more or less the same time as I did. We had each come to Subud separately and were very surprised when we met for the first time in the Subud Hall.

For the next three months we continued with our latihans twice a week and there quickly grew a sense of camaraderie between us as we journeyed along this spiritual path together.

No longer were our weekends spent in the pub. Our lives were changing, sometimes with clear, unexpected experiences, but mostly the changes were more subtle.

Life became a different kind of adventure as we discovered more of our individual inner natures and gained a new understanding of life through experiencing our new found inner existence while continuing to struggle with all our normal outer needs to survive in this world.

Joining Subud and experiencing the latihan together with a few good friends was a lot like setting off on a voyage of discovery. We were the crew; God was the captain.

With the latihan it felt like the first time I travelled to a foreign country and discovered how small and narrow my life had been up until then. Now I began to see there was a whole vast world beyond the borders of my past existence still to be discovered, half of which existed hidden on the inside.

This was the journey of discovery all Subud members embark upon. It was exciting and energizing and I still feel grateful for the company I had on my journey. Companions to this day, albeit we are now spread across the globe. One who has been a true companion on my journey is Ramzi Addison. Even when I was in Indonesia and he was in the UK, and later moved to New Zealand, we regularly kept in touch and offered each other support.

Things Are Different on Different Levels
By the second year after being opened I began hearing about all this 'levels' stuff, which really didn't mean much to me at all

beyond the obvious that a cabbage was somehow on a higher level than dirt and animals were on a higher level than a daisy and naturally human beings are at the top of pile. Quite how that had anything to do with my spiritual progress or the latihan I had no idea.

Now, after some fifty years of following the latihan and listening to many talks of Bapak, I am aware of just how fundamental the existence of these levels are to the whole 'mechanics' of life, both in this world, and the next, as God has decreed.

So, if you are not in Subud, or recently opened, I expect you may have some questions about this subject too. Once again, this is just my own understanding based on a few personal experiences that then has allowed me to expand into some understanding of Bapak's explanations.

God's Power Is in All He Has Created

I assume that if you are still reading this book you also have a belief in Almighty God as the creator of the entire universe. The alternative is to believe that the universe just suddenly happened by accident. That inert material appeared out of nothing and then some of it also just happened to come to life and, of its own volition, evolve into this creature here typing this book, seems a bit of a stretch.

From the point of view of almighty human logic, I would say that neither is a rational belief. Clearly the human intellect is not almighty or all-knowing as some of us would like to believe.

But from a spiritual viewpoint, based on an accumulation of experiences and events, men have seen a glimpse of the reality of God's existence. For me there is no doubt that God exists and that God was the creator of all that is and all that ever will be.

Based on that belief, and supported by modern science, we can see that there is power, a vibration, in all material things on the atomic level. That, to my understanding is the presence of God's power. That God created atoms after creating light also makes sense scientifically. Then atoms formed molecules and molecules are the building blocks of all material matter, from rocks to human bodies. So all things in this material world are really created from one source; matter. That's what feels right to me at least.

But, there is another mystery called 'life', which clearly is able to animate these clumps of energized molecules, this stuff we call 'matter'. To name this elusive phenomena, we in Subud use the well-established term of 'life force'.

This may be a good point to tell you of my first experience related to this subject. This was before I had heard or read any of Bapak's explanations.

A Glimpse of the Life Force in Epsom

One evening Ramzi and I took it upon ourselves to visit our close friend in his flat in Epsom. He had just had a painful break-up with his girlfriend and hadn't been socializing for a couple of weeks. He too was recently opened in Subud, so there may have been a few deeper things going on.

Ramzi and I did our best to cheer him up, and around midnight we all decided to go out for a walk in a nearby public park. The weather was fine and the moon shone bright as we entered the park and made our way along a narrow path. To our right was a large expanse of a grass area that could have included a football pitch. Running along the left side of the path was a long line of huge poplar trees beautifully illuminated in the moonlight.

About half way down the path I looked at one of these enormous poplar trees and was suddenly hit with a very powerful epiphany. So powerful it could hit both Ramzi and myself at the same instant as he let out a "WOW!"

And what was it we both saw. Well, something that sounds quite obvious. Something we all know. But what was different was experiencing the reality that was much deeper than our everyday knowledge.

What we experienced was the miracle of the life force that could turn dirt into wood. So simple, yet so meaningful. That the dirt we walked on could be transformed into a living entity with a completely different nature. A tree! It boggled our logical minds. But in words I cannot do justice to what we experienced.

Ramzi and I looked at each other and we both knew that we had both seen the same thing! God's life force at work.

From this simple eureka moment a whole lot of mysteries began to unravel concerning the different levels of the life force from the material, to the vegetable, to the animal, to the human level, that Bapak had often spoken about.

We returned to our friend's flat and I think he felt better. I have no memory of how Ramzi and I got back to Kingston that night. I guess that wasn't so important for this story.

Unwanted Attention
A Jolly Picnic, With Ramifications

One evening at the latihan hall there was a written notice on the message board announcing that there would be a one-day Regional Gathering in a few weeks for all Subud members in the South East region of England, to be held in Tunbridge Wells. The four of us decided we would attend and we all signed up for seats on the chartered coach, with no idea what a regional gathering was about or what to expect.

We boarded the coach early one Sunday morning and set off with the same enthusiasm of going to the seaside for our summer holidays. On the way down, one of the senior women helpers sitting across from me announced she wanted to put my name down to be the next regional chairman.

Of course we all assumed she was either joking or senile. As a group of young lads we had no interest in the organizational side of Subud and little understanding of what Subud was, beyond doing the latihan and having a cup of tea afterwards with the Kingston group.

We arrived at this very nice place set in the country side. As best I can remember it was a kind of manor house set in quite a sizable estate with a separate large hall and other buildings, that may have been stables once.

The four of us spent most of the day eating and walking around the vast grounds. We had our guitars and there were two visiting French girls from Paris, one of whom was in Subud, but both of whom, we decided, definitely needed entertaining.

It was a few hours later, at around 3pm, someone came out of the main meeting room looking for me and I was informed that I was the new regional chairmen for the Subud South East England region. Me and my friends stood there incredulous. It made no sense.

My first reaction was to ask "Why?" I was enjoying myself being me, and 'me' was nothing like a regional chairman of any-thing.

Apparently the elder lady helper had been true to her word and put my name forward to be tested for this position.

As we ambled towards the large hall this person explained that because I was only eighteen and only been opened a few months it was decided to make me joint regional chairman together with a more mature member.

Unfortunately, I had not joined any of the meetings that day, so I still knew nothing about the Subud organization and had no idea what a regional chairmen was supposed to do. I soon found out it was a purely administrative job and had nothing to do with the spiritual side of Subud, which was a great relief.

I'll Handle This

Not long after that regional gathering I was required to attend the Subud UK National Congress at Swanwick, representing the South East Region. I was a very naïve and shy representative, so I naturally took a back seat in all the meetings, to listen and learn from the more experienced members representing their regions.

On the last evening, before dinner, the regional representatives gathered, together with the many members who attended as observers, in the large meeting hall to receive the National Chairman's report on the state of the Subud organization in the UK. This report was followed after dinner by a Q&A session.

The Generation Gap

It was during this Q&A session that some of the older members raised the subject of Subud's growth in the UK and in the world. They wanted to discuss how Subud was perceived by young candidates and new members and what their first impressions were when they made contact with a Subud group, and what was their impression after they were opened.

These older members were concerned that the next generation, who had grown up in the sixties, may be put off with so many older people in Subud and think Subud is not for the young. This was obviously important for the future of Subud and was considered very seriously.

Looking around the hall it was striking that it was filled mostly with members who were all aged from 35 up to 75 years old. There were hardly any members present who were in their twenties.

It wasn't long after the discussion started that eyes began turning toward me, and soon thereafter the National Chairman asked me to come up on stage to answer questions and describe my experience when joining Subud.

My heart sank as I nervously made my way to the stage. I felt as though I was expected to represent the entire youth of Great Britain in some kind of interrogation session at a time when the UK youth were rejecting so much of their parents' rules and regulations.

This Q&A session was meant to come to an end after an hour, but actually continued past midnight.

The Inner Ventriloquist

While on the stage I was vaguely aware that I was not responding to the many questions as my normal, nervous self would. Words and answers just seemed to flow through my mind and I really didn't need to think much at all.

It was a similar feeling to when I spoke with my mother many years before about her relationship with my father, only in Swanwick my voice was surprisingly stronger. The whole experience for me was not only surreal, but it was in full view of the Subud UK membership.

The next day the congress ended and I returned with my friends to Kingston.

The Generation Gap 'Snap-Back'

That night, back home, I went to bed feeling absolutely exhausted, and my thoughts were still confused about my 'performance', which had made me feel very disorientated within myself.

In addition to that, my body actually ached like I had been beaten up physically. I could think of no rational reason for my physical condition and it just added to my confusion.

The next day was Monday and I was still feeling very tired

and pretty disorientated. "More Subud 'flu perhaps?" I thought to myself that evening, as I made my way to the Subud hall for the Monday night latihan.

My latihan that night was pretty intense with a lot of physical movement. It felt a bit like an inner tempest was swirling around in my stomach and chest. When the latihan ended and we began to move back to the ante-room I was aware that my latihan was still going on inside.

I found that a bit unnerving and mentioned this to one of the helpers. I told him that I thought I still needed to continue my latihan. He called two other helpers over and they were more than happy to accompany me back into the main hall.

This time, in a virtually empty hall my latihan really took off. My movements were less restrained and my voice became even stronger. At some point I began to feel a very deep, almost painful, sadness welling up in me. This sadness continued to grow until there were real tears pouring out.

Eventually even my mind seemed to be thrown into the blender and I could no longer think about what I was experiencing and I just had to let whatever needed to come out, to come out. This intense experience lasted several minutes until I was left sobbing on the floor.

Then suddenly the latihan began to subside and I quickly returned to a relatively normal state, but quite shaken and exhausted. This definitely wasn't a case of 'flu. I could no longer fool myself with that flimsy excuse.

Each of the helpers sat on the floor and started to share what they had received about what was going on in me. They all felt that it was from my experience in Swanwick. They explained that when I was on the stage in Swanwick, answering questions about things my mind did not know, I was in fact in latihan.

You could say that my inner was woken up and rose to the

special occasion by taking the reins away from my ego in order to receive and share something beyond my normal thinking and understanding, about purely worldly things I might add, nothing spiritual.

My worldly heart and mind were relegated to mere observers when confronted by this 'new' force within me. It was like my inner had suddenly turned up on the stage and said, "I'll handle it from here"

Today I also understand that, after returning from Swanwick, my inner had handed back the reins to my ego, because it is the job of the heart and mind to manage my day to day worldly life. Unfortunately, my heart and mind were still in a real state of shock and disorientation and not in a condition to operate as they should.

This was the first major experience where my mind, my ego had really witnessed my inner taking control. This was very scary for the heart and equally confusing for the mind.

What I experienced in the latihan that evening back in Kingston was the reaction of my old self, after my inner had awoken within me, to handle a situation that normally I would have been incapable of handling. From that experience I discovered the huge mess my ego, and all the lower forces, had created within me. I had been shown what I was actually capable of and then fell back to where I actually was in my life.

Confirming Bapak's Analogy
Our Mansion is Full of Servants

My 'being' was like a mansion that had been left to my servants to run alone for so long that they had forgotten they had a master who they were supposed to serve, but instead they had used and abused my mansion as though they owned it.

So many things needed cleaning out because my inner being

was full of a lot of junk and dirt. The intervention or awakening of the inner at Swanwick was far beyond the comprehension of my heart and mind, but through this experience I became acutely aware of many of the mistakes in my character and wrong actions in my short life and this was the source of the intense sadness.

The master had been away far too long. I was only eighteen and had been shielded from most of the lifestyle mistakes so many teenagers were making at that time, yet already I needed a major clean-up. That was a bit worrying.

Now, at Swanwick, it was as though the master had returned and all the servants suddenly remembered their true responsibilities and became aware of how they had failed their master. The level of regret and sadness in the heart is hard to explain.

Those tears were actually my heart, mind and ego asking for forgiveness for how they had abused their power for so many years.

The Swanwick experience was the first time that my heart and mind were shown the proof that 'they' are not the supreme master of my life in this world and that the soul, my soul, is something real and, by God's grace, had executive power and authority over them.

I was happy to hear from my favourite helper that Bapak had often used this analogy of a house and servants many times over the years to explain, very simply, what goes on within every human being. So I felt very reassured that, as a novice, I seemed to be on the right path and not wandering off into some imaginary world.

Before that experience my mind simply thought of the 'soul' as some vague, abstract entity that, although it was somehow part of me, it would only really exist in the next life.

This whole post Swanwick event was a very unsettling experience for me and it took me a couple of weeks to regain, what I would describe as, my comfortable sense of familiarity with myself.

However, I would soon discover that this was just the beginning of a period of training and purification for my heart and mind that would continue for several years.

Only in Subud

As joint regional chairman I was required to attend the monthly National Committee meetings held at the Monmouth Road Subud Hall in London. This really was quite intimidating for me, as an unemployed eighteen-year-old with only six months experience in Subud. To sit in a meeting with these successful men who included the CEOs of major multinational companies and a Senior Underwriter from the oldest insurance company in the world.

The issues discussed at that time were all to do with the practicalities of running a national organization and networking with the international organization in over 70 countries. I had no idea why I was there or what I was supposed to do, so mostly I just listened and learned.

It was in these meetings I learned in more detail that Subud originated in Indonesia with a man called Bapak Muhammad Subuh Sumohadiwidjojo (Bapak, meaning father, is the common, polite way to address an older gentleman in Indonesia).

The reason this came up on the agenda at each meeting was that there was to be a Fourth Subud World Congress, this time held at Bapak's own centre in Cilandak, Indonesia, in 1971, which was still two years away.

It was at the third meeting in London that the subject of chartering flights to Jakarta for the congress appeared on the agenda. After some discussion, the committee agreed that chartering aircraft to bring members from the USA and Europe would be the most cost effective and manageable way to get members to the congress. The alternative was to leave individual members to make their own travel arrangements.

During this discussion, for the first time, I felt moved to say something which was more in the form of a question; "If Subud does charter planes, wouldn't it be good to set aside some seats for Subud members who, through testing, should attend the congress, but may not have the financial means to pay for a ticket?" Everyone present agreed that this felt right and they approved that suggestion to be added to a list of questions for the National Helpers to 'test'. (I will explain more about 'testing' in a later chapter.)

I felt very privileged to attend these meetings because I got to observe how successful, wealthy businessmen discuss issues and come to make some very consequential decisions. I got a sense of what the 'culture' was in that rather exclusive world.

Actually they were all very nice, 'ordinary' people, but with a great deal of worldly knowledge and experience. They were never proud or arrogant and never looked down on me, or treated me in a patronizing way. They certainly did not act as though I had infiltrated their exclusive club. Quite the opposite.

This was a side of Subud that I did not expect to find but, on reflection, it should not have been a surprise because we all did latihan together and we all were walking our own inner path, but to the same destination. There can be no 'separation' based on class, wealth, religion, race or age when you experience the great equalizing reality of God's love and power in the latihan.

Before God we are all equal and the latihan that we experience demonstrates the undeniable proof of that. Our physical and material circumstances must always be considered as temporary, just as our time on earth is temporary.

Making an Effort

Whilst it was true that I was busy having National Committee meetings, organizing regional gatherings and visiting groups in the South East region, it was also true that during this entire time I was basically unemployed. I would not be going down to work in Swanage again and in Kingston there was little work to be found.

I had no qualifications and was very unclear on what kind of work I was suited for. I liked writing songs and playing guitar, but I never felt that my future was as a musician. Since I was a small boy I had always been painting and drawing so I thought that art would be a better direction to go.

I decided to apply to the Epsom & Ewell School of Art and sent in an application and soon after I received a written invitation to present my portfolio at the school.

Being mostly unemployed since leaving school and living a veritable nomadic life, I had no portfolio any more. So on the day of my interview I took the bus to Epsom carrying the only work I could salvage from my mother's flat and other places I had stayed.

The largest piece was painted on a thin plywood off-cut about 60cm by 80cm with an odd bit sticking out at the top which I could not cut off as I had no saw.

Another piece I had painted on the wooden end flap of my mother's discarded kitchen table. One side was Formica, the other plain wood which I had primed with emulsion paint. It was perfectly fine for a painting except it still had the hinges attached.

There were five other pieces painted in watercolour on proper artboard. All these I wrapped and tied up in newspaper and I set off to catch the bus to Epsom.

When I entered the large hall at the school my heart sank.

There were about twenty other applicants who had all just finished High School and were there with their thick portfolios that were overflowing with sketches, pastel works and watercolour paintings. My school portfolio had long since been lost.

Inside the hall I was shown to the last vacant desk that had been set up in a large circle of desks and three lecturers went round to each applicant to review their work. Looking at the other portfolios, I really wondered if I was just wasting my time.

The most senior lecturer approached my desk and introduced himself. I had already untied my bundle and I pulled off the newspaper to reveal my pitiful few pieces of work. He did at least look at each piece as I tried to explain how difficult it was for me to paint and build a portfolio. A general lack of money and no fixed abode being the two main problems I faced.

In fact, for the painting on the large piece of plywood, in addition to the limited colours of expensive acrylic paint, I had also used coffee, mustard and paprika taken from my mother's pantry and mixed with linseed oil to create three additional colours. I simply could not afford to buy more tubes of paint. The lecturer just listened and nodded and then moved on to the next applicant.

That was the point when I began thinking about a career in music again.

About twenty minutes later the faculty administrator thanked us all for coming and explained that we would each receive a letter in the coming weeks to inform us whether we had been accepted or not.

I knew that outside in the corridor there were many more applicants waiting to present their portfolios. Yes, a career in music was looking more and more attractive.

Well at least I had tried, I told myself as I began wrapping up my work. Suddenly I noticed the senior lecturer approaching my desk. He came up very close and in a hushed voice said, "Don't worry, you're in."

I sat on the bus back to Kingston in a happy state of shock, but I knew I had to temper my excitement until I had confirmation in writing. I prefer not to count my chickens before they hatch.

More Than One Iron in the Fire

A couple of months prior to applying to art school I had talked with one of the group helpers after latihan about my concerns with being unemployed and not having any real sense of what direction I should take for my future. I had no idea what I was supposed to do.

He suggested that I write to Bapak in Indonesia and ask his advice as to my true talent and the right work for me. So that is exactly what I did, but, after more than two months I still had not received a reply.

Now, sitting on the bus it occurred to me that I had wasted Bapak's time and I should have been more patient. I was hoping that with a bit of luck my letter had been lost in the post and Bapak had never received it.

Mixed Signals

The weeks passed with no news from Epsom & Ewell Art School or from Indonesia and I was beginning to wonder if God had abandoned me to wander aimlessly for the rest of my life, or was I simply incapable of receiving any guidance for myself.

Each week I would drop by my mother's flat to check on my mother and on the mail. So it was with a great sense of relief and excitement when one day I found several envelopes on the floor inside her front door and saw one with the Epsom & Ewell College logo on it. I immediately ripped open the envelope and read the two very short paragraphs telling me that I had been accepted and should enrol myself within the next two weeks.

I was naturally excited and it felt like a great weight had been taken off my shoulders. My future direction in life was finally settled!

I gathered up all the mail off the floor, opened the front door and crossed the hallway to knock on my neighbour's door. Michael, looking like he hadn't slept all night, opened the door and invited me in.

With a big grin on my face I handed him the letter and as he read it he became almost as excited as I was as he congratulated me. He then went into the kitchen to make some coffee and I went and sat down in his living room.

Holding the other letters in my hand I casually looked through them and noticed one strange, thin blue airmail letter addressed to me. The post office stamp had the word 'Indonesia' on it. Suddenly it felt a bit like Christmas. I carefully opened the tissue thin blue airmail paper and read the faint typing.

It read more like a telegram saying; "Bapak has received your letter. Bapak's advice is, 'Do not study'. Regarding your work, Bapak says you should "do what makes your heart happy."

It was signed Sudarto, who had been with Bapak since the beginning of Subud and now worked in Bapak's administration as a translator for correspondence with members from around the world.

So now I was looking at two letters that arrived together. One letter announcing an opportunity for me to study my favourite subject and the other one telling me not to study.

I showed Michael the letter from Bapak which he quickly read and then burst out laughing! I admit it was funny but, at the time, I was not so amused.

Although it appeared that I had a choice I knew there and then that I would not be going to study at Epsom Art School. I had to follow Bapak's advice. The result of that decision 'not to study' was to put me back to zero again in terms of having a direction for my life because Bapak's advice was simply "Do what makes your heart happy", which was hardly specific enough to identify a career path for me.

I clearly remember thinking to myself that there were many things that made my heart happy, but none of them would earn me a living.

Nonetheless, I accepted Bapak's advice and just had to let go of any plans and ideas I had made for my future. I had to put my trust in God and pray that I would be guided to my right path.

I look back now and see that I was fortunate to have enough sincerity and faith to follow Bapak's advice. This was like a test of my obedience and commitment to God and to correcting my life in the hope that I could find the right path of my destiny.

Very importantly I was not obstructed by a mind that demanded I follow normal, pragmatic logic, which would have seen me arguing with Bapak's advice and going to Art School as my obvious, logical choice.

As will become clear, I feel very blessed to have been given a pretty subservient heart and mind when it comes to matters pertaining to God and faith.

I can see now that this was where, after joining Subud, a new path was opening in my life. It had started with the abrupt end of my ability to consume alcohol and equally abrupt end of my pork eating days, both of which just happened spontaneously without any involvement or objection from my old self.

This 'accepting mind' was nothing I could take credit for, nothing I could be proud of, because it was simply my good fortune to have been born with a mind that was more curious than controlling and more interested in learning than feeling smart. My mind had always wanted to understand people more than to judge them. It seems that is a pretty good thing to have.

I can actually trace the nature of my heart and mind back to my Sunday walks in the forest as a child. What some may call naivety I would call simplicity. I seemed to understand that it is the heart that loves to feel cleverer, smarter and wiser than other people, and so it pressures the mind to analyse and come up with opinions about pretty much everything, and in doing so makes life incredibly complicated and confusing.

Basically this kind of mind, controlled by the ego, just loves to create a lot of highly detailed, but quite irrelevant information, facts, figures and charts, just to be able to feel the glorious satisfaction of sounding and looking like an expert.

The human ego finds it so pleasurable when the heart can feel "I'm smart, I'm superior", and best of all, "I'm right!" that it constantly demands that the mind keeps pushing to demonstrate its superiority over others. This is normal for our ego and lower forces but, following that path is in direct conflict with seeking knowledge of our spiritual life and developing the soul.

But through the latihan these desires can be softened and eventually changed so that a person is only really concerned about how God sees them. And when it comes to being smart, superior and right, there is no competing with God. More about that later.

From Using a Compass to Learning to Trust GPS

I had joined Subud because I believed it was time I returned to the normal, dare I say boring, established road in life and settle down like the vast majority of my old friends from school were doing. Studying seemed to be the best and most logical way to begin moving in that direction. But now I had been told not to study!

So here I was once again feeling lost in the middle of the ocean in my little sailing dingy with no wind and a broken compass. For the next few weeks I diligently did my latihan, which always left me feeling good, but still I had no hint as to what I was supposed to do in life.

Understandably my mind was becoming increasingly restless until finally I went to talk with my helpers and they agreed to do some testing with me.

Explicit Instructions

When testing, it is important to be clear what is the objective and the problem, so that everyone understands the question. The problem that I was facing was somewhat complex, which made it hard to formulate a question. One helper suggested testing about my talents in relation to pursuing a career as a first step.

We started with testing 'how it would be if I pursued a career in art'. Then we tested 'how would it be if I pursued a career in music?'

We all received very similar 'answers'. In both cases it was a very muted response suggesting that either one was kind of OK. It certainly wasn't a definite 'No' but it also was not a definite 'Yes, go for it!' either.

We then ran through a series of questions about various types of work that may be suitable for me. Again we all received very muted responses which was rather disappointing.

Finally, one helper, Sachlan North, suggested we test whether it was right for me to work at all at this time. Once again it was neither yes or no, but more of a 'no'. It was like working wasn't the issue we should be focussed on.

By now it had been about twenty minutes and all three helpers were feeling like they too were in the middle of the ocean with a broken compass.

After a few minutes of quiet pondering Sachlan let out a

laugh and said it had just come to him that we should test "Is it right for me to look for a job?" We tested this and at last we all received very strongly that this was the right thing for me to do.

There was just one problem, which I quickly pointed out. The previous testing had not indicated at all what kind of job I should look for and even if I should work or not.

And so it was the last question we tested that day was "Is it right for me to look for a job, but not take one?" Boom! We all received a resoundingly positive response.

We then did a short latihan and moved back to the ante-room for some tea and biscuits with the other members.

There was considerable talk about our marathon session of testing and the rather peculiar final result. The helpers were in fact apologetic that they had not been able to receive anything more helpful or concrete, but I assured them that in my heart I felt surprisingly happy.

I had my instructions now and they were very clear; 'look for a job but don't take one!' So now it was simple, all I had to do is follow instructions and stop worrying. That is honestly how I felt.

It really came back to the basic 'be obedient and trust in God.'

How to Succeed Without Really Trying

At that time, I was renting a small third floor attic flat in a house owned by a very kind Subud member whose husband suffered with advanced multiple sclerosis. Somehow I had managed to pay the rent for the two months I had been there. I had done a few obscure jobs but nothing long term. But now I had to sit down with her and her husband to explain to them that I would have to move out and resume my nomadic life because of the results of my testing.

To my surprise they both objected strongly and wanted me

to stay. I was really taken aback by their sincere kindness and I felt very awkward about accepting their generosity. I wanted to take responsibility for myself and didn't want to cause them any financial loss.

In the end they suggested, and I agreed, that I would do odd jobs for them, including repairing the roof on their garden shed and a bit of painting and decorating in return for my accommodation, until things got sorted out in my life. This I was more than happy to do.

I soon found that the Subud member who owned the house next door, and their friends across the road, also had a lot of odd jobs to be done. So, very quickly I was able to actually earn enough money for food and for transport to go to job interviews.

In the first two weeks following the testing I had been up to London three times for job interviews. I actually got one of the jobs but, following the testing, naturally I turned it down.

How to Find Your Way Without Looking

The neighbours' friends across the road had one major problem in their life. The wife was 'allergic' to washing up and the first time I visited their home she took me to the kitchen to show me a sink buried in plates, bowls, mugs, glasses, pots and pans and utensils. I could see she felt a little ashamed, but she obviously had a real problem dealing with this phobia.

With my experience working in hotel kitchens, it was not a shock to me and I was happy to come over each day to do all her washing up. When I agreed to do this the look of relief on her face suggested that she viewed me as knight in shining armour.

During the third week she asked if I would mind mowing the back garden lawn, which of course I was happy to do. Actually, I was pretty happy all the time those days. With all these odd jobs my income was quite reasonable. More than what I would have earned at some of the jobs I was interviewing for!

I was half way through the mowing when I saw a tall man in his mid-thirties come out the back door with a mug of coffee. From his general appearance I would have said he was a reformed beatnik from the fifties, or a poet. He introduced himself as the man of the house. This was the first time that I had met him.

He asked me a few of the usual questions just to get to know me and then said that he had heard from my landlady that I was interested in art. I confirmed that was true and he then asked me if I would be interested in becoming his apprentice and learn how to restore old paintings.

Without hesitation I said yes!

He told me to follow him and we went inside, up the stairs and then climbed some 'fold-down' wooden stairs into the attic where I discovered his studio was.

He had installed skylight windows so the studio was very bright. I saw a painting on an easel which I recognized as a Hogarth. I walked over to look at it closely and could see literally hundreds of small white dots all over the painting caused by oxidation of the ground coat of paint that contained lead.

On a large work table behind the easel I saw a Van Dyke and standing in the corner was a life size portrait of an Elizabethan nobleman by an unknown artist. I felt like I was in heaven.

I would now be able to pay my rent and stop going for job interviews. I had a job at last without even looking. It found me! It found me because I was obedient to the testing, as crazy as it may sound to our logical mind. "Look for a job, but don't take one!"

This was the job that would determine the path of the rest of my life, but in a very surprising way. I would note that I still did the washing-up.

I Shall Digress
Connecting The Dots

Over the past forty-odd years, during quieter moments I will often find myself tracing back through my life all the way to my childhood days and connecting the many dots that delineated my path to the present.

This was not done through any mental effort but rather by simply letting my mind drift in a particular direction and, on many occasions, a deeper understanding would rise into my consciousness quite spontaneously.

I made no deliberate decision to review my life. It simply happened every so often and continues today. It is not like day dreaming, but more like passive pondering in a semi latihan state. These dots that emerge bring with them the 'a-ha' moments of insight and knowledge about my life. It is like picking fruit that had finally ripened from a series of trees I passed by long ago.

This period leading up to the testing about my work in life, and being offered the opportunity to learn about art restoration, was one of the most pivotal times in my life both inwardly and outwardly, which, I hope, will become clearer as this story unfolds.

Logic

Just follow your testing, don't worry and put your full trust in God. Be obedient to your inner, not to your heart and mind, provided you feel satisfied inside and you are sure that no one you know will suffer any consequence. That is part of the training.

This kind of counter-intuitive experience is one way I believe the latihan trains the heart and mind to be obedient to our inner guidance. If we give in to the fears and doubts that the mind will create to try and retain control over our lives, we will simply be obstructing, or slowing down, our own spiritual progress, and maybe our material life too.

I say this only if you test with two or three experienced helpers. I do not recommend testing on your own because it is almost impossible to free yourself of the influence of the heart and mind and it is very hard to know where your receiving is coming from. The helpers, being free of the influence of your heart, are better able to surrender and receive clearer guidance from their inner.

Lessons Learned
Hearts Can Get In The Way, Because We Want To Be Good
Looking back forty years now I can see the truth in what Bapak had explained, that our hearts, when filled with worldly desires, can really become our enemy.

Our hearts and minds certainly desire to feel we are good, 'spiritual' people, who believe and trust in God, but the irony is, for many people following various 'spiritual' paths, their egos really do not want, or perhaps are too afraid, to relinquish control and surrender to their faith in God. They want to control their experiences. They have aims and objectives. In many cultures, the practice of 'magic' and use of paranormal powers is very common, and very real. These powers, and forces certainly exist in this world, but not for man to use. But they can be acquired, and that is the temptation. To gain powers that can be controlled. The absolute antithesis of Subud.

But, even people like myself, who have no desire to acquire such powers, often find our hearts and minds, controlled by the ego, want to cherry-pick and decide what spiritual experiences they will receive from God. Even to set limits, hoping to control and manage the inner experiences, because we don't really want things to change too much. We like what is familiar. It's safe and feels solid.

This idea of managing God is clearly absurd, because the mind is completely incapable of understanding even our own inner self, let alone understanding God's will and all the secrets of human life in the spiritual realms.

The truth is that real inner experiences, even minor ones, can be pretty scary for our heart and mind. At least that is how it has been in my limited experience.

Even if we look at the stories of the great Prophets, we read about how they usually experienced great fear when they first received real spiritual revelations. They were not looking for revelations, or expecting them. They come when God decides to send them, not before.

So fear of God is a common, natural response of the heart and mind when a higher force wakes up our inner and we experience things which are way outside of our everyday worldly experiences and earthly knowledge.

We all know how most people would react to seeing a ghost or demon, or even sensing a presence in their house. And that's just something we experience, or witness on this material level, which exists outside of ourselves, while we are still solidly grounded in our familiar worldly life.

So, imagine experiencing things that arise within yourself, that detach you from the familiarity and security of this solid worldly life. Where you are not observing something outside or separate from you. Where the awakening of your own inner self is the experience, and the heart and mind have no handle to hold on to.

When you are given experiences like that, it demands a lot of courage and faith. It also forces the heart to truly surrender and learn obedience. To go through this is to experience the fear of God, or the presence of God's power. But God is all wise and aware of each person's capacity. For many it is a very gentle process that spans many years.

For those who can take it, they may have a period of rapid inner change. But that is rare.

But generally speaking I see the 'Fear of God' as almost a prerequisite to receiving experiences that are truly beyond this world. I obviously lack the courage and capacity for being taken for trips around the universe. But even the experiences we receive in the process of learning obedience and developing our soul requires courage and trust that is the beginning of true faith that guides us on the path of inner progress.

So we are faced with quite a contradiction when we desire to better ourselves, to be a good person, who surrenders to, and worships God, because our hearts, often unconsciously, are afraid to sincerely let go of their safe and familiar worldly life, even for a few minutes.

This, I have observed, can all too often become the status quo in a person's life, where people feel they are not making progress. And that can become a source of frustration and impatience, which in turn can lead us down the wrong path, searching for various tools and methods to develop and speed up our spiritual journey.

Breaking the Status Quo

I began to be aware of a danger or difficulty that exists when a person first starts on a spiritual path during this early period after being opened in Subud. For most of us, we are still running our life based on a heart filled with desires from the nafsu. The usual culprits being our pride in the cleverness of our minds and the desire to be wise or powerful, or any other thing that makes our hearts happy in this world.

If we come to a point where we feel we are not making progress, then it can be very hard to be patient because our worldly desires will not remain passive. They will try and 'solve' the problem, but in a way that they can retain control to speed up our progress.

And there is the irony. Because it is precisely these desires to remain in control of our spiritual progress, that we are not able to surrender, and if we do not surrender we cannot receive the guidance and progress we seek, so we may languish in a kind of status quo!

So our frustrations and impatience will pressure us to find a solution, a new path. This is where we can make some serious errors, because we are all susceptible to the working of our imagination, which can be very powerful and can easily manifest the illusion of being a very spiritual person simply by studying and then imitating others who we believe have some secret mystic knowledge or power that we desire for our life.

While living in the South East Asia, I have met many people who follow various strange paths in the search of greater power and influence over their lives and other people.

It has been my observation that even those who have the sincere intention to become 'holy' by seeking God's guidance through mystic practices and powers, always fall foul of the very forces they seek. If they gain some mystical power that can influence others, they cannot resist using it to their own benefit.

It is the special powers, the ability to affect people or the pleasure of being considered wise that becomes the fruit of their efforts, none of which brings a person closer to Almighty God. In fact, quite the opposite. The well-known saying "Be careful what you wish for!" is very appropriate when looking into the world of mysticism.

Any 'power' or knowledge that can be gained through mystical practices, because they are based on our desires, can only be from this material level. And I can attest that such powers do exist and I understand why they are best to be avoided.

For a person drawn towards that path, hoping to find their way to God, I think it may be better to simply follow the teachings of an established religion. However, I do understand that those 'mystical' powers are like very attractive shiny objects, but I also see how they actually divert us from the true path to God.

Bapak spoke of these things in many talks. And of course his knowledge and experience was complete, whereas mine is has just been enough to know that what Bapak has said is real and true.

Spiritual Pride
An Oxymoron

Pride, in the form of arrogance, is a big enemy. Being British, I have a lot of experience in this area. Misplaced pride is the way people can become fanatical in their beliefs and can even act in ways that are the complete opposite of what their religion and the Prophets teach. Usually this happens when they follow a guru who is himself, consciously or unconsciously, seeking power and influence in this world.

When motivated or corrupted, by pride, rather than serving God, we are actually serving the lowest forces and desires that arise from our heart. The human heart is easily addicted to any satisfying feeling it experiences, including the feeling of being or 'acting' spiritual.

During my time in Indonesia I have met many people who sincerely believe that they are worshipping and serving God by following some 'method' or secret teachings. Some have even tried very hard to 'convert' me to follow one of these strange, mystical paths that they follow.

However, the harder they tried to persuade me the more my inner resisted, because the mere fact that they were trying so hard to persuade me was a clear sign that they were still serving their worldly heart and mind, and I saw the illusion they were chasing.

On this subject, I discovered through several experiences, some small understanding of how the inner can protect and guide us, in the same way I was 'protected' from alcohol and eating pork, as silly as that may sound. Later I will describe some more serious threats where my latihan awoke my inner to protect me. From these experiences I believe I gained two important insights.

It is impossible for a person to act against the will of God when their heart and mind are aware of, and obedient to, their inner guidance. That is, when they are no longer completely controlled by the desires of their ego.

I have seen people struggle their whole lives to get the force of their own desires under control through strange mystical teachings and methods. But success is very elusive without the intervention of Almighty God.

For me that was one of the deeper learnings that I began to understand from my first experience when I abruptly could no longer drink an alcoholic beverage or eat pork.

That change in my life did not happen because of a conscious decision or effort I made, nor was it to do with any religious belief. In fact, it was something my ego didn't want to do and could not understand at the time. On the level of a novice I was shown that if I sincerely wanted to worship God I had little say or choice in what I needed to do and to change in my lifestyle.

If I had tried to stop drinking alcohol, or eating pork, from my own will, it would have been very difficult. I would have been arguing with myself constantly because of conflicting desires. Anyone who has tried dieting will know exactly what I mean.

Another insight I found very interesting was that my first experience showed me there really was some spiritual reason or truth to what religions taught about alcohol and eating pork, and that when the inner decrees a change it just happens with no effort, no arguing and often without warning. It requires no thinking or will.

So from just this single, minor experience, I slowly came to understand that there was more than one 'I' involved in my life. There was the 'I' of my ego, which I was very familiar and comfortable with, and the 'I' of my inner self that had been dormant for many years.

My own inner, my true self, had in just a few years since my birth, become like a forgotten stranger, far from being familiar.

With this understanding I became aware that my description of the conversations with God in Hainault Forest and in Kew Gardens was inaccurate. They were in fact conversations between my heart and my inner self at a time when my inner and outer were more in harmony and could still work together in my life. Today I would say, that for me, when the inner and outer are in harmony, that is when I feel closest to God.

I apologise for that rather long digression.

Back to Restoring The Old Masters

Meantime, I found the work of cleaning and restoring old masters very satisfying. I felt it was a privilege to work on these masterpieces. Scrutinizing the areas of the painting being restored with high magnification glasses revealed so much about the brilliant technique these painters had, and their individual secrets to achieve their artistic goals. Of course I still had to do the washing up in the kitchen as part of my job description. A small price to pay.

A Generous Gift

I was still living in the attic flat across the road and I had made friends with a Subud member, Philip Milan, who was renting a much nicer flat on the second floor. He was a few years older than me.

He worked at a cancer research facility and his hobby was playing classical guitar, which he was getting very good at. Originally he had started with the usual 'folk' music of the sixties and had bought himself a very nice steel-string Hagstrom guitar that had a beautiful tone. However, at some point he felt that folk music wasn't really his thing and what he really wanted was to learn classical music, so he bought himself an expensive classical guitar and stopped playing his Hagstrom.

One day we had been talking in his flat and, as I was leaving to go back to my flat upstairs, he suddenly said, "Why don't you take the Hagstrom…you can have it." My jaw dropped. I couldn't believe what I heard. It would take six months or more of my salary to buy a quality guitar like that and I felt I could not accept his gift. But he insisted that I took it and so I became the proud owner of this Hagstrom guitar and its hard case too.

This was an extraordinary act of generosity on his part and it wasn't the last time he would go above and beyond normal bounds to assist me.

Meantime…

It was soon after I started my apprenticeship that I met an American Subud member from L.A. at a Subud gathering in London. He was quite an eccentric young man in his late-twenties who went by the odd name 'RD'. Just the initials.

He was living a very 'foot loose and fancy free' lifestyle and had no fixed abode. He was a true product of the sixties and the flower power generation, albeit slightly wilted.

One Saturday, after latihan, we were talking in the Subud Hall in Notting Hill Gate and he invited me to join him to go busking on the Portobello Road. Of course in those days, like him, I usually had my Hagstrom guitar with me wherever I went. It was the sixties after all.

This became a routine almost every weekend and through RD I was introduced to many non-Subud musicians and artists living in and around Hampstead and the Notting Hill Gate area. This was another 'in-crowd', similar to the one I grew up with in Kingston.

I think RD and I were considered interesting oddities in this group because we did not drink or use drugs, nor were we constantly chasing girls. But we played some pretty good music and could hold our own in discussions using all the contemporary vernacular of the day, so that made us acceptable.

The Dutch Experience

One day RD and I were at a party and we met with three other musicians. Over time we decided to form a group, because RD had received an invitation from one of the managers of the Paradiso in Amsterdam, to play a gig for 600 guilders. This manager was also a Subud member it turned out. Originally the plan was for just the two of us to play but now we had a band!

To prepare for the gig we needed about ninety minutes of material to perform a full set, so someone arranged for us to stay at a Game Keepers Lodge set deep in a forest far from any neighbours, somewhere near Nottingham. Apparently this was where Princess Margaret and Lord Snowden would spend odd weekends when they were courting. It was a great place for noisy rehearsals.

A month later we travelled to Amsterdam and played our gig at the Paradiso. We stayed on for another three weeks in Amsterdam during which time RD and I did a lot of busking. The Dutch, we found, were far more generous than the English. We were making good money for a couple of hours work each day, busking in front of the opera house.

The band split up with one member, our singer, going to Hamburg and the bass player going to Paris. RD and I returned to London after a month. The band never played again.

The Obedience Training Gets a Little More Serious

One weekend, about three months after returning from our gig in Amsterdam, I was with RD standing on the platform of Notting Hill Gate Underground Station when, out of nowhere, a simple question popped into my head; "How far are you from the light?"

Before I had time to even think about an answer I experienced a sensation of an enormous weight pushing down on me and my mind immediately visualized the tons of heavy London clay between me and the street far above. A vision flashed in my mind of this tiny tube we were standing in being squashed flat in an instant!

This whole experience lasted perhaps three or four seconds, but it left me feeling very shaken. A minute later a train arrived. I had to force myself to stay on the platform and not rush up to the street and instead get on the train. My mind had no idea what I had just experienced and interpreted it as some kind of claustrophobic premonition.

I am sure that any modern day psychologist would dismiss this experience as a common panic attack rather than a spiritual event, and they would certainly be at least half right. Quite simply, from my experience many spiritual and psychological events are often two sides of the same coin. More about that later.

At that time RD could see that I was dealing with something scary, but it wasn't until we were back above ground that I could explain to him what I had experienced. I was still sweating and literally shaking. His response was "Wow, cool man!" almost as though he was jealous! Well what could I expect, it was still the sixties.

The Inner Work Has Begun

The experience in Notting Hill Gate was just the beginning of a long series of similar experiences that continued for almost a year.

I feel I should say here that I have never heard of any other Subud member experiencing anything like this. I say that, not because I think I am anything special, but because it was not at all pleasant and I don't want any new members to feel disturbed or worry that this kind of experience will happen to them. This was just something I had to go through.

A couple of weeks after my underground experience I was sitting on the top deck of a London bus going over Waterloo bridge, minding my own business, when suddenly a question popped into my head; "What keeps the bridge up?"

I immediately felt a physical sensation of falling and my mind was flashed a video clip of the bridge collapsing into the Thames together with the bus. This also only lasted two or three seconds but once again I felt pretty shaken and confused afterwards.

I was not hearing voices or anything else out of the ordinary. I was just riding the bus and thinking the normal kinds of thoughts about recent events, what I might have for lunch later and the like. It was in the middle of these normal internal ponderings that the thought "What keeps the bridge up?" came floating by.

It was not these questions that surprised me or seemed unusual, it was what I experienced in response to these questions that left me shaken and confused. The answers were not given in words or with any explanation, but instead came in the form of quite terrifying virtual reality demonstrations in my mind.

I can't really say I received answers per se, it was more a receiving of the dire consequences if bridges couldn't stay up, if brakes could not work, stairs collapsed or lift cables snapped. The questions were almost rhetorical.

Just a note, for anyone who has experienced severe vertigo, which I did with an ear infection, the experience of being thrown around when the brain cannot interpret the signals from the inner ear, is the closest thing I have felt to compare with the experience on the bus, and a few more that were to come.

Over time these questions became more varied but most of them would still involve a very unpleasant response. At the time I had no idea what was prompting these thoughts or what their purpose was, other than to introduce me to some very scary experiences. It was two or three years later that the understanding began to surface into my consciousness.

Life Goes On

Although I was having these unpleasant experiences once or twice a week, I still had my job to do cleaning and restoring old masters. Life must go on.

The Path is Being Prepared
Provenance

About two months after I returned from Holland Philip came up to my flat to ask me if my boss would be interested in buying an old painting from his brother. He told me it had been hanging in a sports club next to a dart board and was full of tiny holes. Clearly the club members were amongst the worst dart players in the UK.

I asked him how much did his brother want to sell it for and he said he wasn't sure, but I could make an offer.

A few days later he brought the painting home and I looked

at it. It was filthy with a thick layer of nicotine from years in a smoky bar and indeed it was covered in hundreds of pin prick holes.

All I could tell was that it was early nineteenth century and the subject was a fairly standard English landscape with cows in a field. As best I could see, the technique of the artist was certainly beyond that of an amateur, but I could not find any signature. I said I would show it to my boss and see what he thought.

The next day I brought the painting up to the studio and examined it under proper lighting with my boss. He rolled his eyes at the amount of damage. He confirmed it was early nineteenth century, but with such a common subject and no signature that we could find, it was pretty hard to make an evaluation.

I returned that night with the painting to my friend and said that my boss couldn't give an evaluation, especially without a signature, and the amount of restoration it would need made it a very risky proposition to buy. My friend didn't seem in the least surprised and said his brother would be happy with fifty pounds. "The frame might be worth that much," he suggested.

The next day I told my boss that we could buy the painting for 50 pounds. My boss thought for a minute and then came up with a proposition for me. He would buy the painting, but I would have to clean and restore it. If it was good enough to sell to one of his clients then we would split the money with me, fifty-fifty. I was more than happy to take the risk.

After cleaning the painting, I was able to discern a signature, 'Mark Fisher'. My boss was not familiar with the name, but that day he was picking up a painting from Christies in London and said he would ask the expert on 19th century British Artists if Mark Fisher was a listed artist.

It transpired that Mark Fisher was a German artist who was quite well known in his day and had a patron, the Earl of

Portsmouth. There were a few collectors of his work, and a painting, if properly restored, could fetch up to five hundred pounds at auction!

I felt bad with my downstairs neighbour because we had only paid fifty pounds and now it was valued at possibly ten times that amount. I explained to him what happened and suggested he tell his brother and we should agree to pay a higher price. My neighbour immediately rejected that idea saying a "deal is a deal" and his brother was already very happy with the 50 pounds, so there was no need for further negotiations. This was now the second time he showed an unusual spirit of generosity.

After having the painting relined at Christies, it took me more than two months of concentrated work in my own time to complete the cleaning and restoration. A photograph of the restored painting was placed in Christies' auction catalogue and Christies made sure that all the known collectors of Mark Fisher's work were invited to the auction at the end of the following month.

Things Happen in Parallel
Whose Plan Is This?

At the time the painting was due to be auctioned, Bapak was touring several countries on a world trip and that July he was visiting the Subud members in Holland. One of my best friends, Ramzi, who had joined Subud just before me, had managed to get to Holland to join their congress and to listen to Bapak's talks and do latihan with our Dutch brothers.

When he returned to Kingston he was so exhilarated by the experience that he decided he must follow Bapak to America where Bapak would attend the Subud USA gathering at Skymont in West Virginia in August 1970.

When I met him he spoke enthusiastically about how great it was seeing Bapak in another country, because he was treated like a guest too. He then insisted that I should join him on this trip to America in August.

What with the strange and mostly scary experiences I had been having I really did not feel comfortable in myself about travelling to America at that time. Ever since the Notting Hill Gate incident I had been having more experiences and they were becoming increasingly frequent. The result was I was developing a growing feeling of insecurity.

But now my problem was I had no rational or acceptable reason to say no to Ramzi. I was not willing to talk about the weird experiences I was having at that time.

I tried to comfort myself with the knowledge that neither of us had any money for airfares and accommodation, so I was pretty sure his plan would never happen. That brought some relief for my nervous heart.

In fact, Ramzi tried very hard to raise the money for his trip. but with absolutely no success. Meantime I got news from my boss that our painting had sold at Christies auction for 1,400 pounds sterling!!

My boss knew there was some plan for me to go to America to attend a Subud event and he also knew it would take a few weeks for the money to come through from Christies, so he said he would advance me 400 pounds and give me two weeks off work.

Far from feeling happy my heart slumped and I was beginning to feel pretty nervous that I could end up going after all. I just knew that if I was going, Ramzi had to go too. I was not going to travel alone. Meantime, Ramzi still hadn't been able to raise any money and he was beginning to have doubts.

With 400 pounds sterling, I had more than enough to book tickets for both Ramzi and myself. As I said earlier, if I was going to America, I definitely was not going on my own! So a week before we were to leave we went down to Thomas Cook Tours and I paid 50% on two tickets.

As the days passed and my friend still had not managed to raise any money for the trip, he decided to test with the helpers if it was right for him to go. The following Thursday, after lati-han, we asked the group helpers to test for both of us.

When the helpers came out of the latihan room they looked sadly at my friend and said their testing had indicated that he definitely should not go. As for me, according to their testing, I absolutely had to go.

My heart sank to the floor like a quivering mass of jelly because I was still dealing with these very unnerving experiences and the sense of fear and insecurity was accumulating in my heart. I really did not want to go.

Remember what I wrote earlier about the need for courage.

Now I was in a dilemma. The testing had shown that I absolutely should go to America but my nervous heart was saying "don't go!". My heart was not being obedient because it was afraid, which I knew was wrong. So my heart made a deal with God. Very simply the deal was; If God really wants me to go to America I will go, but I will not do anything to help or make it happen.

That's how foolish the human heart can be!

I did have one fall-back fact to cling to like a security blanket, which was that this was Thursday night and my flight was booked for Monday and I had made no preparations beyond booking the tickets. I had no idea what other preparations I needed to make, but I was fairly confident that there was not enough time left to arrange everything and I would have to cancel the trip. That thought felt so good it actually calmed my heart down. You see how the heart and mind can manipulate us, without us really knowing?

Who is Running this Show?

That night, when I got home, I met Philip at home and told him about the testing. He asked me if I had been to get my vaccinations, that were still required by the US in 1970. "No," I replied.

Have you got your visa for the US? "No."

Have you got your ticket? "Yes. But I haven't picked it up yet," I said unenthusiastically.

He looked quite shocked and told me that I must get up early the next morning and have my passport ready.

The next morning, he actually came upstairs before 7am to wake me up. By 8.30 am I was sitting in his new MG sports car and we set off for Tolworth Towers to get my vaccinations. The next day, Saturday, I would have to pick up my official Government Issued Yellow Vaccination book, which I would need to show US Immigration to get a visa.

After getting my shots, he then drove like the wind to Thomas Cook's so I could cancel my friends booking and collect my ticket. We then raced all the way up to Grosvenor Square in London to the American Embassy, as only an MG sports car can do.

We entered the embassy and found our way to the visa section, which was a very large hall with rows of benches like church pews, and all of them were filled with people waiting either for an interview or to get their passports back after getting their visa.

My friend made his way through the crowd and returned to the back of the hall clutching the application forms. Apparently the embassy would not be able to process any more applications that day so we would have to return the next, which was Saturday.

That night Philip filled in the forms for me. He just read the questions and then wrote in the answer that I gave him. I was keeping to my side of the deal with God, neither helping or hindering.

We were a bit stumped at the question 'What is your purpose for visiting the United States?' Eventually I said, "Put for spiritual reasons."

As I sat in the MG sports car the next morning my heart was feeling much calmer. The reason for this was the note at the bottom of the form that said something like; 'Allow three working days to process your visa request'.

Saturday was a half day, Sunday the Embassy is closed and at 4pm on Monday my flight took off. There seemed little chance of getting a visa and making the flight now. Oh what joy and relief for my cowardly heart.

Monday was also the day that the Subud meeting started in Skymont, so there was little point catching a flight later in the week. The more I thought about it the more it looked like there was no way I would be going to the US.

So I felt a lot more relaxed as we set off for Tolworth Tower again to pick up my yellow vaccination book and then from there we drove straight to the American Embassy.

We arrived at the Embassy by mid-morning. I had my passport and the application forms in my hand as I made my way down the aisle between the pews to the long counter where the immigration officers were receiving and checking the passports and forms, stacking them up and passing them through a small hatch in the wall behind them to more immigration personnel for processing. The hall was full of people and I was happy to see there were multiple stacks of passports all along the counter.

I gave my passport to an officer who quickly checked my passport and the completed forms. I was applying for an eight-day visa to visit America for spiritual reasons. He gave me a quizzical look and then told me to go and sit down and wait to be called for an interview.

As I made my way to the back of the hall I looked at what

must have been more than a hundred people waiting, and they were all ahead of me. I was beginning to feel even more confident that it was not God's intention for me to go to America at all, and the helpers testing must have been wrong, when, suddenly, I heard my name being called out.

I turned around and went back to a different immigration officer who handed me my passport. I asked him what was wrong and he took the passport back, flicked through it and handed it back to me saying, "Nothing's wrong."

I flipped through my passport and then saw a large green and red ink stamp that almost covered the entire page. My heart sank and the anxiety returned as I said a meek "thank you", turned, and slowly walked back to Philip. He saw me holding my passport and assumed something was wrong too, until I showed him the visa. It was a multiple entry visa, valid for three years and I was allowed to work! ...IMPOSSIBLE!!

This whole trip was not my plan, and I had no desire to go to America or Skymont. But, there definitely was a plan and it worked perfectly, with no assistance from me. All I had promised was 'not to resist' and just keep following, even though the result was against the wishes of my heart.

I did not realize it at the time but this was an important lesson in being obedient to my inner guidance and to stop just following the wishes of my heart or trusting the logic of my own mind.

A Rough Ride

I spent the next day, Sunday, with my Subud friends, all of who were excited that I was going to attend the Subud USA gathering during Bapak's visit. Some were even jealous in a friendly way. As for me, I felt nothing but impending doom. I felt like a lamb being led to slaughter and I really did not want to die!

The next day my dear neighbour drove me to Heathrow and

dropped me off at the departure entrance. I was dressed in a suit, carrying a small suitcase in one hand and my Hagstrom guitar in its hard case in the other. I had $200 in cash for my eight-day trip.

Like a zombie I walked to the check-in and then proceeded to the departure lounge. My anxiety was making me feel like I was in a bubble and I was hardly aware of anything else going on around me.

I remember boarding the plane, a 707, and feeling how crowded it was. I sat down and tightened my seat belt. My heart was actually filled with fear and I had no expectation of ever reaching my destination. I sat there silently praying to God as the cabin crew closed the doors.

I was praying for a miracle when I heard some disturbance towards the front of the plane and I could see the door was being opened again. A man from the airline entered the plane and was calling my name looking for me. My heart soared with relief thinking that something terrible must have happened, like my mother had been rushed to hospital with an in-growing toenail, which would mean I could get off the plane and go back home. A miracle!

I raised my hand and the man quickly came up to me and thrust a small piece of paper into my hand and left. I unfolded the piece of paper and saw a name and a New York telephone number scribbled in biro and a second number for Skymont, near Front Royal, West Virginia. At the bottom was the signature of a Subud member from the Kingston group who had come to see me off but had been delayed and just missed me.

It was then I realised that I had no idea where I was going other than Skymont West Virginia. I understood in my head that not knowing where I was going could be a problem, but my heart was not bothered, because I still had this deep feeling of doom which my heart assumed was a premonition that I wouldn't ever make it to the US anyway. This sounds comical now but at the time I was within a millimetre of having a panic attack.

Not long after that we were airborne and I just continued with my silent praying, expecting something bad to happen at any moment. About three hours into the flight my brain was exhausted and just about numb with fear when a question popped into my head; "What keeps the plane in the air?"

I won't describe what I experienced. Enough to say it was very unpleasant and left me more convinced than ever that I would never land in America.

Three hours later the captain's voice came over the speakers informing us that there was a bad thunderstorm over JFK airport, so we were diverting to Boston. The turbulence increased and the plane was getting buffeted around as the night sky lit up with lightning flashes, which just fed my fear that something bad was going to happen.

In the end it turned out that we had been circling in a holding pattern waiting for the storm to pass and we landed at JFK two hours late. I was still alive but feeling very disorientated as I picked up my luggage and followed the other passengers out into the main TWA terminal.

Because we were so late, the terminal was actually closing for the night and in just a few minutes every passenger had magically disappeared into taxis or had been picked up by family. I stood on my own in this huge hall wondering where I should go as one by one the lights were being turned off.

Suddenly a young man stepped out of the dark and came over to me and asked me, somewhat ironically, "Where are you going?".

We spoke for a little while and then he asked me if I wanted something to eat or drink, because he could go over to the Pan Am terminal that was still open and buy me something. I said I would like a cheese sandwich and a coffee with milk and I gave him ten dollars. After about twenty minutes it occurred to me that I was probably a victim of a scam.

I then went to the toilet which, fortunately, still had some lights on. Not only lights but there was music being piped in to the toilet, which I found pretty surreal. Musical toilets hadn't arrived in England yet. I went back outside and sat down on a long sofa like seat. About an hour had passed since I handed the stranger my ten dollars when suddenly he appeared with my sandwich and two cold coffees.

My faith in mankind had been restored. We sat there until dawn when he said he had to go. Soon after he left some airport staff began arriving. I asked one of them how I could get into the city and he suggested I took a taxi as there were no buses until eight o'clock.

An hour later I arrived at the Greyhound station in New York where I bought a ticket to Washington. New York looked just like it did in the movies, but it smelt awful. I had arrived in the middle of a strike by the sanitary workers and rubbish was piling up on the residential streets all over the city I was told.

I realized how ignorant and stupid I and my friend in England were when we booked the tickets. I should have flown direct to Washington because I now had a sixteen-hour bus ride from New York to Washington ahead of me.

I tried calling the New York number written on the scrap of paper but there was no answer.

The Greyhound bus left late in the afternoon. The ride was uneventful, but I had the opportunity to see some stunning scenery on the way. After sixteen hours, the bus finally entered the terminal in Washington the next morning and I asked about a bus to Skymont near Front Royal. At the ticket window I was told there was only one bus a day to Front

Royal and it had already left.

Then I remembered my friend who had scribbled some information on a small piece of paper and got it to me on the plane. I retrieved the piece of paper from my jacket pocket and called the Skymont number.

I was a bit taken aback when I heard the voice of a child answer. I asked if his dad was there and he said his dad was outside somewhere. Then a slightly older voice came on the phone and I explained my situation. He sounded about ten years old and his only suggestion was that I take a taxi because it's not that far, or stay the night in Washington and take the bus the next day.

I found the taxi rank outside the bus station and a driver got out of the lead cab and helped put my suitcase and guitar in the trunk. I got in the back of the cab and he asked me where I wanted to go. I gave him the piece of paper with the address and saw him hesitate. He said, "That's a long way, are you sure?" I just shrugged my shoulders and said "There are no more buses today."

He started the engine and we set off. As we travelled out of the city I sensed he was pretty tense. It wasn't long before he suddenly pointed at the sun visor and in a pretty aggressive voice said, "I keep all my money up here!"

Somewhat startled I didn't quite know how to respond, so I just said, "Oh, why?" He answered that he didn't want any trouble. If someone wants to rob him they can just take the money. He then went on to explain that the previous week his friend had been stabbed in his taxi and later died, because he wouldn't hand over his money.

I finally understood that his nervousness was because he thought I might have a plan to rob him on some quiet road outside the city.

I simply said to him, "We don't do that kind of thing in England" and almost immediately I felt his tension go down. Up until then I don't think he realized that I was English.

Soon after that he started telling me about his family, his son and three daughters. He told me his dream was to save enough money to buy a small boat so one day he could take his son fishing up at the lake and maybe even buy a small cabin there.

I was quite astonished how, in the space of two minutes, he had gone from being a very tense, aggressive and unsociable African American taxi driver to a relaxed, happy husband and father working hard for his family and his dreams.

After about an hour and a half driving he announced that he was hungry and asked me if I wanted anything to eat. I had only eaten a muffin on the bus from New York so I was certainly ready for some lunch. He pulled over at a restaurant and asked what I wanted. I said a hamburger with French fries would be fine. He said I didn't need to come in with him and about five minutes later he returned with two huge cheeseburgers, French fries and a small salad in two large paper bags one of which he handed to me.

I asked him how much I owed him and he said it was on him. I insisted that I should pay for it and he insisted lunch was on him. So we sat in the cab and ate our lunch and chatted. I could see this guy was a very decent human being and how stressful and damaging it must be for him to live in such a harsh city environment. America was pretty rough, particularly for a black American like him.

After more than three hours of travelling, we finally turned into the driveway of Skymont and drove up to the large cabin that was being used for the reception and admin office.

I looked at the meter. It read $98. I looked at the reception area where there were about half a dozen kids running around and I wondered which one had suggested I "take a taxi because it's not that far".

I did not begrudge at all paying the taxi driver but it did mean after paying him and the Greyhound bus ticket and one muffin and a coffee at the airport, I now only had $8 dollars left for my eight-day stay in America.

I guess it was fortunate that I was still in this very disorientated and detached state because it didn't even occur to me that I no longer had enough money to get back to Washington, let alone to JFK in New York, perhaps because, at the back of my mind, I was now convinced that I would never see England again. The 'doom and gloom' anxiety remained and my brain could only interpret it as a premonition of my imminent demise.

The Hippie Wild-West Spiritual Picnic

After finding one of the adults in charge of accommodation I was escorted back down the driveway and across the road to a large field with many tents and parked vehicles. It was there that I was introduced to the group from Subud Cincinnati, who kindly agreed to 'accommodate' me for the week.

They had come to Skymont in a yellow school bus which they had converted into a make shift camper van. The bus was reserved for the women and children. The men slept in tents.

It never occurred to me that I would be camping out for a week in the hot and humid air of the Blue Mountains.

I put my suitcase in the tent where I would sleep and my guitar went in the bus for safe keeping. I had been wearing a suit for three days since I left Kingston and had no opportunity to shower. I had only managed to shave in the men's room at the Greyhound station. I had one change of trousers, a couple of shirts, three T-shirts and some underwear and socks.

On this side of the road with all the tents and young people, it definitely had the feel of a mini-Woodstock, especially when it rained, which it did quite often. The shower facility befitted the general conditions of the camp.

I remember very little about that week in Skymont. I know the Cincinnati group were very generous in their hospitality, and I later discovered that they were very aware that I was going through some pretty intense inner turmoil, which in those days was usually described as a crisis.

A Few Words About 'Crisis'

A 'crisis' as I understand it, occurs when a person's inner-self awakens and takes back control from the familiar and comfortable 'ego-self'. This 'ego-self' is the sum of everything a person relates to and projects to the world when they say 'I'.

There are several different ways we may experience a 'crisis' and most are wonderful and uplifting, but there is a process of purification that can be less pleasant.

That was what I started to experience towards the end of my first year in Subud. As best I can describe it, this kind of crisis is when the 'ego-self' suddenly experiences the presence of the inner life force which immediately gets to work sorting and cleaning things out, which, if it is deep and intense, will put the heart and mind in to a state of shock and considerable confusion.

Some Comfort, I hope

I would like to note here that it is many years since I have met or even heard of anyone experiencing an intense period of 'crisis' like this. For most people this process of separating and reintroducing the 'inner-self' to the 'ego-self' happens slowly and gently, and although it may take many years of gradual purification, this slower pace will not cause the ego to experience any great shock or disturbance in the member's everyday life.

Back in those days I believe the world was very different. The state of the western countries and their societies during the fifties and sixties allowed many Subud members to go through some pretty intense periods of purification without too much disruption to either their day to day lives or to those around them. I know that many of my friends from those times could all write their own very interesting books about their experiences after being opened. Probably more interesting than this one!

As I was young, single and basically unemployed at that time, during my first two years in Subud, my inner and the latihan pretty much had free range to push ahead with whatever intense purification and re-education of my butler and servants that my inner deemed necessary. I certainly believe that we are only given as much as we can handle, and our outer situation is always a factor in our inner progress.

Purification, Education, Rehabilitation

As an analogy, it is like the master of a large country estate returning home after being away for many years, only to find that the butler and servants have taken over the house as though they owned it. This situation had gone on so long that the servants had even forgotten that the true master really exists as a separate entity or that the butler was simply the head servant.

For most of us it gets to the point that our butler firmly believes he is the master! These servants occupy, influence and often control the heart and mind completely. They make all the decisions in our life according to their 'needs and wants' alone.

They judge what is good and bad and they will determine our fate, but they know nothing of our destiny.

This is how it is for human beings who have lost contact with, and forgotten that there is a true master within every human being, which we call the soul or inner self. They are under the control of their heart that is itself controlled by these lower entities or servants.

Actually I believe we can all see that this is the common condition for almost all human beings in this modern world.

Indeed, for most people, by the time they become teenagers the 'head butler' or 'ego' will have already usurped the position of the inner master for so long that they become convinced that the inner self, the 'real master' is no more than a mythical character or at best an entity called the soul, that will exist only after they die.

Even many of those who are seeking or actively following a spiritual path, do not realize that it is often their heart and imagination that desires to find God and wants to become a good, spiritual person, without realizing that it is impossible for our heart and intellect to find, let alone understand, Almighty God.

This is because their inner is not involved and is not able to guide them to the right path, as only the inner can. (Not to say that God, with His infinite grace does not intervene to save people from their fate and open a path to their destiny. There is no limit on the grace and generosity of Almighty God.)

Over time the butler and all the servants, when left unsupervised, will allow the stately home to fall into disrepair. In the worse cases the ego would allow endless parties to go on with all kinds of strangers allowed to roam freely through the house. These entities invariably use and abuse anything they find. Some of them, although strangers, even take up residence.

Letting strangers in would be the effect of promiscuity on the inner; drugs, gambling, pornography and pretty much anything that damages or soils a person's inner feeling, which will often damage the physical body too.

Most of the servants have forgotten what their true duties are, so nothing gets cleaned, nothing gets repaired and from the inner point of view the mansion descends towards the level of a slum. This becomes the level of our inner self, living in a slum.

However, for the servants it is a magnificent slum and a fantastic life, so they certainly don't want anything to change. It feels so wonderful to be in charge, free to do whatever you like, put off doing your work without getting into trouble. Enjoying many excesses without restraint or guilt.

So of course they will panic and even resist if the true master suddenly turns up one day, out of the blue, and starts inspecting his home and seeing all the damage the servants have caused. The leaks in the roof, broken furniture, piles of dirty clothes and rubbish left all over the house and strange, dark entities acting like they belong there.

This is a metaphor for the inner state of many human beings by the time they are in their mid-twenties. Most will not be aware of this, because they identify themselves with their ego and servants. They participate in the self-destructive activities from which their heart and mind derive great pleasure.

In a human being the damage and abuse these servants cause can be the result of drugs, alcohol, multiple intimate sexual relationships, unbridled greed, pride and anger, lying and being deceitful and all the other negative excesses many people tend towards as teenagers and young adults.

To build on this metaphor, I would add that the mansion may look wonderful from the outside just as a human being can look attractive and be dressed as a good, kind, successful person worthy of respect, but inside the servants are in charge and it is a terrible mess that gets worse the deeper into the mansion you go. So be careful when you choose to knock on a door of someone you admire.

So in a crisis it can be like the butler is suddenly confronted by his master and caught red-handed, failing in his duties. The butler is powerless to do anything in the face of the inner authority and will be in fear of losing his job, and let's not forget that his job is literally his life on this earth, which is to maintain this one coarse body so that it will live for as long as possible on the Earth, as a place for a human soul to reside.

Something else I learned from my crisis was that the 'ego' generally associates the inner self with death. This is why an experience that truly comes from the inner realm of the human soul can be so disturbing or scary, because the heart and mind generally assume this is a sign that their time is up and they are about to meet their maker, not in the human realm, but in the realm of servants.

Unmasked in America

At the end of the Skymont gathering, Bapak and his entourage left to return to Washington and most of the Subud members packed up their tents, loaded up their cars and started making their way back to their home towns. By any normal standards I should have been in a total quandary watching the Cincinnati group dismantling their tents. I had no idea as to what I should do now.

I was down to less than $4 and had no way to get to JFK for my flight back to England. But before I could even start thinking about those practicalities the Cincinnati group had already decided that I was going to be their guest in Cincinnati.

I remember little about the journey from Skymont to Cincinnati with about a dozen adults and kids in the yellow school bus. I felt like an actor in the wrong film, sitting in the bus with all these adults and children bouncing down the highway. The scenery was quite beautiful I remember, and we got to Cincinnati after dark.

In Cincinnati the bus stopped in front of a very large two

storey house where several of the Subud members lived. There was not a spare room for me but they kindly made up a bed for me in the entrance hall at the bottom of the stairs by the doorway into the living room and dining room.

I should explain here that during my stay in Skymont my feelings of anxiety had mellowed somewhat, and by the time I arrived in Cincinnati I was more in a state that I can only describe as 'stunned acceptance', or resignation to whatever was going on with me in both my inner experiences and my outer circumstances.

It is hard to describe this state, but while my heart and mind felt very disorientated and disconnected from my surroundings, I had at the same time a very deep understanding of what was going on around me, especially what was going on in the lives of the people I was meeting. Especially things they kept well hidden. These were insights that simply popped into my mind seemingly out of nowhere.

During this period, as a person was talking to me, any person, I would hear and be able to follow what they were saying in normal conversation, but simultaneously I would also hear my own inner voice giving a kind of dispassionate running commentary to me about the true state of that person as they talked.

I would spontaneously become aware of some problem or fear that person had in their current life, or more commonly from their past, and was keeping well-hidden or buried deep within themselves. Things they did not want to face or were not fully aware of themselves. Often these things were like log-jams in their lives, or important decisions that were being delayed or avoided, and that were holding them back in life or causing great pain.

The most common issues I saw that seemed to be the biggest obstacle to people's progress both in their spiritual and their worldly, material life, were not to do with lack of money, unemployment, accommodation or other issues we all consider key problems in life.

Almost every problem and insight my inner voice would describe to me dealt with people's relationships and how much damage was being done in bad relationships, both current and in the past, where lust was commonly mistaken for love. In addition, there were so many painful problems between young adults and their parents that they could not resolve.

Parents & Children

For many people I would see terrible knots between parents and children that were filling people with pain, anger, insecurity, loneliness and great sadness, that they buried deep in their hearts, like trash in a toxic landfill covered with a thin layer of top soil. And then they suffer and get frustrated, because they can never find a way to make their own heart happy as they try to build their life on a foundation of landfill trash.

I cannot describe the myriad of different problems young adults had with parents and vice-versa, but I know that, as they were in the middle of introducing themselves and making small talk, I was frequently prompted to cut them off and make some reference to an issue or event in their life, which was completely unknown to me and indeed meant absolutely nothing to me, but would immediately touch a nerve in them. The common reaction would be for them to burst into tears. This was quite perturbing to me, and even more so for them.

The words of advice that spontaneously flowed quietly out of my mouth almost always involved suggesting they needed to find the courage to go and ask forgiveness from their parents, regardless of whether they thought the problem was their parents' fault or not.

I can say, looking back now, that to follow that advice really did need courage because it meant swallowing pride, letting go of anger, letting go of pain and blame and any sense of 'injustice'. I do know that for those who were able to follow the advice it brought very positive results and they kindly made a point of letting me know that.

Lovers & Strangers

This was the sixties when "Make Love not War" was the slogan sweeping over many of the youth in America and the rest of the western world. So there were plenty of 'bad' relationships that teenagers and young adults in western cultures had got themselves into.

Indeed, many young people had suffered a string of bad relationships and 'one night stands,' not realizing the awful consequences to their own inner life. A situation which I believe is even more common today.

When was the last time you heard a friend talk about promiscuity? These days it is so common and acceptable that promiscuity is no longer considered 'a thing' in most western societies. I know I must sound like an archaic prude, but I am only sharing what I was shown by my inner.

When I met a person who was in such a relationship, or had been damaged by such relationships, I was never prompted to say anything to them directly. What would often happen though is the person would start talking about themselves, quite uncontrollably, and suddenly seeing their own mistakes and at some point start crying, also uncontrollably. Two, I remember even collapsed in tears to the floor in front of me in a similar way that I found myself crying on the floor after the Swanwick Congress.

If I had not been in a state of crisis I am sure I would have found this extremely alarming, but I was so detached from outer events I had no reaction at all except to wait for instructions from

103

my inner. All I was doing as far as I knew, was 'witnessing' their 'confession' and purification, while I continued to surrender to God. Whatever they were experiencing was entirely between them and God, and none of my concern.

Quite a few couples I met during the three weeks in Cincinnati, I heard, ended their toxic relationships and parted ways in the weeks after I left Cincinnati. Well, three couples I know of. Coincidence? Well, maybe. It really doesn't matter. Personally I remain very grateful to all those people, because they showed enormous generosity, and patience with me during my stay in America.

Socializing in An Alarming Way

During my stay in Cincinnati, several Subud members who I had never met before would drop by the house and would introduce themselves to me and start talking about the usual kind of things people share when making new friends, when suddenly, out of the blue, I would ask them a question or make a statement about an issue they were struggling with, completely unrelated to what they had been talking about. But nothing to do with relationships.

Naturally that would, if not shock them, certainly surprise them. Very often these strangers would just spontaneously start crying, as though some big knot had been untied or some dam had been breached deep in their feelings.

When things like this happened I was acutely aware that I was simply a passive witness. My ego had no control over these insights. There was no thinking involved nor even a desire to engage in a conversation with any of these people. So this was not some special ability I possessed or controlled. I could neither make it happen or stop it from happening. So do not think I was doing anything that I can take credit for. I was no more than a ventriloquist's dummy. I can gladly report such things rarely happen like that these days.

I later came to understand that this is an ability I am sure all human beings can and will experience when they are in the right state. But I am not sure if there is a way to deliberately 'put' oneself in the right state. I certainly can't.

It is something received and I would say it is received only when needed for something important. The difference here was that I was in crisis, which means the latihan was strong and continuous within me all the time.

That state I mentioned is the submission of the ego to the Inner-self. If this happens while listening to a person talking, then while we remain able to listen and respond normally to what the person is saying, at the same time we may hear another conversation between our inner-self and the other person's inner-self that I believe is far more important.

So while a person would be happily talking about something in their day to day life that they find exciting or interesting, and that we would all describe as 'normal' conversation, their inner may be crying out for help and lamenting something in their situation that they were keeping well-hidden, or perhaps were not fully aware of themselves. In the inner world there are no secrets, no lies, games or manipulations.

Hearing the inner voices of others, whether friends or strangers, is not a very pleasant experience. Many people think it would be fantastic to be able to know other people's deepest, personal secrets, like reading their minds any time you want, as though it was some kind of superpower. But it is not like that. Not like that at all.

The Screw Is Tightened

Perhaps I can give a partial explanation for this state I was in not mentioned before. It was whilst in America that I received the answer to all those questions that popped into my head in England about underground trains, bridges and planes. The fear and near panic I experienced with those questions pale in comparison to the answer.

A very simple answer. The tunnel didn't collapse, the bridge stayed up and the plane could fly... "because of God's power". When the reality of such a simple answer is received as an experience, it is overwhelming. That God's power is expressed in the nature of every material He created, in every law of physics that determines the possibilities and limits of all that is done on earth... I shuddered physically in awe of that reality.

A tiny glimpse of the almighty power of Almighty God. And if God wanted to change the nature of stone, or metal, or any law of physics, or any other material object then, in a flash, this entire world would cease to exist as we know it. In a flash! That easy. That scary. That is how much we, all of humanity, are dependent on God.

And then a special announcement for me. That inner voice delivered a warning to me; "If you forget God, He will forget you!"... "And if God forgets you, you will cease to exist. You will cease to ever have existed. Your mother will have no memory of giving birth to you. Your friends will have no memory of knowing you. Every word you wrote, every word you spoke will be erased. You will become nothing."

That was quite a terrifying reality to receive and experience in my feelings. So terrifying that I immediately found myself silently repeating the name of God in my heart, truly believing that if I stopped, even for a moment, poof! I would disappear and no-one would even notice.

And yet I was still able to walk around, talk to people, eat and take care of myself, but never stopped repeating God's name in my heart. This was the state I was in when blurting out comments to people that would set them off crying. I was actually totally consumed with my own imminent demise to be concerned whether they had cheated on their wife or were harbouring some evil desires.

The other Subud members in Cincinnati understood that I was going through something particularly intense, and were very gracious in their readiness to create a place for me to have this experience, rather than having me carted off to a psychiatric facility.

Super Powerless

I shall try my best to explain later why, based on my experience, the idea of acquiring 'super spiritual powers' is so wrong and potentially dangerous. This is important to mention because I believe the idea of 'spiritual powers' is relevant to the much broader motives why many people desire to start on a spiritual path in this life. Others, including myself, are more inclined to seek 'spiritual guidance'. A desire to change their life and character for the better.

But that is quite another subject which I will come to later. I certainly did not understand any of this during my stay in Cincinnati in 1970. I was basically just a hippie in a suit with a guitar and no idea what was going on inside me other than I must not forget God for even an instant.

The Kaleidoscope of Life

I spent a total of three weeks under the care of the Cincinnati Subud group. This was not a holiday for me but more like a safe retreat to undergo some pretty intense purification that could only happen in these or similar circumstances, as I was incapable of really functioning in a normal way.

It would take far too long for me to fully explain everything I experienced during my three week stay in Cincinnati. So I think it is enough simply to summarize a few of the 'highlights' because my reason for writing this book is to focus on the Subud experiences I had after I was opened, as they are part of a universal inner life that I hope will be relevant for newly opened members and a confirmation that at least some of the things Bapak explained in his many talks are real and can be experienced by simple, ordinary people like myself.

So please do not mistake this book for an autobiography and certainly not a work of fiction either. The following are incidents that happened to me during my month in America, and something of my understanding about them.

The understanding always came much later, sometimes years passed before I was able to peel the onion and get to the core of the experience. I hope that through the peeling of the onion, going deeper and deeper in understanding I may have achieved some small degree of wisdom that may be useful to others.

Rapid Fire from the Inner

Whilst having dinner at home with all the occupants of the house in Cincinnati, both grownups and children, I would be asked odd questions about Subud UK and other aspects of my life. On two occasions I felt as though my tongue was suddenly swelling up and it felt so big I could not continue talking, so I would have to stop, in mid-sentence! Fortunately, this group at the table had already decided that I was in some kind of crisis so, after a short pause, they would start a new conversation amongst themselves and I would continue to finish my dinner, which didn't seem to be hindered by my swollen tongue sensation.

I lost my hearing for a day. It was not that I went deaf and could not hear, but when people spoke, their words were just meaningless sounds that my brain could not interpret. So again people would speak to me, but I could not answer because my ears and brain were not functioning correctly.

I had had a similar experience in England with my sight. Suddenly colours and shapes didn't exist as solid references to my surroundings. This was very short, only five minutes, but long enough to raise a momentary fear that I was going blind.

As I mentioned earlier, I slept on a sort of camp bed in the hall at the bottom of the stairs and, as usual, in the morning people were coming down and passing me on the way to the dining room. They would greet me as they passed, if my eyes were open.

One morning my eyes were open and I got a series of greetings followed soon after with calls to have some breakfast. But this morning I could not answer. In fact, I could not move my body at all.

After breakfast, all but two women left for work or school until lunch time, when some returned. I was still in the camp bed. I heard their greetings but still could not respond.

That evening everyone was home and it was time for dinner and one of the children came to ask me if I wanted dinner. I looked at him but could not answer. About half an hour later the man of the house came out of the living room and asked me, "Do you want to come to latihan tonight?" Immediately I sat up, said "yes", took some clean clothes to the bathroom and got ready.

These experiences were pretty straight forward. This was just a rather speeded up form of purification. I learned that as the latihan penetrates our physical body it not only 'cleans', but more importantly, can influence the functioning of our body.

I now know that it is not uncommon to lose the use of a faculty or even a talent while it goes through the process of purification and repair.

The result of these events in Cincinnati was very similar to the first experience of my inner penetrating part of my physical body, which made it impossible to drink alcohol or eat pork.

These experiences in America had an impact on my daily life that made it impossible for me to use swear words, impossible for me to gossip or speak badly about people, or tell lies. My inner would not give me permission to do these things.

My tongue/speaking was being purified. The same for my hearing. My ears would hurt if people argued, gossiped, used swear words or said hurtful things. I can only describe it as being similar to how many people feel when they hear chalk squeaking on a blackboard. Perhaps not quite so bad as that, but unpleasant enough.

The day I spent not moving in my bed was the beginning of quite a long process of my inner penetrating and cleaning my entire body. I shall come back to this later.

Of course I can write about this now in a very calm and matter-of-fact kind of way, but at the time it was not like that at all.

It is also important to remember the state I was in throughout this time. My mind had been trying to rationalize what I had been experiencing ever since the incident on Notting Hill Gate underground station. I had this great sense of doom and gloom well before leaving to America.

After a couple of months of scary 'questions and answers', my heart and mind were pretty much exhausted from still trying to maintain what they knew as a 'normal' life, but it was an incredible struggle because there was this force acting within me that my ego could not control or predict, which kept throwing my heart and mind off their familiar pedestal.

By the time I got to Cincinnati that exhaustion had finally worn my ego down to some form of submission to my 'fate'. I no longer had control and I was going to have to accept that. So if my tongue swells up and I stop talking mid- sentence in front of people, then so be it! I had nothing left of my ego to even feel embarrassed or shocked about how I appeared to others, including my friends and family back home.

And besides, by this time, in my mind I was convinced that I would never see England again or my parents or friends. I had to just let it all go because nothing mattered any more.

Sometimes a tiny part of me would pray that all this really was God's will for me and not some mental aberration. But I knew that all I had done, back when I got opened in Kingston, was simply state my belief in God and my willingness to surrender and worship Him. I wasn't doing anything else or following some strange, mystical guru. I wasn't following any man made method like Gurdjieff's in Coombe Springs or Transcendental Meditation.

From my opening it had just been me and God. In fact, that is what attracted me to Subud in the first place. No rules, no guru, no method. Just God.

An Ohio Set-up!
Inside out, Outside in

One Friday, a Subud member from New York turned up at the house. He and another Subud member in Cincinnati were off-road biker fanatics and they invited me to join them for a weekend trip of off-road biking. In my state of submission where I seemed to have no will of my own, I of course said yes.

That evening they loaded their two trail bikes on to the back of their truck and we set off on a long drive to some forest in Ohio. We drove deep into the forest following a barely discernible trail. Eventually they stopped near a small stream and made camp on a high ridge above the stream.

I helped collect wood for a fire while they put up two tents.

After the fire was lit they went back down to the truck to check their bikes when I heard some loud swearing, which my ears did not appreciate.

It transpired that they had forgotten to buy gas and the jerry cans were empty. So they shouted up to me that they were going back to buy some gas and left me to guard the tents and equipment.

I had an idea how far back it was to the highway and last gas station, so I knew they would be gone at least an hour.

If I felt full of doom and fully disorientated in Cincinnati you can imagine how I felt now, alone in some strange forest, literally miles from anywhere, in this foreign country at eleven o'clock at night.

After about half an hour I stood up on that high ridge with the small fire burning a few feet behind me. As I stared out into the darkness I started to physically vibrate; it began in my legs and then my stomach and spread to my torso until finally my whole body was vibrating. I felt very scared and my heart was pounding. "What now?" I thought. "Am I going to die now, here? Alone?"

As I stood there, I started to experience a sense of slowly rising up. My body was still standing firmly on the ridge but my 'sight,' my view, was definitely moving higher and higher. I could see the blackness of the tree tops stretching far out ahead, blacker than the sky.

As you can imagine the fear was increasing by the second and I was thinking that this really was the moment when I was going to die. Instead I just rose even higher until I began to see what I assume were the lights of a city far off on the horizon.

Suddenly it was like I was shot way up higher and I heard a loud bang or explosion, seemingly in my head. In that instant my entire awareness of self, my whole being, was like a tiny, expanding ball in the pit of my physical stomach, which grew and grew until it filled my coarse physical body and I was back to where I started, except severely shaken.

This was one of the most dramatic, frightening and yet amazing experiences I had ever had. At the time I was both terrified and confused. My mind was still trying to rationalize these experiences and in this case my mind's logic was grappling with this question; 'With such fear and premonitions of death and doom that have culminated in this experience, why was I still alive!?" I asked myself. "What was the point to be that afraid, and apparently even leaving my body, if I was not to die?"

I had barely recovered and was still mulling over that question when I heard the truck returning. The two Subud members were soon up on the ridge and to my surprise they started packing everything up. They had failed to get gas for the bikes and decided to return to Cincinnati that night.

I look back on that event and can't help but think the whole thing was a set-up by God to get me to a place where I would be alone and in a sufficient state of surrender to allow me to go through that experience without any chance of interruptions.

A six hour round trip into the forest with no gas for their bikes was a complete waste of time for my two Subud brothers. I was the one who had the experience, they simply drove me there and then drove me back.

Coincidence? At the time I was too shaken to really think about what was going on, or have any sense of the irony. I also did not mention my experience to them for fear of their thinking I was crazy.

These days it is considered more believable that you have seen a UFO and been abducted by aliens than if you have had a spiritual experience.

Taming of the Shrew
Now I think I should explain more about the purpose of this fear

that had become a permanent feature of my life at that time.

Before this trip to the U.S., there had been an underlying sense of fear building in me. By the time I left England, my mind interpreted this fear as meaning I was not going to return from America. From that assumption my mind had no alternative but to be convinced that I was going to die on this journey. That was how desperate my mind was to stay in control. It could not accept that it could not figure everything out. Such is the foolishness of our minds. Well, mine at least.

After the experience in the forest, it came to me that not only would I need to accept death, but I was expected to accept there was no England, literally; there never had been an England and my life in England had never happened, and it was all a figment of my imagination. No England, no family, no friends. No past and no future. Just me remembering God now, for as long as God allowed me to exist.

That sounds crazy and part of me knew it was crazy at the time, but what was happening was I was being forced to be obedient to my inner. If I refused to accept that England doesn't exist, then the fear would just increase until I finally accepted that idea as being the truth.

It took a couple of years to realize this, and that the principle is pretty much the same as in Shakespeare's play "Taming of The Shrew." In my case it was my inner that was taming my ego, my heart and mind.

On my return to England I discovered another purpose for the fear in regard to my life in England, which I shall explain in a later chapter.

All Good Things Must Come to an End

So eventually the time came to think about returning to England, even though in my heart I was convinced that God had no intention of letting me make it back to the UK. Still I knew I had no choice but to play this scenario out to the end.

Of course by now I had nothing left in my wallet except my plane ticket. Once again the Cincinnati Subud Group came to my rescue. They bought me a Greyhound Ticket to New York and gave me some extra cash to get a taxi to the airport. The lady of the house where I stayed very kindly made me some roast beef sandwiches and put them in a brown paper bag for the long bus trip.

It was just before dawn and everyone from the house came to the bus station to see me off. Perhaps they just wanted to make sure I got on the bus and left Cincinnati. They were good people and I am very grateful for all the help, hospitality and patience I received from them.

After something like 18 hours riding in this bus I finally arrived in New York. It was already dark, so I quickly looked for a cab to get me to the airport, because I was running late. It was 7.30 and my flight took off at 9.00 that evening. I put my guitar and small suitcase in the boot and got into the cab and asked the cabbie to get me to the airport as quickly as possible.

After about twenty minutes I began to feel very uneasy and then I spotted a sign to JFK Airport, but it was pointing in the opposite direction to the way we were going. I immediately complained to the cabby who said, somewhat apologetically, that he was just making a short detour to pick his daughter up from her dance class.

With my best British voice I told him the time my plane took off and that his daughter would have to wait for him because the plane won't wait for me! Reluctantly he turned the cab around and finally got me to the terminal with only minutes to spare. At least so I thought.

I rushed to the check-in counter only to find there was just one young check-in lady and she was closing up the counter. There were no other passengers to be seen. I told her what flight I was on and with sincere regret she informed me that the plane had already left the terminal. I had missed my flight!

Just then her supervisor appeared and after explaining my situation to him, he said not to worry, I could get the same flight the next day. He then asked to check my ticket so he could make the booking.

My ticket had been folded up, in my wallet, in my back pocket the whole time since I first arrived a month earlier. It had been very humid in Skymont and pretty hot in Cincinnati so that when he took out the ticket he had to peel it open. He then had to hold it up to the light to read it. After a minute he said, "Your ticket is only valid up until midnight tonight so, you will have to pay an additional US$120 for the flight tomorrow."

Still in my submissive, doom and gloom, disorientated state, I didn't quite know how to react. Some part of me was thinking that God's plan must have gone a bit haywire here. I was pretty sure I was supposed to catch this plane and just disappear somewhere over the Atlantic, never to be seen again. Now I have to wait another night to meet my doom. It didn't seem right.

As funny as this sounds now, this was actually what was going through my mind at that time.

I then told him I did not have $120 and I proceeded to produce all the money I had, which totalled $3 and a few cents.

I was now concerned that maybe both he and the check-in lady were thinking more about getting home than worrying about me and I would be left to sleep in this huge dark terminal alone, and have to sort this problem out the next day.

Then suddenly the manager perked up. "One minute, let me check something," he said, as he grabbed the phone on the counter and made a call.

He put the phone down and with a big smile turned to me saying "You're in luck. A 747 broke down earlier in the day, but it has to be in London for the return flight tomorrow. It leaves at 11.58 tonight so your ticket is still valid!"

And so it was that my bag and guitar were checked in. I thanked them for their kind assistance and went to find a seat for the 2 hour wait before boarding.

Now, for someone who's heart is convinced that their doom awaits them and they will never see England again, just the idea of flying was already scary. So the idea of flying on a plane that had broken down earlier that day was quite terrifying. But I had to play this story out to the end and meet whatever fate God had prepared for me.

Finally it came time to board and a stewardess came from the plane to call me. She then quickly returned down the tunnel back to the plane. I nervously proceeded to walk across the lounge and through the metal detector.

Out of the corner of my eye, in the dimly lit lounge, I noticed something move. Almost immediately I was sprawled on the floor with a man's forearm on my throat barking at me, "What's in the bag!!?"

He grabbed the bag and slowly opened it. The uneaten beef sandwiches were wrapped in aluminium foil which, apparently, had set off the metal detector. I guess this security officer must have been pretty fed up having to wait until midnight just to do a security check for one passenger. He straightened his jacket and apologized gruffly.

I stepped into the plane. This was my first time on a 747. It was huge compared to the old 707s. Not only huge but also empty, except for eight stewardesses who all sat right up the front.

Like a true Englishman I sat cowering about fifty rows behind them at the back.

As I sat there my nervous mind was still fixating on God's doom and death plan. "How clever of God to put me on a plane with no passengers. That's a sure sign that this plane will never make it to England," I thought to myself. I did however feel sorry for the stewardesses and crew and wondered what twist of fate had brought them all onto this doomed flight.

As an aside this was a prime demonstration, and warning, about how amazingly creative the human mind and imagination can be. My fears turned out to be just a personal 'conspiracy theory' that I totally believed. Beware of conspiracy theories sold by people who are totally convinced they are right! How wrong I was, but for me it was a necessary part of the process.

About two hours into the flight my fears suddenly increased greatly when the plane hit some very bad turbulence. Because I was sitting at the back of the plane and all the galley curtains were open I could see right down to the front where the stewardesses were sitting and what really raised my fears was that I could see the fuselage was actually twisting slightly like a corkscrew back and forth in the turbulence.

As I sat there gripping my armrests, a stewardess made her way back to me and explained that to save time and fuel the pilot was flying within the Arctic Circle, much further north than the normal flight path, because it's a shorter route; she also apologised that it might get a lot bumpier.

So I spent some two and a half hours gripping the arm of my seat, refusing all food and silently praying constantly while waiting to meet my doom.

And then, suddenly a ray of sunlight burst through the windows and I gathered all my courage to look out, and down. We were over Ireland and I was truly amazed at the patchwork of tiny fields that were clearly visible. Even more impactful was the colour. The deepest, luxuriant greens of Ireland, uniquely different from the greens of America.

I could feel that cool green colour, like pure water flowing into me. It filled me up because I was like an empty vessel. This was the true meaning of the feeling that my heart and mind had interpreted as 'never seeing England again'. What it really meant was that this inner force of my latihan was cleaning out all the rubbish from my history in England so that I could start a new life with a relatively clean sheet of paper. That was one example of the result of my intense purification.

Not long after that we landed at Heathrow and I meekly thanked the eight Stewardesses as I left the plane and made my way to immigration and baggage claim. I then went through customs where I was stopped and had to open my little suitcase and guitar case.

The customs official then asked me a question that seemed right out of Monty Python. He looked at my guitar and asked, "What's that?" I said, "My guitar."

He paused to think up his next question and then asked, "How do you know it's not a banjo?"

I wondered if he was making a joke but his expression told me that he expected a serious answer. "A banjo only has five strings and a guitar has six or twelve strings," I replied. He seemed a little disappointed that I had an answer as he closed the lid and drew a squiggle on the case with a piece of chalk.

I stepped out of the Terminal feeling physically and emotionally exhausted. I had 3 dollars but no British money, so all I could think to do was take a taxi to my best friends, Ramzi and Aisjah's house in Raynes Park, some hour and a half drive away. I was just praying they would be there and would have enough cash to pay for the taxi.

They did!

Meeting Myself Again

So my Skymont trip was over and my feet were back on British soil, but it didn't feel like it because the fear and disorientation were still with me.

I had a very hard time trying to explain everything that had happened over the past month in America to Ramzi and his wife. There was so much to tell that it was hard to organize my thoughts and be coherent. Fortunately, this was my best friend in Subud who was like a brother. In fact he was the one who originally wanted to go to Skymont and dragged me into his scheme in the first place. I think paying my taxi fare was poetic justice.

His friendship and patience was immensely valuable during the extended period of my coming down, back to earth and discovering my new self. I also have a debt of many fried egg sandwiches and quite a few plates of spaghetti that I owe his wife, which helped to keep my body functioning over the weeks and months that followed.

Dear Reader – please forgive my intrusion here. Reading through David's account of his early experiences, which saw him in a state of real fear for an extended period, two things occur to me. The first is that I was a witness to this and he is not exaggerating! Secondly, in common with many members, I have been through quite a lot of very interesting experiences myself (see my forthcoming book), but never anything as intense as David's early years.

So, lest a new or prospective member is alarmed by this account, let me say that in my long, fifty-four years experience, both as a member and as a helper accompanying members, I have not come across any one experiencing anything quite like this.

The other thing I, and many other long time members

have noticed is that the new generation of members over the last twenty years or so do not seem to have to go through any kind of similar experiences. Why this is I do not know, but it is possible that the kinds of souls seeking the latihan in the world today are different, so their experiences are different. Ramzi Addison

The Training Continues, Post America
Finding A Balance

After returning from Skymont and Cincinnati to my small attic flat, my experiences moved into a new phase. I was being shown through my inner instructor something about how my ideal life style should be. This was far more pleasant than the previous weeks of only fear and disorientation.

Unfortunately, it transpired that the ideal way to live for my inner at that time was pretty extreme.

Another important insight I gained during that period led me to throw out what little junk and clutter I had and keep the flat as clean and tidy as humanly possible. This mirrored what had been going on inside of me. I wasn't getting neurotic about cleanliness, it was all very calm and matter-of-fact, and I barely thought about it. Keeping things clean and orderly just came naturally and I just obeyed the feelings that arose in me.

It was during this period that I could clearly feel the strong influence that objects and our surroundings could exert on my inner feeling and ideally how I should manage my environment. I began to see on a deeper level that while I should respect and value the material objects that provide me with comfort and convenience, I should not be 'owned' by them to the point that they end up occupying and enjoying my home more than I do. If that happens then I would be serving them. That's another way the servants can take over my mansion!

By not filling our home with an over-abundance of things, and stuff, but keeping our possessions closer to what is necessary for our life, and when we have the means, be modest in acquiring the extra things that make our heart feel happy. That is when our life will come into balance between the inner and the outer. That, at least was the lesson for me in what I experienced.

Of course it will all start again when we get married.

So, soon after returning from America, it seems my inner demanded this high level of cleanliness and order. I was being taught the correct way I should live; the ideal way, from the inner point of view.

However, I was aware that this level of extreme cleanliness and tidiness could not go on forever. Not if I ever wanted to get married and have a normal life. I don't think any woman could put up with living that way, unless they were completely neurotic germaphobes, or in a crisis like mine, and a crisis is not forever.

What I also learned from this experience was how we are further influenced and polluted in other ways by material objects, and this happens by the material forces outside interacting with the same material forces that exist within each of us.

I got this understanding when, during this part of my crisis, my relationship with material things 'stopped working' and I no longer felt any influence or had any interest in any but the most essential material objects. It was a very liberating and enlightening feeling that lasted for several weeks.

Items that I used to desire and even dreamed about possessing, like a Harley Davidson Electra Glide motorcycle, a Gibson guitar, expensive branded clothes and the like, no longer meant anything to me.

To have my own transport would be nice, but I didn't care if it was a 1200cc Harley or an old 250cc BSA. We all need clothes but it no longer mattered to me, that is, I no longer desired or hankered for any particular brand. I simple stopped having those kind of aspirations and desires. For me, if I had enough to meet my needs, that was good enough.

I certainly did not have the money to buy anything branded anyway, so it was just as well I didn't desire them anymore. I was grateful and content with what I had. What a blessing that is and to a large extent remains with me to this day.

So these changes I went through, that just happened to me, were a large part of what I experienced over about two or three months after coming back home.

However, although my experiences were expanding to new areas, the fundamental tool of education was still fear. It may sound strange but during this stage of my crisis virtually all my desires were stripped away or at least thoroughly subdued for a considerable time by the constant fear of God's wrath if I stepped out of line. It really put things into perspective and changed priorities.

Time for a related issue. The cheaters, abusers, liars, thieves, molesters, philanderers that we all love and trust.

Shiny Objects, Rusty Interiors

So I began to see how a person can take ten showers a day and look squeaky clean and be smartly dressed in their branded clothes, and act very appropriately, like true ladies and gentlemen, as they were taught to do since childhood, but, if their heart and mind are still filled with their lower desires, the low forces, then their character will still be on the level of those lower forces.

Without the guidance from a clean, active inner, a person's thoughts and actions will always be serving their heart, their desires and ambitions. Their inner self will have become encased in layer after layer of lower forces, that will have accumulated and hardened over the years, like tons of London clay between them and their inner light.

Well, this is a kind of analogy for what I came to understand by seeing the inner and outer of many people during this period. More important, it was what I came to see and experience in myself.

Show Me How To Find You

Sadly, I constantly observe how so many people are easily fooled by a person's outer, 'squeaky clean' appearance, when in fact it is their inner character that is far more important to know, albeit far more difficult to examine.

Throughout history, people searching for a spiritual path have discovered that it is exceedingly hard, if not impossible, to change or clean one's own character by the effort of our own will, simply because the one in charge of making the effort is the one that needs to change and be purified. It's like expecting the washing up to clean itself.

Too often it is our desire to make an effort that is the biggest obstacle and a major part of the problem to making progress in the spiritual realm. It may take many years before a person is able to truly surrender their will, their need to be in control, and let go of those desires trying to force themselves to be better.

It's hard for our ego to understand what we can do alone, and when we need to get out of the way so that we can receive something that is truly from the inner, our own, custom created, true cleaning expert!

Hence, as Bapak has explained many times, why the proverbial hermits in caves on the mountains are trying to escape the influences of all these worldly forces within themselves. They want to clean up the inner mess so they try to remove themselves from all the shiny objects and temptations of modern life that are always disturbing their heart and mind, hoping to receive a good cleaning from the grace of God.

But making all that effort and self-deprivation is not the way of Subud. That is why the latihan of Subud is such an amazing gift, because it just happens spontaneously. We can receive spontaneously what those hermits were looking for. No years of meditating and fasting. No hours of chanting mantras. No need to forgo the conveniences of modern life.

If we use the analogy of a car, what human beings need in order to purify their inner, their engine, is a mechanic, an expert who can be trusted. And who better to trust than the manufacturer. In the human context that means we need God's help and His power to manifest within us, to awaken our inner self and start the cleaning and repairing of our engine. That means the purification of, and raising of our true inner character to the highest quality God intended for us.

That at least is my limited understanding from my own experiences since being opened. Like all my Subud brothers and sisters, I received that inner life force within me and, in my case, immediately it began to get to work with that first simple change in my life of "No more alcohol or pork for you, lad!"

Storm Clouds Gather

Although I had survived my trip to America and safely returned to England, the feelings of impending doom had not left me. In fact, they were becoming more intense.

Then came that experience again, where I was shown that, if I forgot God, for even an instant, then in that same moment God would forget me and I would cease to exist, completely and entirely erased! Gone from the universe. But more than that. God could make it be that I never had existed! Even my own mother would have no memory of me as though she had never given birth to me. Every photograph, piece of clothing, school books and toys I ever had would all cease to exist. They never existed.

Every relative, friend, neighbour and acquaintance would have no recollection that I had ever existed. Indeed, there would be no-one in the universe to ask any question about me. No one ever knew me.

In these written words, it sounds over dramatic, but if the words are allowed to return to feelings, you will have a sense of the awful reality of God's unlimited, irresistible power.

Receiving that kind of truth was truly terrifying. To feel, to the extent that I was capable, the absolute power and authority of God over all things and how inconsequential I am, was far worse than the idea of facing death.

Soon after this I tried to explain the experience to my good friend, who was also in Subud, and he had to stop me half way. I could see that in this crisis state my voice was able to carry the truth of this experience, so it touched his inner and it was freaking him out. He obviously did not need to be shown this in the same way I had to experience it. Lucky him!

To get just a faint taste of the reality of God's power, a power that is 'absolute,' is extremely unnerving for the heart and mind.

So it was with this fear of forgetting God that I tried to carry on a normal life, while inside I had to maintain a form of *zikir*, that is, repeating the name of God silently, but constantly.

The understanding I was getting was, if I stopped and forgot God for just a second, it seemed I might just go pop and cease to exist. Cease to ever have existed. It sounds ludicrous to our worldly mind, but I didn't feel like arguing!

Human Annihilation

So in those weeks after I returned from Skymont my crisis had stepped up a notch or two. I would find myself being woken at night in a state of great fear without understanding what was causing it. I was safe, at home, in bed, in England and everything was fine. And yet I had this feeling of impending doom welling up from the pit of my stomach for no good reason.

This was a great test for my mind, which was desperate to have some kind of rational reason to cling to that could explain what was making me feel so afraid. Over a period of several days the level of fear just got more intense, especially at night.

Finally, one night it got so bad I went down to my friend Philip on the second floor and woke him up. He kindly offered to drive me to the house of the helper who opened me, and I gladly accepted his offer. We arrived at the helper's house at about 1.30am. Thanks again to Phil's MG sports car.

I knocked on the helpers front door, and after a few minutes he came down and opened the door in his dressing gown. He invited me in and we went into his living room where I began to try to explain to him the horrors of what I was experiencing. After ten minutes his wife came in bringing tea and biscuits to us in the middle of the night. She then said goodnight and returned to bed.

These night time visits became fairly regular as my level of fear increased. In total I must have woken up Philip and his MG, and the helper and his wife more than half a dozen times in the space of about three weeks.

I feel very grateful to my Subud brother, Philip with the MG, even more so to my helper, Sachlan North, and of course his wife, Miriam, who never complained and happily brought us tea and biscuits in the middle of the night.

Sometimes I would stay about one hour until I felt calm enough to manage my fear, and Philip would drive me back home. Other times Philip would return home alone and I would stay with the helper until day break, when finally, the fear would subside and I would catch the first morning bus home.

Who Orchestrated This?

One night the familiar feelings of fear began to swell around my stomach. After perhaps half an hour, this swirling fear reached a point of near panic and I was completely at a loss what to do. There was nowhere to run to, no escape because it came from within me. Somewhere in my brain I was thinking I cannot wake up Philip or the helper again, because I went through that last night. But this sense of fear had reached the level when politeness tends to be trumped by panic.

So it was that half an hour later I was with my helper again, trying to convey what I was feeling. He was drinking his tea and remaining very calm and normal as he always did. A solid rock I could cling to in the midst of this storm.

I told him with a shaky voice that this feeling of fear was so real and so intense that the only thing I could think of that would scare me this much would be a premonition of a third world war.

It sounds ludicrous now and probably did to him too, but I was deadly serious. I was so afraid I could not even drink my tea. I didn't care about anything to do with my worldly life, because I was being confronted by possible annihilation in a nuclear war. It truly was that real and that bad.

A few minutes later I thought I heard a large explosion off in the distance. A moment later there was another distant boom. That one Sachlan noticed. Then a third and fourth boom.

Sachlan's wife had come down stairs and looked in to ask if we knew what those sounds were. Then we heard people coming out onto the street and the helper looked through the curtains. A lot of people were standing in the road in their dressing gowns looking off into the distance.

I was now literally shaking in my chair, basically incapable of doing anything other than surrendering my fear and fate to God.

In the back of my mind I could hear my heart saying, "This is the doom, I knew it was coming!" as though all my doom and gloom experiences really had all been some kind of convoluted premonition about a third world war.

"Yes, that all made perfect sense now; World war three! What a clever mind I have." (Remember what I said about our brilliant minds coming up with ridiculous conspiracy theories)

The helper drew back the curtain and even from across the room I could see a red glow on the horizon above the roof tops, with flashes of yellow followed several seconds later with a loud, distant boom. He then went out into the street and talked with some of his equally confused neighbours.

When he returned he was no more enlightened than when he left. He looked at me and I looked at him and I am sure that there was a bit of a question mark in his mind that perhaps I really was receiving a true premonition.

He then turned on the radio and immediately we heard the sound of heavy machine-gun fire followed by a grenade exploding.

A BBC reporter was now describing how he could see an armoured car coming around the corner. There was more machine-gun fire and explosions. Out of the window the sky was being lit up even brighter and the distant booming noises were almost constant now.

That was the final straw for me. If the BBC was reporting it and we were witnessing it outside our window, then it must be true! What other conclusion could my ever-trustworthy heart and know-it-all mind possibly come to?

My heart was now about to explode with fear and my mind had almost short-circuited, when abruptly the voice on the radio changed and an announcer said to the reporter, "Thank you for that live report from the war in Yemen's capital, Aden…" he then continued, " We are just getting reports of a large fire at a Calor gas factory in Mitcham, Surrey. We have no further details at this time..."

On hearing those words my heart rapidly deflated as the fear evaporated and I slumped exhausted in the chair.

My helper looked at me and I think he felt a little relieved himself. He then said, tongue in cheek, "If no one has died or been hurt in that fire, then I think God orchestrated this show just for you!"

Finally, after a few minutes I was able to drink my tea and before dawn I was walking back home to Norbiton, arriving in time for an early breakfast before getting some sleep.

About ten o'clock later that morning I was woken up by my landlady because I had a phone call. I went downstairs and I picked up the receiver. I heard the rather jolly voice of Sachlan, who said he was reading the morning paper and it was reported that several houses had been destroyed in the Mitcham fire, but the only casualty was an Alsation guard dog.

This event, whether orchestrated or just coincidence, was the pinnacle of my 'Fear of God' crisis that started on an underground train station in Notting Hill Gate several months earlier. From this point on the element of constant fear slowly subsided and my life became more settled, but no less disorientating.

So, What Was the Point?

At the time I was having these intense experiences I was too overwhelmed to be able to gain any understanding or wisdom of why I was going through this, or what the purpose and meaning of it all was.

In fact, the process of receiving those insights and understandings, and perhaps a little wisdom, took several years of passive contemplation, like peeling an onion; and, over time, the understanding went deeper and deeper. These insights came without any effort or even desire on my part, in exactly the same way that all the early experiences simply happened, starting with losing the ability to consume alcohol and eating pork.

Just like when the strange, innocent sounding questions spontaneously emerged into my mind on underground stations, buses and airplanes, they just came out of the blue.

The difference was that now it was not questions, but answers and understanding about those experiences during 1969-71 that would spontaneously emerge in my mind. Something that continues until today.

I very much hope the description of events above provides some context of the normal day to day world that I was living in, whilst at the same time experiencing this phase of my crisis.

For me, at that time, it was as though I was living with one foot in this material world and one foot in that inner world of the latihan.

I hope that I have managed to describe these events in such a way that anyone reading this can also sense the reality that those two worlds do exist, in parallel. The reason we are not aware of those two separate realities is because, from the moment we are born, they become mixed together within our being.

It's a bit like a cup of coffee. We can taste the coffee but not the water. And while we live on this earth our hearts and minds will always crave more coffee, and then we discover milk, sugar and even cinnamon. At some point most of us forget everything about the taste of water. We cannot separate the heart and mind from our inner self with our will, or through things like meditation, because that is like the cup of coffee trying to unmake itself.

Even if that were possible, the moment the coffee separated from the water it would become a lifeless powder, unable to move, swirl or pour. In fact, it would be dead.

That is where the Latihan differs from all those other methods, because the latihan arises from the inner by the power of God. The latihan is able to separate the inner and outer elements so that, over time, we can recognize the coffee, sugar, milk and cinnamon. But most importantly we begin to taste and recognize the water. What is quite miraculous is that during this process, the coffee, milk and sugar do not die.

This process of repeated separation also exposes other impurities which will be filtered out and removed. The goal is to be able to enjoy our cup of coffee, but be aware of the pure water as much as the other ingredients all the time, not just when we intentionally do latihan.

I feel I should emphasize how the inner process that was going on in me happened in the midst of all the hustle and bustle of normal life on this earth. I say that to assure anyone that has doubts that the latihan is at work within us twenty-four hours a day, not just for two periods of half an hour each week.

I was not living like a hermit monk in a cave up some mountain, meditating and fasting for weeks on end trying to attain some spiritual experience. I was living in the midst of this modern world with all the noise and excitement those hermits are trying to escape from. That also makes the latihan such an amazing gift from God. It truly is beyond anything we can imagine.

Finally, I must reassure you that of the thousands of Subud members around the world, I have never heard any stories of any of them experiencing the type of crisis I had. The many various stories I have heard from, or about, other Subud members have been very different in nature with no elements of fear involved. But that is how it should be. The latihan should progress in a calm and orderly way and not disturb our life. Why I had to go through what I did, I have no idea. I just don't think about it and the question never arises from within.

Who Is 'I'?

The story above is like describing the experience of the outer vessel or vehicle that I was given at birth for my journey on earth and how those early latihan experiences have impacted on my heart and mind. In other words, my heart and mind looked at all these events as a naïve bystander caught up in something they could not comprehend.

But, as a story it has little value without understanding the content. It is in the content that I discovered the meaning, purpose and benefit of all that I experienced during those early years, and all the years that have followed.

I cannot, and perhaps should not try to explain all the understandings and insights that I have discovered, because I'm sure it would be very boring and they may only be true for me.

Other people will discover their own truths. But I shall attempt to summarise the key insights that have come to me over the past forty odd years, because that is what may have a value and be a benefit to others who are considering joining Subud.

But more important perhaps, I hope my modest experiences may be useful for those who are newly opened in Subud, who may have similar spontaneous experiences that come to them before they have any clear understanding that their heart and mind is able to grasp about what the purpose and benefit is.

I hope here to give some of the inner context to these events, as they were relevant to me, and I hope others will be able to find the relevance and reassurance that the inner life is a reality, as they begin their spiritual path, and to allay any doubts and increase their faith. The life force of the soul working in our worldly life is no myth or fairy story. The latihan is exactly as Bapak has explained it.

Lets Make One Thing Clear Again

When I first felt moved to write this book, my first response was, "Who am I to write about spiritual matters? I am not special, nor have any desire to be any kind of guru."

Then I realized that was the point. A simple, average sort of person, by the grace of God, through the latihan, can experience the kind of things that previously were considered beyond the reach of ordinary people. This book was to be one of many that exist as proof for anyone who may have doubts that we are all created by Almighty God and we can all receive his grace.

I have heard many stories over the years from many Subud members about their experiences, which I feel are far more ethereal and uplifting than what I have experienced. I only wish they had all written books too. Perhaps they will.

The fact is we are all unique and have our individual needs as we journey through life. I write this book simply to add one more small piece to the kaleidoscope of human experience related to the Subud latihan that brings the inner reality of God's infinite creation into the realm of our own individual journey in this material life, as I have experienced it.

I have prayed that my words would be guided as I write and that I may be forgiven for any mistakes or shortcomings that slip through.

First Signs of Progress

As I mention at the beginning of this book, I always look to Bapak's words and explanations as my reference. To both confirm Bapak's explanations and increase my own faith in my journey. Here I offer my recollection of Bapak's explanations about purification. This is, note, not a quote, but a summary of Bapak's words as I recall them.

The early signs of purification after being opened are the

changes in a person's character and habits. Slowly, over time the desire to tell lies leaves us; the desire to win and feel superior goes; feeling jealous of other's success leaves us; indifference becomes empathy, anger becomes patience, worry becomes faith etc. That is the gentle way, the normal way of progress in Subud, with patience and faith, without disturbing our outer life.

In fact, often other people may notice these changes happening in us before we do.

A Summary of The Big Picture So Far
The Chain of Events

If we consider life as a journey, I think it is useful to identify the 'stepping stones' of events, like the stations we pass through on a train journey. In this way we can see certain threads that show we have travelled 'a prepared path' rather than a random 'throw of the dice', fateful life. I will do my best to provide some explanations of how I see the latihan experience related to these stepping stones.

But remember, this is simply my understanding, which may not resonate with you. I am like any other flawed human being on a journey. Our journey may not be the same, but our intended destination is. Some may travel by train, others by car, bicycle or jet plane. Each will have their own experiences. The kaleidoscope of humanity. Together we journey on.

Here I summarize the key stepping stones that I have identified in my life from the age of eleven up to this point in the story.

My mother moved from North London to Kingston on Thames in South London when I was 11 in 1962.

She later bought a flat in Norbiton Hall when I was 13, where our next door neighbour, who was ten years older than me, was a Subud member and an ex-Gurdjieff follower at Coombe Springs.

Coombe Springs was the first place Bapak went outside of Indonesia on his mission to bring the latihan to the world. Bapak arrived at Coombe Springs in the early fifties, and it was where he started the first Subud group, with many of the Gurdjieff followers becoming the first to be opened in the UK.

My neighbour in Norbiton Hall, a member of Coombe Springs, brought me to the 'Subud Kingston Hall' to sign up as a candidate member and serve my three months' probation, just in time to be opened the day after my eighteenth birthday.

After my first two latihans my body would no longer accept alcohol or pork:

This was, for me at least, undeniable proof that human beings really do have an inner self or soul which, if it is woken up, can over-ride the desires of the heart and mind and thereby truly guide and protect us.

This inner self or soul, by the Power and Grace of Almighty God, is quite capable of altering our conduct and even our character, that forms our inner content.

This was also the first small proof for me that the coarse, material human body really was filled with a host of 'entities' that together formed the worldly 'ego 'and personality that people recognise as what makes us uniquely who we are, what we are familiar with and refer to as 'I'.

This ego and these entities almost always become enamoured with, and very easily influenced by all the shiny objects and delights of this material world. These entities are commonly described as 'passions' and 'desires' that collectively we can call the lower forces. In Indonesia they are referred to as the 'nafsu'.

These 'entities' reside within our being and influence our human heart and mind and are given to us when we are born. They come with the body. They are the tools we need to live and progress in this world and so are really our internal servants and specialists to operate our material body, heart and mind.

These nafsu quickly start exerting their influence after we are born. Initially there is the entity that creates a sense of hunger. There is an entity that causes us to cry out when we are in discomfort. There is an entity that has the nature of curiosity, which is a very powerful tool to drive our intellect to learn and discover what we need to know to survive in this world.

However, as we grow up we almost invariably fall foul to the pressure of the desires that do not just push to get fed, to drink and sleep and get attention, but also want to know what will happen if we steal those cookies, what if I tell a lie, what happens to me if I kill this bug?

There is even a 'nafsu' that, if it is sad and hurting inside, will get angry with anyone around, or over time turn that person into a bully.

As we get older, these nafsu will stop wanting ice cream and instead will start to want lots of money. They want cars, clothes, diamond rings, big houses and all the best things in this worldly life.

They also want the satisfying feeling of being respected. They love the feeling of being superior. They love the feeling of being loved, and they can even fain being meek and humble in order to get love.

As the intellect develops and we become aware of the satisfying feelings of 'joy and pleasure' verses 'pain and frustration', these forces become very attracted to toys, dad's toolbox, ice cream and getting attention when we want something.

As they get older, there is an almost endless list of things the heart will discover and desire. In fact, anything that can be labelled 'NEW' can quickly replace what then becomes 'old'. And marketeers understand this. Thus the iPhone 13.

I believe I have met all or most of these entities and desires within myself. At fifteen, I remember how pleasurable it was imagining owning a Harley Davidson. Riding it. Imagining the reaction of my friends and enemies as I pulled up to the curb in front of them.

Best of all, how all the girls would melt at my feet as I sat 'side saddle' on my parked, Metallic Blue Electra Glide with white wall tires and vertical chrome fishtail exhaust pipes rising from behind the saddle bags. Oh it felt so good!

The power of the imagination mixed with the seductive force of a material object, even though, basically, this object was just a pile of iron and rubber. Imagine, I was worshipping iron and rubber, the most basic element on the material level, which we dig out of the ground.

How was that possible? How could a lump of iron produce such a powerful feeling of pleasure?

There is a third, and essential element hiding in plain sight. That element is the investment of qualities that raises that lump of iron and rubber to a higher level. And that is the creativity, intellect, skills and effort that come from the human level. In other words, the people that design and manufacture motorcycles were creating something to resonate with my desires. And that was not a bad thing. That was their talent. Their servants working to provide for their needs in this world. That was their job!

That human input is what raised the lump of iron from a worthless element of the earth to a powerful object that can affect and influence human beings. The same goes for every object man makes that we either desire or own. Everything from polished diamonds to fish hooks, cars, knives and forks, furniture and fabrics. Even instant coffee and sliced bread.

Unfortunately, that human talent, driven by just our worldly 'will', can also be used to create guns and atom bombs as well as spears for hunting and nuclear power stations.

Elements taken from the material, vegetable and animal levels, or kingdoms as they are sometimes called, when mixed with the human force of creativity, intellect and effort, will acquire, to a greater or lesser extent, the power of attraction and can have a great influence on human beings. For better or worse.

Well that was quite interesting to me when I began to see the mechanics of how these forces work. Especially when I ended up working in advertising. However, it was when I suddenly was shown that the same applies to what is above the human level that I reached the limits of my mental faculties.

If a force or entity from a higher level invests something of its qualities into a human being, then that human being will acquire qualities that raise that person's being above that of normal human beings. They may be able to do things that others would call miraculous. I'll leave you to expand on that thought and how it answers many questions about historical religious figures.

The last thing that fell into place for me, so far, was realizing that the one who had invested their creativity and power in the creation of human beings was God. Because of that, it becomes eminently clear that every human being must have a link, a connection, and potential to resonate with Almighty God. Wow!

Back to the Everyday Stuff

I think we can all agree that there are quite a few people in this world who really desire to experience the self-satisfying feeling that they are 'holy' and 'spiritually on a high level,' which is the height of irony. Obviously anything that is "self-satisfying" comes from the self, not God.

This is the nature of a child who become ruled by the desires of the lower forces that influence their heart and mind. Many will grow up still being controlled by these forces, which, in fact, is most of us in this world. That may sound bad, but the truth is we cannot live in this world without these forces. This is why, on the spiritual path, we are all vulnerable to giving in to our desires for as long as we live in this world.

Eventually, if we are not mindful, our whole life is taken up with what we, that is our heart and mind, like and don't like. How to get what we desire and how to avoid what we don't like. But this 'we' is really just our ego and all those forces who have taken over our being.

Eventually we get to the point that, as human beings, we become cut off from the most important element of who we are, our inner, and we end up serving these lower entities and their desires our whole life.

Our own inner voice becomes overwhelmed and lost in all the hubbub going on in our heart and mind as we chase the things our heart wants, and we become completely controlled by the desires of these entities residing in our heart instead of their being guided and controlled by the inner voice of our soul.

In this state, people happily engage in all kinds of activities which are actually very harmful and dangerous to themselves, simply because they cannot resist the influence of the forces that drive the desires of their hearts.

In this way, for much of their lives, human beings are simply servants of their heart rather than the heart serving the human soul. The result is that the soul is degraded and corrupted and can become one with the ego that is dominated by the lower forces.

This can result in that person's soul being so degraded that it may not actually be on the human level by the time their life ends. That is why all religions teach us a way to live that restrains the more damaging desires of the heart.

The Mind working for the Heart

The pressure of these desires can be enormous and will often cause the mind to use the gift of thought and analysis to create all kinds of clever justifications and excuses for engaging in wrong behaviour. The mind can even create brilliant false logic, which can absolutely fool the self, and persuade others. Many successful politicians are very adept at doing that.

This isn't just about the big things like drugs, drink and gambling but also the small things like being impatient, being angry, being easily offended, being greedy, being arrogant and telling lies.

The mind can always find a justification for why "I know it's wrong but my case is different", or "Just once won't do any harm", and of course the old favourites "Well they're all doing it", and "This is how my parents taught me".

The mind can come up with all kinds of arguments why, in their case, these very destructive and negative actions are justified. When people act like this, unfortunately it is confirmation that a person is still firmly under the control of their heart, and that their heart is still filled with the lower, material forces.

All this is explained in far more detail in the books written by Bapak. I would firmly encourage anyone who feels drawn to Subud to buy or find Bapak's book *Susila Budhi Dharma*. There you will discover a wealth of knowledge that will confirm just how little I know. But a little can go a long way.

Whatever understanding I have gained did not come to me at the time of my early experiences, but slowly emerged over the following two or three years. Indeed, I still learn things and have insights related to those early experiences even today, after fifty years.

I shall repeat myself here by saying that you can find much deeper understanding of these things described in Bapak's talks and books. I can only add from my limited experience, confirmation that, what to me once seemed quite esoteric in Bapak's explanations, is true and actually very logical.

This works the other way too. After many years of doing latihan it is reassuring to come across a talk from Bapak that describes what I and others have experienced, as it confirms that we are still plodding down the right path.

Now back to those stepping stones.

Swept Up and Slammed Down

Within six months of being opened I found myself being selected, through testing, to be the Regional Chair for Subud UK South Eastern Region, with the largest number of UK members. Because of my youth and newness to Subud, it was decided to make me co-chairman with an older, more experienced member.

As Regional Chair, I had to attend the annual National Congress where, on the last evening, I was called on stage as a representative of 'British Youth' and peppered with questions about my perception of Subud and how could more young people be attracted to join etc.

This session lasted several hours and I felt myself being thrust into a position that I was not prepared for, but somehow the answers came and flowed quite spontaneously into that hall, full of my Subud elders.

On returning to Kingston I was in a state of disorientation and the next night, after group latihan I felt I needed a special latihan with the helpers in which I spontaneously burst into tears. This crying continued for five or ten minutes and when it was over I felt completely drained and emotionally exhausted. This experience left me wondering who is in charge of 'me' and my life. Who made me cry?

Who Is Driving My Car

Again, this event in Swanwick is, for me, real proof that the cleverness of my brain is not always up to the job that needs to be done. It doesn't have all the answers. On the other hand the inner appears to have an endless source of knowledge and when awakened can take over from our ego, our familiar self, and use our heart and mind as tools to do or say what is required, what is relevant and what is real.

When this first happens in a very sudden or surprising way, it may not be easy for the heart and mind to accept, because initially at least, they cannot comprehend what is happening and they certainly do not understand that having this inner force providing guidance and knowledge in our life should actually be the normal way for human beings to live.

In my case my ego reacted as though it had secretly been slipped some mind bending drug and I felt very disorientated and confused. My familiar self, that is my ego, was not yet ready to really surrender control to that inner life force that had, on several occasions, taken back all the authority and status from my ego.

When the Real Racing Driver Puts Us Back
in the Driver's Seat

After my experience at the congress, when the inner was no longer required to take charge, it returned control back to my heart and mind to 'carry on as usual'.

That is when there was quite a big reaction within me, because that experience on stage had shown me how I should be, all the time, with my inner participating in my life, even taking the lead, and my heart and mind working as servants. The inner should be the benevolent master, guru and supervisor of the ego, heart and mind.

Once my inner returned control to my ego, I felt as though my inner had abandoned me, like a parent abandoning a child on the side of the road. It left me to experience the reality of how 'low' and useless my familiar ego was and how poorly my heart and mind were at doing their job of managing my life in this world, both my inner and outer life.

It was like being given a taste of how it is to become a 'king', and then be sent back the next day to being that mere lowly servant again called Ego. A servant who had spent years acting so arrogantly, thinking it was so smart, sure it was in control and making great decisions, whereas, in fact, it was now obvious that the nafsu, the servants, had just been abusing and misusing the precious gifts given by God for my physical life on earth.

The ego had not only lost touch with my inner but mostly had forgotten the existence of a soul. I still believed in the soul, but I could no longer identify it within myself because it had been dormant for years, but dormant no more since being opened.

Recognizing the reality of my own uselessness, and how far my ego had lead me down the wrong path was the cause of the uncontrollable tears, desperate for forgiveness and pleading for a second chance.

That was the meaning of the tears as I understand it now, and the primary reason I had needed this experience at congress was to learn that valuable lesson: the 'I' that I was so familiar with was totally useless at guiding me through life, if I wanted to reach my true destiny!

I also came to understand, over time, just how hard it is to realize this fact for people who had a lot of success in their outer lives. People who had been given a brilliant intellect and were 'straight-A' students, or had become self-made millionaires. The idea that their ego, seen from the outer, was not doing a good job, sounds pretty preposterous. Why do they need to follow a spiritual path or need purification, they may ask.

Going Deeper for Additional Answers
I Shall Digress Even Further

Actually what my heart and mind experienced with that collapse into tears, was also an integral part of the congress experience.

It was a lesson from my inner, to start to break down the pride and arrogance of my ego. That same pride and arrogance that I observe we all have, however well-hidden; it might be behind veils of politeness, generosity, good manners, meekness and caring disposition that we may show outwardly in our day to day life and identify as 'I'.

That's how we fool the world and fool our own selves about who we are and what kind of inner character we truly have. It's inevitable really, unless, or until, we receive something from a higher source that works through our inner to reveal or expose our true self, warts and all, and hopefully our inner self can begin to change and improve our character.

But He Seemed So Nice!

Someone may be seen as a good person but it is important to know how deep does that goodness go.

I find it a great irony of life that man is so determined to know what is real and true and to separate truth from what is fake, and yet at the same time we are so good at avoiding mirrors. One of the greatest gifts we have, that also can create huge obstacles, is actually 'built in' to our ego. That is we are so adept at mimicry.

On the one hand mimicry is an essential tool that all babies use to develop their life skills in this world. Parents and teachers depend on children's ability to mimic for their development, and so parents try to lead by example. But in later life the result of this skill can be the cause of great suffering and damage to one's

145

self and to others, when what we mimic is not compatible with our true inner nature.

This ability to mimic the good character of others explains why we frequently find ourselves shocked and disappointed by people who we have admired and respected, often for years, and suddenly one day they are exposed for committing horrendous crimes, sometimes over the many years that we have known them. Only then do we realize that all the time we had known them they had only been mimicking the qualities and character that we admired.

We have all seen the stories in the news. Respected religious leaders who abuse children, doctors who commit murder, judges who subvert justice for financial or political rewards, law enforcement who intimidate rather than protect and many other people in positions of trust, not to mention politicians, who dress to play the part but whose true inner nature and character so often falls far below the required minimum for the position they hold.

As my good friend Shakespeare said "All the world's a stage...". With the help of the right clothes, haircut and accent, very bad people can skilfully mimic the character and personality of very good people, both men and women... until they are caught!

When we study a subject, we are using our mind to mimic the mind of someone else. So if we try to study spiritual matters we will only end up mimicking our teacher, not experiencing and owning our own knowledge. Unless, in the process God steps in and sends an epiphany.

So it seems to me that it is very important to recognize what we know and believe that has been borrowed from others, and what has truly come from our own source of knowledge within, through the grace of God.

Levels?

When goodness is simply imposed on a child by education and upbringing, it will only penetrate the outer heart and mind. In effect our heart and mind will go through life simply mimicking the ways of a good person, following what has been taught them.

For living and being successful in this world, this form of education and upbringing can be more than adequate, but not for developing and improving our true inner character. Only God can change the quality of our inner self.

This mimicking, while useful for our worldly progress can also become like camouflage for a soul that is in fact still on a low level and still easily influenced by the lower forces.

No amount of education or intellectual arguments are able to change the quality of a person's true inner character, and that person is still going to be very easily influenced by the lower forces, regardless of their education and upbringing.

That is why an apparently nice, well educated person from a good family can, in a flash, spontaneously become a cheat, a liar, a shoplifter, an abuser, even a murderer. Their low inner character will cause them to react very badly to some external event or opportunity. They cannot resist. This is because they are controlled by the sub-human forces that come from a lower level.

Further, at the moment they act in a bad way, they will not have a sense of doing something wrong, because many things which are forbidden on the human level are not felt as wrong on the lower levels. Self-restraint is not in the character of the lower forces.

I would like to take this opportunity to peel this onion a bit further, which means I am leap-frogging many years ahead in the story line, to include here some insights that the latihan has given me regarding the influence of the material forces, which includes the vegetable and animal forces in this world.

There is a well-known saying in the medical profession which is; "Doctor, heal thyself". Recognizing that when doctors get sick they need a doctor. And so many of us, who have some interest in the mysteries of life and death, go through life with the challenge; "Human, know thyself". That is a far greater challenge than for doctors to heal themselves.

Because of this we inevitably end up seeking wise men and studying books of philosophy and religion, but none of them can show us how to know our true inner self. That knowledge depends entirely on receiving a kind of epiphany. And no book or wise man can show you how to do that.

That is why I feel so blessed to have received this latihan of Subud because through surrender, slowly, bit by bit I can find that knowledge and guidance that I need, custom made for my life, arise within me. The same as every other Subud member can receive for their own unique life.

So that is why I include here some of the inner lessons I have had about life. Not that you should accept them as true, but as an illustration of how the latihan can work to progress our understanding. In doing so I have found my views and attitudes towards many things in life have evolved and changed from my time of mimicking those around me, including adopting the beliefs and ideas of my culture, without ever understanding why.

Who Said That?
Crime and Punishment

In 1972 I thought I heard Bapak say in a talk that criminals shouldn't be punished... That can't be right! The world would be in chaos if we can just go around stealing, and worse, without any repercussions! It's clear I wasn't very bright in 1972. I was still locked in my rigid Britishness.

But I didn't reject the idea that Bapak had planted in my thoughts. I just put it on the back burner.

Over subsequent years, however, I have had several experiences that lead me to some surprising conclusions about 'right and wrong' and 'justice and punishment', that from the point of view of worldly human society would be quite unacceptable. The best I can explain what I have been shown is to say "murder is permissible on the vegetable and animal levels".

I came to understand the obvious, that it is not a sin for an animal to steal from another animal. It is not a sin for one plant to steal the sunlight from another plant. We do not say that animals murder other animals or plants murder other plants. This is because they are simply following their nature, and it is their instinct that guides them. This is all in accordance with God's will.

Animals only do what needs to be done, including to kill other animals in order to survive, either for food or to protect their territory or the gene pool of their group. That is the basis of their life in this world as God has ordained.

Only human beings commit murder, but, with rare exceptions, they only do this when they are taken over and under the control of a force lower than the true human force. In other words, they are judged as humans because that is their outer form, but inwardly they may have a nature on a sub human level, dominated by animal or even vegetable forces.

Perhaps this explains the words of Christ on the cross "Forgive them, Father, for they know not what they do."

When I mention the vegetable force, please don't imagine a cabbage or turnip. The vegetable force is the life force on the level of plants or flora. It is the force that drives growth and survival and is the essence of their nature. On this level there are hundreds of thousands of different species and each with a different nature. It is that life force and nature that enters human beings when we consume plants and vegetables.

For the most part we are only aware of the taste and texture of the plants and vegetables we consume, and we are not able to feel the effect of the nature and force of these plants that will influence our own nature. Although magic mushrooms and marijuana might give you a clue.

Bapak has actually written extensively about this in his book, *Susila Budhi Dharma*. I have to admit, when I first read about this many years ago, I found it way beyond my understanding and put it in my 'Sleeping dogs' file. But I am very grateful for Bapak's book now, because in the following years, as I began to have my own little revelations about these forces, I was able to refer back to Bapak's explanations and at least feel that what I was seeing was not just coming from my imagination.

For those who are as confused as I was, when I first read about 'vegetable forces', I can offer you this pointer regarding the different natures of plants and how they can exist and influence us human beings, as I have seen it. Sort of 'Vegetable forces for dummies'. We have already established what an excellent dummy I am.

We all know people who are very selfish, ambitious and relentless in their pursuit of their goals. Great for work and doing business, not so much for spiritual progress. They have little or no empathy or compassion for anyone around them and will happily push people out of their way to get what they want. Where does that nature come from? What force is dominating their inner character.

Now think of Bindweed. Doesn't bindweed have that same nature.Having bindweed in your garden is just as annoying as having a selfish, ambitious colleague in your office. Just ask any gardener.

From this you may be able to feel the nature of potatoes compared to rice and get a sense of how the nature of each influences a person who consumes either over time.

Well, if this subject is of interest to you, I suggest you read Bapak's book for a far deeper and comprehensive explanation of what I can only hint of here.

Back to Murder

So, I remember listening to Bapak back in the seventies when he said something like, "It is actually wrong to punish a thief or murderer, because they are only following their nature."

And for many years my heart and mind struggled to understand how that could be right, but eventually I began to see there are different laws on different levels. It took a long time to be able to separate myself from a lifetime of education about right and wrong in this world and receive some sense of the inner reality that Bapak was explaining.

This is what came floating into my brain:

From the viewpoint of the inner, we should not condemn a person who commits a crime, if they are only following the natural instinct of their low inner nature because, like an animal, it is not a sin or a crime in 'their world', on their 'level'.

However, for the greater good of society, just like wild animals, it is best to keep such a person caged.

But some wild animals can be domesticated and trained. For them there is hope for freedom.

This little insight answered a lot of my big questions about justice in life.

It's clear that we all have those lower forces within us because, if we did not, we would not be able to kill animals and plants for our own survival. The human race would be short lived.

My understanding of what Bapak had explained is; We have

those forces within us because we consume them in our food. The foetus grows on the food that the mother consumes, so even before we are born, those worldly forces are already an integral part of every human being. We can't escape them. Our very flesh is sustained by the vegetable world and our bones are formed from earthly minerals. The lowest level of all.

Someone with a human soul that is awake and active will be able to command and control those lower forces in themselves so that whatever animal or plant they kill is only out of necessity and they will consciously honour the sacrifice that those animals and plants make to sustain our life in this world.

In return for that sacrifice, and to fulfil one of our duties in this world, we invoke the name of God to bless our food, both when we kill an animal and when we consume our meals. Through this blessing, as we consume the inner content of our food, we human beings can raise those lower animal and vegetable forces, which themselves contain the lowest material forces of minerals, to a higher level.

If we don't bless the food we consume then we are acting on the level of animals and plants. That will bring the content of our soul, our inner quality, down toward their lower level, with severe ramifications for our life both in this world and in the hereafter.

This, I believe, and have been shown, is partly how a human soul can be brought down to a lower, sub-human level.

Without blessing our food we are in a way murdering that food twice. Once when we kill it and again when we consume it. This is the action of a person who is greedy, or at best unmindful of what they are doing as they go through life simply satisfying their desires.

In today's frantic world of 'fast food', GMO farming and mass market processed foods with strange additives, the importance of blessing our food can sound like a very quaint, irrelevant idea from some past era.

My experiences tell me something very different. I believe that it is even more important these days to be mindful of the consequences of all our actions for the sake of our inner progress and that includes our relationship with the food that sustains our life in this world. It remains important to bless and respect everything we consume.

In Bapak's book, *Susila Budhi Dharma*, Bapak explains the influence of different kinds of food on human beings. How the nature of each type of food will influence the nature of the person who consumes it. Things like the nature of fresh water fish verses that of fish from the ocean. I have mentioned a little about this here, but my experience is still exceedingly limited.

And while I still have many unanswered questions about these forces, it makes sense to me. Just from my earliest Subud experience I got a good indication. The first two things I had a lesson about, namely alcohol and pork.

One made from plants and the other that consumes plants, but both have a powerful effect on human beings.

It Might Take Time

During the seventies and eighties I recall hearing Bapak talk about all these forces and levels and how they influence our lives, and I have to say that at that time it all sounded like a very complicated and convoluted 'theory' that was way beyond my understanding.

Not that I rejected it, but my mind definitely was not capable of understanding the reality and truth about these forces. You could say that it was a lot of facts about sugar but I wasn't getting the sweetness.

Today I can see some small part of the truth about those forces and the 'nafsu' because of so many of my own experiences, where I have had certain forces within me separated out so that I could 'see', or feel them as individual entities that live with me, inside my body, and that they belonged there. They were my servants, there to help sustain my life and earthly body.

Without them I could not work, eat, paint, think, write, laugh, joke or make music or have a family. But they can also make life hell.

This broader understanding took many years to become clear and today my mind has no problem understanding and confirming the truth of Bapak's explanations for myself. That is not to say I have a complete understanding anywhere close to Bapak's, but I have enough to know I can believe and trust what Bapak has said and written.

I hope everyone who is just starting to do latihan will also be able to confirm these things for themselves in time.

Forgive me for this long digression, but this seemed to be the appropriate place to write about these things.

Back to the Journey. Stepping Stones
The Corridors of Powerlessness

So, back in 1969-70, as a Regional Chairman I had to attend a monthly meeting of the National Committee in London.

At one meeting in 1970 the agenda included the subject of Chartering aircraft to take members to the 1971 congress in Cilandak, Indonesia. During this discussion I raised the idea of setting aside some seats for members who 'should' go but financially were not able to afford to travel to Asia for 5 weeks. Later, testing indicated that 10 seats should indeed be set aside.

This was the only meaningful contribution I believe I ever made in any National Committee meeting and I never thought about it again.

In May of 1971, almost a year later, I received a call from my friend Sachlan North to tell me that I had been selected by testing to go to the Fourth World Congress in Indonesia, with a free seat on the plane.

I have to ask myself, was that regional congress in Tunbridge Wells, the dear Woman helper putting my name forward and the testing that made me a co-Regional Chairman all just a coincidence, or was it part of my destiny to get me to the 1971 Congress in Indonesia, when I definitely would not be in a position to pay my fare? Those are what I call 'stepping stones.'

But I am getting ahead of myself again because between serving my term on the National Committee in 1969-70 and flying off to Indonesia in July 1971, I had to go through my Skymont and Cincinnati experience.

The 'Crisis'. What Was that All About...
Why All the Questions?

Regarding the first question on the platform of Notting Hill Gate Underground: "How far are you from the light?"

In my mind I saw and felt a hundred feet of heavy, wet London clay pressing down on a little tube in which I was standing. A tube that could so easily be squashed flat in an instant. That's the worldly understanding.

But the true meaning is fairly obvious. The question was really "How far are you from your inner light. The clay was a representation of the layers of material forces, sins and mistakes that had accumulated within me over the few short years of my life, that formed this impenetrable prison around my inner. Now that was scary!

The second question came while sitting on the upper deck of a London bus going over Waterloo Bridge:

"What keeps the Bridge from falling down?"

In my imagination, but with a frighteningly realistic sense of physically falling, I experienced the bridge crumble and collapse, sending the bus and other cars crashing into the water.

The meaning of this question was to force my ego to give an answer that defied worldly logic. It appears that my ego wasn't very smart and it required several more terrifying experiences like this, including "How can a metal aircraft get off the ground, let alone stay airborne for hours?, What keeps boats from sinking?, Why don't skyscrapers fall over? What keeps this lift from falling to the basement? And many more similar questions before I finally understood.

Of course I had learned physics at school and could answer all those questions based on the basic laws of physics, but those scientific answers would not satisfy this questioner. This was another case of 'different laws on different levels.'

Today I can say that all the questions after Notting Hill Gate, had the same answer, that did not reveal itself to me until I was on my way flying back from America.

The answer to all of them was the same:

"Because of God's power".

This process of questions and received experiences was not some kind of theoretical exam. I actually experienced, to the extent that I was capable, what would happen if God withdrew His power and cancelled or changed His laws of physics. These short experiences lasted only seconds and I think they can be compared to putting on a pair of goggles and experiencing virtual reality.

What this meant was, that all of man's cleverness and skill in building and creating these fantastic things would be impossible without God's power and God's laws.

God makes the laws and sets the limits. Man then discovers those laws and tests the limits. One sign of man's folly and arrogance is, that when a man or woman discovers a new law, it is often called by the discoverer's name like 'Newton's law of motion' and 'Einstein's law of relativity' as though men made the laws.

We also say these are the laws of nature or the laws of physics, but in fact all these laws existed before man was even created on earth, and they are all God's laws.

Through that series of questions, followed by very short bursts of terror, I finally got the message. Everything, and I mean EVERYTHING, is dependent on Almighty God. That real safety and security for us in this world is in the laws and power of God. God the creator and benefactor of all mankind.

This again put the human ego, my ego, into perspective. However smart or talented we are, we are incapable of creating anything in this world without the certainty and stability of God's laws. God's power is infinite and the life force, that is God's power, permeates everything in the universe. If I ever had any doubt, it had been well and truly knocked out of me by the time this period was over.

Allow me to continue a little more on this subject

Scientists now know that every material substance that they can test and measure is made of identical particles simply arranged and grouped differently. Scientists can also confirm that every particle vibrates in a unique way.

Through the configurations of these particles, each infused with the vibration of God's life force, every substance, element and material is created in the universe with its own consistent, unique nature for a time appointed.

A material can be hard like a rock, steel and diamond or as soft as a flower petal. It can be a fluid or a gas. The finest of all is light, and I believe that light is the highest form of physical existence on this material level.

All these materials can return to pure energy and reform as another material. This is all the working of God's power in the material universe which today man calls physics on the subatomic level.

Scientists have even ventured into 'Quantum Physics' where they are discovering God's laws that are beyond man's powers of logic. In fact, to believe in many scientific theories these days actually requires a greater leap of faith than to believe in God and religion.

And it is because of God's Grace that these laws do not change from day to day, because if they did, all life would be impossible and the universe would be in constant, eternal chaos.

It was through experiencing this long series of 'Why' and 'How' questions during my early years in Subud that I finally understood that all living creatures have no option but to bow down to God's infinite greatness and, in my case specifically, left me no choice but to throw most of my ridiculous pride out the window. Most, but not all.

It is clear that I had to learn to be inwardly humble towards God, and not just give unconscious lip service with false modesty and fake subservience, which, sadly, I observe, is the all too common attitude to take these days, even within religious communities. Not to say there are no truly devout, holy people in the world, but I think it is safe to say, they are in the minority. But who am I to judge? Only God knows the truth of all things.

This process of education that I had received had been very effective because, by this point, after two years in Subud my heart and mind had been truly humbled by experiencing just a tiny taste of what God can do and what would happen if He decided to withdraw or change His will for the world! The entire universe would cease to exist! That's really scary when you receive and feel just a hint of the reality of that possibility.

Man Must Work
Stepping Stones. Trust Your Testing

When in late 1969 I became concerned about having no direction in my life I asked the Kingston helpers to test about my talent and possible career. I was not expecting to receive what we all did.

Bapak had advised me not to study and instead "Do what makes your heart happy", which I found hard to put into practice. In fact, this was a wrong translation of Bapak's words, which I found out a few years later.

The testing, as best we could interpret it, seemed to say "Look for a job, but don't take one!"

Somehow I found this very satisfying and not the least bit confusing.

By following this testing, quite unexpectedly, I came to be offered a job as an apprentice learning to restore paintings by Old Masters. The job came to me.

My friend in the flat downstairs brought me a very badly damaged painting of dubious value and with no providence, which his brother wanted to sell cheap. My boss gave me the 50 pounds sterling to buy it and after I had restored it the painting sold for 1,400 pounds. 50% of which was mine for the restoration work.

The money from this sale made it possible for me to attend the congress in Skymont.

Against all odds and without me even wanting to go to America, thanks to a Subud brother and his MG sports car, I was able to arrange my ticket, my vaccinations with documents and visa to America within one and a half working days.

I had applied for an 8-day visa to visit America for spiritual reasons, but was given a multiple entry visa valid for 3 years and I was allowed to work.

I had asked my helper to test, with some other helpers, whether it was right for me to go. My friend Ramzi had also tested and his answer was a definite NO. My testing was a resounding YES.

My helper told me many months later that he saw an image of me in the testing where I turned into a glass vessel with a human shape. Inside me were all these swirling colours in complete chaos, that slowly settled down into neat layers like a kind of horizontal rainbow.

He said he knew then that I really had to go, but didn't tell me in case I got scared. That was a bit redundant. I was already as scared about going as I could get.

Once again I have tried here to identify the series of key events that formed a clear path for me to go to Skymont, whether I liked it or not!

Of course the truth is I could have refused to go and scuttled the whole Skymont thing, except to do that would mean I was not sincere in worshipping God and was not prepared to be obedient to my inner guidance.

It would have meant giving in to the fears of my heart and putting a stop to my inner progress. That then would beg the question 'Why did I bother getting opened in Subud in the first place'.

So I did not resist, but I was extremely passive and made no attempt to help myself get to America. That was how I put the theory to test. If God really wants me to go He will arrange everything and make it happen. And so He did, using the good people around me. How foolish I was, as if I could test God!

And so I Arrived in Skymont
Clean as you go
My month in America was all about freeing me of my British her-

itage, or British baggage. The habits and beliefs I had acquired growing up and many of the values and principles peculiar to my British culture, but most important of all, to remove all the support for my ego that only existed in England. The comfort and familiarity of the past that makes changing oneself so difficult.

This went far beyond any loss of emotional or psychological support that one would normally call being 'homesick'.

The fear and disorientation that I experienced penetrated deep to my core. This was a continuation of the series of experiences I had with the 'Why' and 'How' questions, except there were no more questions, just answers and more enigmatic experiences.

I think I have explained most of the experiences I had whilst in America. It was a mixed bag of scary purification, basic education and a sprinkling of startling insights.

The scary stuff I think I have covered enough for now. The basic education was when my faculties underwent purification and as they became clearer they began to perform as they should and were becoming more obedient to my inner. The process of purification for me was quite intense and to my mind, at that time, quite inexplicable.

The sudden inability to continue talking mid-sentence.

The loss of hearing, in the sense that I could hear people talking but my brain could make no sense of the noises they made.

And there was the day I could not get out of bed or talk or make any kind of movement until it was evening and time to go to latihan. (It is clear to me now that all these experiences were caused by the action of the latihan working from my inner to purify each of these faculties. At the time I had no idea what was happening to me.)

My experience of standing alone, deep in a forest in the middle of the night, when I discovered that everything outside exists or can be reached from within. The soul can rise up and reach to the stars while all the time remaining within the core of ones being. It felt like I was going to die at the time.

One other little incongruity that stands out from my time in America was being able, in my state, to drive a Subud member from Cincinnati to Lexington, having never driven a car on a road before, and then, while that Subud member enrolled themself in the University, I went alone and, on their behalf, I was able to purchase a refrigerator and gas stove, have them installed and get the power and utilities put on at their apartment, all in the space of three hours.

As a foreigner with no experience in these matters I am still amazed at how it was possible for me to do that.

In Case You Were Wondering

Through all these experiences I was too preoccupied with my own inner turmoil to worry about what other people might think. Thank goodness I was with Subud brothers and sisters who at least knew I was going through some intense inner purification and sorting out. Anyone else, outside of Subud, would probably have taken me straight to the psychiatric ward of the nearest hospital.

Actually, somewhere in my brain the fear that, "if anyone really knew what was going on inside of me, they would declare me insane!", was a genuine concern that I had that just added to my fears.

As an aside, I wonder sometimes how many people may have had a spiritual experience, perhaps on a bus crossing a bridge or on the platform of an underground station and ended up being taken to a doctor and forced to take horrific, mind bending drugs, in an attempt to bring them back to their 'normal' selves.

That too is a bit scary.

How well do doctors understand the difference between a damaged brain or chemical imbalance requiring treatment and medication, versus an intense inner experience that will resolve itself without any special care or mind-altering drugs?

This is why a person suffering from mental illness may not be opened in Subud. It could result in enormous confusion for that person as a brain that is malfunctioning can react very erratically to stimuli that arise from within, which will have all the appearances of a crisis, except it could continue for as long as the mental or psychological problem exists.

They may indeed experience some deep insights into life and the inner world, but they will not be able to benefit from such experiences, if their brain cannot function in a logical and stable way.

Post America Summary

When I returned to England I felt like an empty vessel and very disconnected from everything that once was so familiar. In a sense I had died in America and so much of what I thought was my 'self' was now buried in that land.

All I had was a pile of fragmented experiences swirling around in my mind, which made it almost impossible to explain what I had been through. It took months and years for that inner whirlwind to settle down to a point where I could begin to explain things relatively coherently.

Back in the UK, whilst the obedience and training of my heart continued, I found I was also entering a new phase of purification and education that started very soon after my return.

The focus of my crisis now expanded to include the purification of my physical body and home environment in terms of creating a balance between my inner condition as it was becoming cleaner, and my outer, material condition. The lifestyle I had to adopt was pretty extreme, but very liberating. Indeed, during that period, I felt a degree of peace and calmness that is exceedingly rare in this modern world.

The irony is that the other side of my obedience training was about to come to its zenith. Just prior to this period of purification of my personal life, the level of my inner fear reached my maximum limit. One night I was experiencing a degree of fear that sent my mind reeling trying to rationalize the cause.

My intellect finally settled on the conviction that I was having premonitions of an apocalyptical third world war, as the only rational thing that could generate so much fear in me. That was the best I could come up with. Doctors would describe this as a series of panic attacks and no doubt would prescribe anti-anxiety medicines to help me avoid this experience.

I am quite happy to accept panic attacks as a good description, but I can look back now and say that I am glad I went through this experience without doctors or medicines. One outstandingly patient and understanding helper and a generous neighbour with an MG and the moral support of a few good friends was all the support I could ask for and I owe them much.

I do also feel I have a debt to one Alsatian dog who may have made a supreme sacrifice.

I will mention here one difficulty that was important for my conscious faith, which was my mind asking, "are my experiences really being guided from my inner? Is this really 'from God'?

Another irony was that for a few months up to the Merton fire and as my levels of fear were rising, when I went to latihan, I would often stand there feeling completely normal, free of all fear, and I would end up just sitting down on one of the chairs that were lined up against the wall, calmly having a cigarette while everyone else continued doing latihan.

It was during latihan that I lost all sense of fear and could fully relax and feel comfortable while I pondered about my life in what I would call a normal, familiar way. As soon as latihan was over, the feelings of fear would slowly return and it was back to my inner training.

After the night of the Calor gas fire in Merton, the feelings of doom and gloom subsided quickly, and I began the process of familiarizing myself with a new 'Me'. I was now slowly able to 'enjoy' some of the rewards of what I had been through for the past year.

Going For A Spin In My New Car

I can't really detail all the examples of how my new self could do things my old self could never even imagine. What I can do is choose the most relevant events that best illustrate how my new self-operated. These stories are not in chronological order because there were often overlaps where two or more things were happening within the same period.

Twists and Turns
Lose Your Job, Win an Award

Several weeks after the Merton LPG Factory fire my heart and mind were finally settling down to accepting my new 'self' and I was feeling that I needed to work. Since returning from America I had been in no state to work and had been supported by friends and even the Subud UK organization.

And so it was, I happened to visit a friend who was renting a flat in the house next door. It just so happened that her boyfriend, Roy, was there and we talked about my situation. To my surprise he offered to try and get me a job in the company where he worked which was within walking distance from Manorgate Road, where I lived.

The company, amongst other things, produced specialized, innovative educational materials and textbooks for the MacMillan Publishing Company. For about two months I worked on producing charts, diagrams and illustrations for my boss, Roy. The last job Roy gave me was to create a diagram that would describe a manufacturing process from the arrival of the raw materials to the shipment of the finished product. I can't even remember now what that product was, but the process was complicated, and the diagram had to explain it to children aged between 8 to 10 years old.

I knew that three previous diagrams by other designers had been rejected, so this was quite a challenge. I recall it took me a whole week to complete my diagram and it was submitted to Macmillan's.

Now, it just so happened that this company was called Structural Communications Inc. and had been establish by Mr. John Bennet of Tibetan dance fame. Most of the employees were his pupils from Coombe Springs, who all knew something about Subud, but had chosen to continue to follow Bennet and the teachings of Gurdjieff.

Perhaps it was because I was still in quite a strange state that soon after I joined the company more and more of the staff would come and chat with me. They wanted to know more about Subud and my experiences after being opened. I did my best to convey my experiences, although I still had little or no understanding to explain what I had been through.

I have no idea what I said to them, but I know a small group of them were well on their way to joining Subud when, one morning I was called to see Mr Bennet in his room. It was a short but pleasant meeting. He basically said he was sure I would understand that I really was not compatible with the aims of his company and so it would be better if I resigned.

I completely understood his meaning and accepted my generous severance pay; we shook hands and I walked home. Three months later Roy dropped round one lunch time to let me know that my last diagram had won some internal Macmillan's award.

I would have felt vindicated then, except I could not because I didn't have those kinds of feelings anymore since returning from American. They did slowly re-emerge like a distant echo over the following years, but when they arise, they are only fleeting. I really do not like those kinds of painful feelings.

I would like to say that I found John Bennet one of the most sincere and gentle souls I have met. Acutely intelligent, well read, and compassionate, he worked tirelessly to achieve what he believed was his mission and had a great impact on many people's lives. He provided the first home for Subud outside of Indonesia and is an important part of the history of this brotherhood.

A Test Run
Bon Voyage and Back

Earlier I mentioned that at the first regional congress I attended in Tunbridge Wells, that we Kingston lads were busy entertaining two lovely young French girls, one of whom was in Subud, in the beautiful Kent countryside.

Now, eighteen months later I got an invite to visit Paris to stay with one of those young ladies in her parents' home in Paris. What prompted this trip was the news that Pak Brodjolukito, who was a secretary to Bapak, and was accompanied by his French wife Ulfiah, would be visiting the Paris Subud group and Pak Brodjo would be giving a talk.

As one of Bapak's assistants, Pak Brodjo had a lot of experience in the latihan and because I was now feeling in a good enough state to appreciate hearing his stories and explanations, I thought I would venture out into the world again. Pak Brodjo would be the first Indonesian I ever met up close and I was also curious to get to know how Indonesians were.

And so I left for Paris. I arrived at Gare du Nord station early in the evening and I had the young lady's address in a Paris suburb written on another one of those small pieces of paper.

My problem was that I only spoke about ten words of French and half of those were rude. Adding to my problem, I discovered that the French seemed to have a real aversion to speaking English. So, it took quite a while for me to get directions I could understand as to what train to take and what station to get out at.

Finally, I was standing at the front door of a large, quite old Parisian house and I knocked on the door. After a minute Monique (not her real name) holding a large towel that was curled on her head, opened the door.

She was clearly embarrassed to be caught having just washed her hair, but she invited me in and I was introduced to her mother and older brother. I would not meet her father until the next day at breakfast.

I soon discovered that Monique and I were the only people in the house who could speak English.

I was shown to my room and I settled in and after an excellent dinner we all retired for the night. I was happy that I was not having any strange doom and gloom feelings, which had been a nagging concern before leaving England.

The next morning, I came down to breakfast and took my place at a large table in the kitchen opposite Monique's father. Two feet behind me was the cooking range which was a very large Arga range that used coke instead of gas or electricity. It also heated all the hot water for the house.

Monique's father was of Italian descent and very conservative. He did not look happy. Apparently, I was not the first young

Englishman that Monique had brought home and he did not approve of my presence.

At this time, I was still coming to learn about my new self and one thing that was very clear was that I could not get into any kind of relationship with a girl, but there was no way I could explain that to him, or to Monique for that matter. She was not in Subud.

Monique's mother had served us all large bowls of strong coffee and then she reached down and opened one of the smaller oven doors right next to me and removed a pair of well-worn slippers, which she took round to Monique's father who immediately slipped them on.

I looked at Monique and she stared back at me, slightly embarrassed, as she took a sip of her coffee. I then said to her, "In England we use those (ovens) to bake bread!" She immediately burst into uncontrollable laughter, spraying her coffee on to the table in front of her.

I really didn't think my little joke was that funny. By the look on her father's face I didn't think he thought it was funny at all, as he gruffly demanded she tell him what I had said. Monique translated my comment and after a short pause he burst into laughter, too. Amazing! I had achieved détente with a single silly British joke.

After breakfast Monique's father insisted I follow him into the back garden where he had a large wooden structure in which he kept about thirty prize homing pigeons.

We spent half an hour trying to communicate with each other using sign language and broken words, but at least he smiled a lot. Monique told me later that showing me his pigeons was a great privilege because her father was a very private person. That slipper joke had worked like a charm.

Later that day the second young lady from the Tunbridge

Wells congress turned up. I'll call her Michelle. She was the Subud member and she had a car and had said in her letter that she would take me to the Paris Subud Hall for Pak Brodjo's visit. But as soon as I mentioned visiting the Subud group her expression turned sad.

She then explained that, not long after the Tunbridge Wells congress, she had gotten into a relationship with a French medical student and had become pregnant. The student had left her before she gave birth and she was now a single mother.

If that wasn't already bad enough, the older, ultra conservative Paris Subud members at that time had been so critical of her for getting pregnant out of wedlock that she had virtually been ostracised and so stopped going to latihan.

This was a fundamental problem with deep rooted, judgemental cultures. Add to that the generation gap of the sixties and their attitude could be expected.

So, she really did not want to visit the Subud hall, however, she felt bad for me and agreed to drive me to the hall at the end of the week, when Pak Brodjo would give his talk.

Over the next few days Monique, Michelle and I took sightseeing trips in and around Paris. As the days passed, I became aware that I was speaking a lot of French. In fact, by the end of one week I was able to converse with Monique's father and even make more British jokes about his pigeons, but in French.

Two years of learning French in school had resulted in me being able to say about three sentences, but now, after just five days, I was becoming pretty fluent.

On the day of Pak Brodjo's talk, Michelle picked me up and Monique came along for the ride. After about forty minutes we arrived at what I believe was the Latin Quarter of Paris. Michelle began driving very slowly and I sensed she was actually very nervous about meeting the Subud members.

Suddenly she pulled over and stopped. She pretended that she could not remember where the hall was and started apologizing to me profusely. Spontaneously I reassured her that there was no problem and no need for her to worry. I told her to stay in the car as I opened the door and got out.

My New Legs Had Autopilot!

I stood on the pavement and my legs just started walking. It is hard to explain if you have not done latihan, but almost every Subud member will know how it feels when we allow our body to be moved in latihan.

About thirty meters ahead I came to a T-junction and I looked to the right and then to the left. My legs wanted to go left so I went left. After another thirty meters or so I came to another T-junction and my legs took me across the road, turning right.

All the buildings along this street were very old houses behind tall walls with large, cobbled stone forecourts. The entrances had huge, double doors large enough for a horse drawn carriage to pass through in the olden days.

Suddenly my legs stopped, and I was looking at two huge closed doors wondering what I should do now. I then felt the urge to turn around and, when I did, I noticed the entrance doors on the opposite side of this narrow street were slightly open.

Through the gap between the doors I could see across the courtyard, on a pillar, was a very small blue sign about 20cm square. I looked again and realized it was the Subud symbol. My legs had brought me to the Subud hall.

Monique and Michelle had been slowly following me in the car and had stopped a few meters back. I suggested to them to just leave me there and go off wherever they wanted, but if they could, please pick me up in two hours.

This part of the Paris trip was my first experience of what

Bapak meant when he said the latihan purifies our whole being so that our inner can penetrate every part of our body. So that is why many members walk around, seemingly aimlessly, when doing their latihan. My legs were able to be guided by my inner with no involvement of my mind or will. My inner knew what my mind could not.

This was the result of all the spontaneous movements during my latihan and the more intense experiences I had in America. The proof that my inner, to some extent at least, could be active in all aspects of my earthly life and, if I was mindful and obedient, it could truly determine my movements, voice, sight, feelings and even my thinking.

Over time I began to really understand what Bapak was talking about, how our spontaneous movements in latihan were how we were both purified and then trained to follow our inner guidance. I could even begin to see what was meant in the Koran about how, in the afterlife, our own limbs will testify against us.

If we misuse our bodies, we damage that part of our soul, which will become obvious after death when only our soul will continue. The same with our faculties. But I am getting ahead of myself again.

I remember little about Pak Brodjo's talk and the following latihan. I do remember introducing myself to a few of those old, conservative members and sensing how they were not that happy having this strange, long haired, nineteen-year-old boy from England suddenly turn up. They probably thought I was one of those weird British Hippies they had read about!

Michelle and Monique had kindly returned and were waiting for me and together we all went back to Monique's home. My GPS legs were never mentioned, but I could tell from their subdued voices that my actions that day, finding the hall, had unnerved them somewhat. I said nothing.

Having the inner move the body in this way was to save my life two times in the future, which I will come to later.

Help! I'm Turning French!

A few days after visiting the Subud Hall in Paris I was preparing for my trip home. I spent some time in the garden with Monique's father and his pigeons. We discussed several things about life and laughed quite a bit. He even said, to Monique's amazement, that I was welcome to visit again.

On my last night, I was lying in bed and in my mind I was going through all the steps I would need to take the next day to get myself back to Kingston.

I suddenly realized that I was thinking in French!! I laughed and thought to myself what an idiot I was because I couldn't go back to England speaking French. I would never live down the shame! The trouble was, even that thought, I was thinking in French.

That sent me into a bit of a panic. I had lost my English!!

I tried forcing myself to recall the English words for various things like naming fruit, place names and conversations I had with friends. It truly was a struggle for my mind and left me wondering what I was going to do.

My mind did still like to worry sometimes.

So, it seemed that my clever little inner had even penetrated my 'thinking' and in less than two weeks had cunningly substituted the standard English dictionary in my brain with a French one. I was not amused!

Once again, I was being shown how the inner has extraordinary access to knowledge and the power to insert that knowledge into our conscious thinking mind. In terms of my words, accent and even the way I moved and so on, I had basically become French. What worse punishment for an Englishman could there be!

This was further evidence that Bapak's explanations about how the latihan can purify the mind, after which the inner can actively provide real, practical, worldly information that was actionable, was not a theory or made up claim.

I think this mental language swap was the most extreme example of this that I have ever experienced.

The next day, on the channel Ferry, I finally felt the 'Frenchness' leave and the 'English me' being restored the closer we came to England. Only then did I appreciate what a wonderful experience that had been. Never to be repeated in that way again.

In Case You Are Wondering
An Obedient Heart

In the state I was still in, I could be nothing but a perfect gentleman towards Monique, even though she made it clear that I had every opportunity to embrace her very warm hospitality any time I wished. Why had she invited me to stay with her after all.

She had tried quite hard to persuade me to join her in St. Tropez for the summer, where she had been offered a job by a music company that was opening new offices and a studio there.

I was confronted with a choice; St. Tropez or Cilandak in Indonesia. A summer with a beautiful young French woman on the French Riviera, or five weeks in a very hot and humid compound, living in a bamboo long-house with two thousand Subud members from all around the world surrounded by about two million mosquitoes?

It was hard for me to see her disappointment when I gently declined her offer. But of course, I did not really have a choice. I had to do what was right according to my inner, not what my heart may desire. No shiny objects for me. That was the result of my obedience training.

The Long Goodbyes

Having returned safely to my attic flat in Manorgate Road, I was now counting the few weeks left before I would be taking off to the congress in Cilandak.

During this time I met with many of my relatives for what turned out to be a last goodbye. That didn't make a lot of sense at the time because I was only going to be away for five weeks.

The Shiny Objects for the Boys

During the months between returning from America and my departure to Indonesia, I had received five proposals of marriage. One happened in France as you may have guessed. These proposals came from young women, two in Subud who I had known for some time, the others were virtual strangers. Their ages ranged from 23 to 28. whereas I was just 20 at the time.

This sudden popularity perplexed me at the time because, as I have explained, I was basically unemployed, had no academic qualifications and certainly no money in the bank. In fact I didn't even have a bank account. Everything a woman doesn't look for in a husband.

All I can say is, I did have an obedient heart, which seemed to be what was attracting these women to me. And this is the catch-22, because when the heart is obedient it makes it impossible to take advantage of people, in this case, very nice, attractive young women, simply to satisfy my lower desires.

I will not enumerate the number of opportunities I was offered to satisfy my lower desires without even the complication of a commitment to marriage. To all those young ladies I had no choice but to decline their offers. After all the fear and purification I had been through, I really didn't want to make any mistakes.

There is, I believe, a very important lesson in this for all young men. While I came to understand why these ladies were attracted to me, I knew none of them were the right woman for my life, nor was it the right time for me to get married. On that basis, any relationship would not only be pointless for both of us, but also would not last long. Such relationships would also result in a lot of damage to the inner, as I had seen in many young people when I was in America.

What was clear was that many women are attracted to men who are not driven or controlled by their desires and yet, ironically they will work very hard to try and get such a man to make an exception in their case, and follow those very same desires with them.

Obedient Hearts Are Often Misunderstood

One of the changes that took place in me as my heart learned to be more obedient was that I did not react or panic about events in the way most people would expect. If I lost some material possession, or a person broke a promise, I would not get upset. My heart would appear to be almost indifferent.

If a person had lost someone close to them I would feel the compassion in my heart for them and their grief, but at the same time I would also feel a prayer that came from beyond my heart for the person they had lost. So I would not be so solemn or sad.

Even the loss of my brother and my parents, after a very short period of sadness, did not cause my heart to mourn or grieve for any extended period. Indeed, I felt closer to them than in life and a feeling of joy and love for them arose in my heart that quickly overwhelmed my sadness.

For those who observed my apparent lack of grief, many often interpreted it as being heartless. But this balance between grief and happiness I know is a common experience for many Subud members who have good, compassionate hearts.

Worldly Relationships of the Heart

My experience has been that generally people who are ruled by their hearts, especially teenagers and young adults, will think a person with an obedient heart is pretty strange, but the fact is, just like me at that age, they are not yet able to understand or feel the difference between a heart filled with powerful desires that dominate a person's life and a heart that, for the most part is obedient to a person's inner.

This is very pertinent when it comes to first impressions when men and women meet.

In general what most people judge in an encounter with someone they are attracted to, is how that person's heart responds to their advances. And they will judge, or read a person's responses based on their own experience, what they have been taught by parents, friends, films and magazines, and these days of course we must add 'social media'.

So, to respond to a person's advances in a different way to what Hollywood and all the other external influences say is the 'normal' response, is very confusing.

Unfortunately films and magazines are written very much to attract and entertain the nafsu and so they inevitably reinforce the culture of the nafsu, the so called 'natural' desires. They are the creation of the material nafsu in the minds of the people who produce them, and money is the underlining motivation.

The result of this, especially in the last century, has been to break down the values and fears of acting in ways that damage the human soul. You could say it has been a form of moral corruption, but I won't say that because I begin to sound like my grandparents, except of course they were right.

This erosion of moral values has caused a tremendous

amount of pain and suffering which young people have great difficulty to avoid. The problem is, those forces from the nafsu are very strong and persistent. Even with the cultural restraints and higher moral values of the past it is clear that man has struggled to control the desires of lust, and love of wealth and worldly power since the beginning of civilization.

Now I Am Going to Sound Like an 'Old Man'

If a woman displays her desires, she expects the man to respond positively, as many men will happily do. But if a man does not respond most women look for a fault in the man, to excuse or cover their own embarrassment. This shows that deep down they are still aware that their actions are not motivated by their inners, but by the lower forces of the nafsu that reside in their heart.

They may feel deeply hurt at being rejected and wonder if there is something they lack in terms of attractiveness, but the inner reality is they are feeling shame for following their desires. They cannot easily accept that a man's desires can actually be restrained by his inner guidance. In fact that is the duty of every man to not only restrain his own desires, but also those of every woman. A very difficult duty to perform.

Many young women may consider a man's lack of response as a fault or insult. This is a sad fact of modern life that so many girls grow up with little understanding of how a 'good' man acts, and that leads to so many problems for so many young people who follow, and respond to, the desires of their heart with no inner guidance.

This works both ways. How many men actively seek out women to despoil? If their attempts at seduction fail then they immediately find fault with the woman and criticize her to protect the embarrassment felt by their own ego.

The irony is that many women are attracted to a man who has an obedient heart, but, if he gives in to his lusts, which those women will tempt him to do, he will lose the very thing that made him attractive to them in the first place.

The man will also experience a decline in his spirit and he will lose his inner peace if he gives in and follows his base desires.

That situation is what is known as a 'catch 22'. The more a man restrains his desires the more attractive he becomes to many women, who will try very hard to make him give in to the force of his lust, and thereby lose the very thing the woman admired. Such a man, you would think, might never get married or even have a girlfriend for very long.

Of course this does not apply if both the man and the woman are dominated by the nafsu. A woman who may appear as pure and innocent can in fact have very powerful nafsu that will be attracted to the nafsu of some very unsavoury men. Life is complicated!

Another story that illustrates this in the Bible is the story of Joseph.

Joseph, who had been sold to Potiphar, an officer of the Pharaoh, came to be trusted and honoured in Potiphar's household. He was, however, falsely accused by Potiphar's wife, Lempsar, of trying to violate her, after her attempts at seduction had failed. Joseph ended up in prison on these false charges which was both Lempsar's revenge for rejecting her advances and her way of hiding her sin from her husband.

I believe the story of Samson and Delila in the bible illustrates the same thing, in a roundabout way. If a man's heart stops being obedient and he follows his desires, or succumbs to temptation, the temple will be destroyed for both the man and the woman! I can see how 'The Temple' can be a metaphor for their souls being brought down.

In a way, looking back, that was the test I was confronted with in Paris., albeit in a far less dramatic way. Fortunately, I was in a state of naivety and did not realize I was being tested at the time. Ignorance is bliss, as they say, except for Joseph, apparently.

But I had a lot more to learn about this in the years to come. The relationship between a man and a woman, husband and wife, parents and children, are the most influential and complicated matters for both our inner and outer lives. There is much I am still learning even today.

From these experiences I came to understand the truth of Bapak's words that, without the help of God, it is virtually impossible to change our inner state. We can make efforts to control the weaker forces that urge us to tell lies, or be boastful , to reduce our criticism of others and avoid gossiping etc.

But to actually change our character and train those more powerful nafsu cannot be done by our own willpower alone, because those very same forces we want to overcome are present in our will and are part of our character.

This is the benefit of the latihan. From the time we are opened, these forces start to be separated and become recognizable to us. As we progress, these nafsu begin to change through the working of the latihan without any involvement of our will other than to surrender.

Eventually these forces are sorted out and will become obedient through the power of God. In this way our character will be improved and old habits and desires will, as it were, evaporate.

*

The Djameechoonatra at Coombe Springs, and below, the magnificent stained glass window.

Bapak at Coombe Springs in 1958.

*Bapak with his wife, Ibu Siti Samari, in the garden
at Coombe Springs in 1958.*

PART 2

All the World's a Stage

Indonesia

In July of 1971 a chartered Caledonian Airlines 707 took off from London filled with excited Subud members heading for the Subud Congress in Cilandak, Indonesia. Most were from the UK but there were also quite a few Americans and Europeans.

After a long flight, including a refuelling stop in Karachi, we were approaching Kemayoran airport in Jakarta. As we came into land, we noticed we were flying parallel to the runway, not over it. I then saw a large fire truck parked at the end of the runway and wondered what was up? Suddenly the plane banked sharply and did a 'U-turn' over the truck and bang, we were rumbling along the runway.

It transpired that Caledonian Airlines had not been able to get landing rights in time and the Indonesian airport authorities had tried to block our landing. The pilots were arrested and were held for a week in a hotel. I won't go into the details of why landing rights had not been granted except to say it was to do with business.

Once in the airport we saw many police standing around carrying what looked like AK 45 automatic rifles. This was the first time I had seen such weapons in public. Apparently, we had arrived in the middle of Indonesia's first election and security was high.

We quickly got through immigration and customs and exited the building. Outside several buses were parked, which we quickly filled, and we set off in a convoy with a police motorcycle escort. We kind of felt special and a bit nervous at the same time.

It took about half an hour to arrive at the entrance to Wisma Subud. As we drove through the large gateway, it was like entering a carnival. There were banners and flags everywhere. There were small kiosks and many temporary restaurants built of bamboo. And then we saw the big two storey bamboo long-houses in which most of us would be accommodated. It all looked quite magical to me.

Later that first evening, as the sun was going down, I walked back to the entrance and stood looking across the street at the banana trees and a few small one storey houses down the road. Everything looked so strange and different to anything that I had ever experienced, but inside, I had this strong feeling that I had finally come home.

My First Contact

Whilst standing there on the side of the road, an attractive, middle-aged Indonesian lady dressed in traditional Indonesian kabaya stepped out of a rare taxi and walked in through the entrance. She stopped, and with a typical warm, welcoming Indonesian smile, she turned to me and asked me my name and where I came from. Her English was surprisingly good and she asked about my home Subud group as I walked with her back into the compound.

She then asked me, out of the blue, if I had already eaten dinner, just like a mother would. I said, "Not yet," and she invited me to join her at one of the many temporary restaurants that had been put up for the congress.

That evening I had my first taste of sate ayam with lontong. It was excellent and unbelievably cheap. Actually free. The restaurant owner knew this woman and didn't charge her anything.

Some of the older English Subud members who saw me with her acted quite strangely when I met them later. It was then that I found out that she was Ibu Mastuti who, for many years oversaw the preparation of Bapak's food, and was always in his entourage when he travelled overseas. I had no idea.

This was when, sadly, I became aware of a common human

characteristic that genuinely surprised me. A form of jealousy to do with status or power. From one or two of my Subud brothers and sisters I could sense some resentment and suspicion, as if I had orchestrated my meeting with Ibu Mastuti in an attempt to get closer to Bapak.

It took me a while to understand that some people, even Subud brothers doing latihan, could still think like this. It was so far from my own approach to life that I did not recognise what their problem was for quite some time.

There were a few other brothers and sisters who had the opposite reaction. They were really happy for me to have this chance meeting, because maybe I could get close to Bapak. This seemed equally wrong and perplexing to me. It seems my two years of crisis had left me in a state of extreme naivety. But I don't want to judge. I have plenty of my own faults to work on.

Two days later I met Ibu Mastuti again when she visited a small, temporary, combination food stall and shop that her sister was running in the area of the long house where I was staying. She was happy to see me and started a conversation. I was surprised she even remembered me. I found her to be completely normal with no affectations or arrogance at all. She was just like an ordinary mum. Her close proximity to Bapak was not something she felt made her special.

Although I was twenty, I looked about seventeen. Perhaps that is why she kind of took me under her wing. She invited me to join her and her children on a day trip later that week to the mountain town of Bogor, and on other occasions I was invited to join them on some sightseeing trips around Jakarta.

Unfortunately this only added to some people's feelings I can only describe as envy, which I found so out of place. But it is a valuable reminder that when we get opened in Subud we do not immediately become perfect people. It's a long, long process of purification and education by our inner, that Bapak's daughter, Ibu Rahayu, said will go on even in the next world.

A Different Kind of Opening

The congress was opened about a week after we had arrived. President Suharto attended the opening ceremony and gave a speech welcoming almost two thousand foreign Subud members to Indonesia and congratulating Pak Subuh for the important work he was doing to bring spiritual awareness to the world.

The congress really was a kind of celebration of humanity with international cultural events, workshops, socializing and a dazzling array of Indonesian cuisine. But the foundation of the Congress was the exceedingly strong latihans and many talks given by Bapak, often with testing.

I could feel many similar things rising up in me that I had experienced in America during my crisis, but not with the same level of fear. After Bapak's talks and testing I would see many members walking around in a kind of shell shock state for an hour or two. Something I was very familiar with.

Luckily, they only felt that way for a short time before they could get back to feeling their familiar selves, albeit slightly changed. That is preferable I think to the intense changes I experienced. So now it was my turn to feel a little envy.

A Second Beginning

After five weeks, the congress came to an end and it was time to go home. For me this was a difficult time. Since that first evening, standing by the road at the front of Wisma Subud, I had felt like I was home, even though everything I saw around me was alien, it felt familiar. Because of this feeling of being in the right place, the idea of returning to the UK made me feel like I was being sent away, far from home. I really wanted to stay. But that was a big decision.

I decided to ask Ibu Mastuti if she could ask Bapak if it was right for me to stay in Indonesia. Her answer was quite perplexing. She simply asked if I felt it was right to stay in Indonesia and I said yes. Then she said, "Well stay!".

So, when the English members gathered to coordinate arrangements to get to the airport, I announced that I would not be joining them. My seat on the plane was given to a young English Subud member who I heard had hitchhiked from the UK to Singapore and then taken a boat to Jakarta to get to the congress. Now he could fly home.

The next day, as the British members boarded the buses to the airport, one of my friends came to me and gave me thirty thousand rupiah that they had collected for me. That was about US$80 at that time. He said "Don't come back to England after just one month. Stay until you have done everything you need to do!"

I had no idea what I needed to do. I had no idea what lay ahead of me. Fifty years later I still haven't done everything I need to do it seems.

A Test of Faith

I watched as the convoy of buses left and I was sorry to see them go. I had Thirty thousand rupiah, a small suitcase with a couple of shirts, a pair of jeans, socks and underwear, a razor and toothbrush and absolutely no plan. Everything I needed to start a whole new life in a foreign country, apparently.

My heart certainly felt apprehensive at the challenge before me.

Fortunately, many members extended their stay after the congress and there were still about 300 members from all over the world staying in the compound. I was not alone.

The last of the bamboo long houses in the compound remained in place for about five years, which provided shelter for several single Subud members, including me, on and off for several months. Three of us never went home again.

Now, fifty years later, I live in Wisma Subud in a large four-bedroom house with my wife and daughter. My eldest son is married and living in America, and my youngest is studying in New Zealand. So, a lot has changed. That little suitcase was sufficient after all. There must have been a plan, it's just I wasn't allowed to see it at the time.

But this is a story about my experiences related to the latihan, not an autobiography or travelogue, so I shall focus more on the events and experiences I have had in Indonesia, which I see as the stepping stones of my inner progress, and how it has been expressed in my outer life. And perhaps, the plan may be revealed, in retrospect.

Many of the smaller things, I believe, it is best to skip. Your life is too short to be bothered with those details. I shall focus on the things that really stand out for me, both for my inner development and outer progress and how I see there is synergy between the two. Hopefully it won't be too boring.

The Early Years. Stepping Stones
Initially I stayed outside of the compound in the middle of the city with a family who came from Padang, an area in West Sumatra. They were friends of a Subud member, but were not in Subud. I was there to teach their children English in return for room and board and basically pocket money.

Padang food is amongst the hottest of all Indonesian cuisine and I used to joke that even the water was chili hot.

I often felt very homesick there, but it never shook my belief that this was the path I have to travel. I rarely went out or met any English-speaking people and they were not too happy about me going twice a week to Cilandak for latihan. Quite honestly I felt like a well looked after captive.

The man of the house owned the second largest travel agency in Indonesia so, when it came time to extend my visa, he took me to meet his friendly contact in the central Indonesian Immigration Office, who turned out to be the head of the department for foreigners.

I sat before this senior officer while my 'employer' explained my situation. The officer took my passport and flicked through it. He stopped and commented in English, "So, you have been to America." He put my passport down, looked at the Travel Agent and said, "I can extend his visa, but... he hesitated briefly, he has to move to my house!"

My 'employer' looked shocked and a bit annoyed, but he knew he could not refuse because he needed this official to keep his business, bringing in foreign tour groups, running smoothly. And so that evening a Mercedes turned up at the house and I was driven to the immigration official's house in West Jakarta, with my little suitcase and guitar, of course.

What joy! My newly adopted family were Javanese and the food was wonderful. The immigration officer had three children, none of whom were interested in learning English, but he also had several companies involved in some big government projects. He was very glad for my inputs translating letters from foreign companies and writing replies.

He was also very interested in Subud and had been involved in the immigration issues for the Subud Congress. His family were good Muslims and prayed five times a day most days, but in no way were they fanatical. We would stay up late talking about Subud and Islam and I saw how their religion formed a foundation for their family and daily life.

After about three months I felt a genuine desire to become a Muslim. He was both surprised and overjoyed when I asked him what I had to do. He basically said, "Leave it to me," and two weeks later, on my 21st birthday, there were three hundred people from the local area in Slipi, and a senior figure from the Ministry of Religion, all gathered in his house and under awnings in the garden, who had come to celebrate my entering Islam.

After a very short ceremony I received a Koran in English signed by the Minister of Religion and then the celebrations went on into the night with entertainment for the local 'village' people who gathered in the street in front of his house. Everyone got food and refreshments and I was left amazed. I have no idea how much he spent for this celebration, nor did the subject ever come up. I am very greatful for his unusual generosity.

Meantime...

During this time, I was given a job in a newly established advertising agency that was managed by a wonderful English Subud member we called Mr. Pollard.

Each morning one of the art directors who lived close to Slipi would pick me up on his 90cc Honda moped. Clinging to him on the back of the tiny machine, my European sized body must have looked very comical as we made the thirty-minute ride through Jakarta to the office, rain or shine.

Just for some context, it was 1972 and back then someone from the office would have to go to Singapore every month to buy supplies of felt pens, layout pads, paste-up glue, plastic rulers and set squares and even pencils and Rapidograph ink, which were not yet available in Jakarta. There was no TV advertising and no glossy magazines, so there was no real modern advertising industry.

A few months after I joined Islam, I moved from the house in Slipi because I had an offer to share a room with another very kind English Subud brother, Robin, who had set up and ran the first independent international marketing research company in Indonesia. Although I was back in Wisma Subud, I still visited my Muslim family regularly and, for the next four years, I never had any problems with visas. And that was a true gift! I consider that part of the secret plan I was blindly following.

How to Disappear

One afternoon I was sitting on the open guesthouse porch having a coffee. There was a sister from America sitting across from the round coffee table and a few other people sitting and chatting at other tables.

I was feeling very light and calm, pleasantly empty while looking out at the trees and probably pondering one of those weird questions that seemed to just pop into my head when, suddenly, the young lady opposite me let out a loud laugh and then turned to the group at the other table and said, "Look at David, he's so quiet even he doesn't know who he is."

She continued to giggle to herself and I could only grin back at her. Unfortunately, I knew what she meant. She had caught a glimpse of something else I always thought was well hidden. We didn't speak about it but, as you can see, her comment stuck with me all these years. Someone caught a glimpse of me. Well at least it made them laugh, which is good.

A Mystery Invitation

One day in 1973, I was checking my mail and there was a fancy looking envelope in my mailbox. I opened it and it was an invitation to be a judge for the annual Popular Song Festival of Indonesia. I had no idea how they got my name or why they thought I could be a judge.

The festival took place in the only 5-star hotel in Jakarta at that time. After watching about twelve contestants I gave my vote and a winner was announced. Not the one I voted for. The next night there was a post-festival party where I got to know the other judges and a throng of people, best described as the Jakarta élite.

All the contestants attended of course, plus film stars, fashion designers, artists and even political personalities. Suddenly I was thrown into a completely different world that I found quite extraordinary in a country struggling to make it into the twentieth century, and which was still considered a 'third world country' at that time.

Two people I met at that party have remained good friends to this day. One was the highest paid film star, Rima Melati, when she was at her zenith and the other was the leader of a music group from Bandung, who were the group I had voted for at the festival. They each represented two completely different worlds and lifestyles that exist in most countries, except I hadn't expected to find it in Indonesian society.

Rima's mother was a leading fashion designer, and I was quickly engaged as a free-lance set designer for her fashion shows, a job I had absolutely no experience in. I was paid an incredible amount of money for pretty ordinary work during this time. Not that the staging materials and lighting equipment were available in those days to do anything particularly special.

The first project I was given was to design and build the catwalk and backdrop for a fashion show to celebrate the birthday of Ibu Tien, the influential wife of President Suharto. At that event my network amongst the rich and famous of Indonesia grew even bigger.

Through Rima's mother I was introduced to an organisation

that was established by Ibu Tien. This 'non-profit' organisation was preparing a tour to promote Indonesian batik in Europe, and they needed help to produce promotion materials in English.

After a few days working there one of the group of women running the organization asked me if I had a work permit. Something that was very difficult to get in those days. I said no, I only had a visitor visa.

She told me to bring my passport the next day, which I did, and she took it in the morning. At 4pm she returned my passport with a one-year visa and a work permit. A process that normally takes about three months was done in seven hours.

This, I began to understand, was how Indonesia worked. If you were accepted into the right circles, just about anything was possible and problems and red tape could be made to disappear.

If you were just an ordinary member of the public, then anything needed from the government meant long queues, reams of forms and endless trips over weeks, or even months. I should point out that things are very different for the Indonesian public these days. Indonesia has come a long way.

From my time as a set designer and consultant for promotion work, I learned a lot about this class of people, but I never considered myself part of the élite. I saw myself as a guest and simple observer, as usual, but I did enjoy the ride. I made many good friends during that time who I remained close with until today.

One thing that really stood out and stuck in my memory was one day, when I was talking to three of these women who ran the foundation, and who I believe were wives of senior government officials, I mentioned a large suburb of Jakarta near Cilandak and only one of them had heard of it. But ask them about Tokyo, London or New York and they knew exactly where all the best shopping districts and hotels were.

I recalled, before the music festival, going to see my 'adopted Muslim father', the immigration official, to extend my visa. It turned out it was pay-day and in his office I watched as he was signing a huge ledger and receive his monthly salary in an envelope. Before the junior staffer could take the ledger away the official turned the ledger around and pointed to his name and the monthly amount he received for me to see.

It was only thirty-four thousand rupiah! Not even enough to feed his family for a week, and yet I knew how big his modern house was and that he owned five cars, including a Mercedes, and his son was going to study overseas. He must have been one of the 'business' élite in Jakarta, not just a civil servant.

Fasting In The Fast Lane

In 1974 I was staying in Wisma Indonesia in the Subud compound. It was the month of Ramadan, which is the month that Muslims fast from dawn to dusk. No food, drinks, cigarettes or anything else should pass the lips.

I had tried fasting before, and it was very difficult for me, because in a very short time after beginning to fast each day it was as though my heart and mind simply surrendered and I could do nothing. My brain would just go fuzzy and I would feel like I was in a dreamy state of suspended animation. This is not what is supposed to happen!

Indonesians, who had started to fast in Ramadan since they were young children, were able to function normally for the most part. They could work and think and have meetings just like any other day.

This Ramadan seemed no different at first, and by the third day I was finding it difficult to even get out of my room. I should say that luckily I did not have a real nine to five job at the time. I was doing the staging for one or two shows a month and made

195

enough money to live fairly comfortably. During Ramadan the shows and other entertainment stopped.

Then on the third day I began to feel a kind of compulsion arise in me. It was very insistent and it soon became clear to me I was being told from within that I had to say my prayers. Unfortunately, since joining Islam I had not had the opportunity or perhaps the inclination to learn the Islamic prayers off by heart.

On the third day of the fast, I was sitting on my bed when suddenly I felt something arise within me.

I understood that I was being instructed from within to perform my Muslim prayers, so I went out and bought three large sheets of thick paper and, with a marker pen, I copied out the prayers in big letters from a little book I had been given by my pop singer friend on a visit to him in Bandung. I wrote the pronunciation of the prayers phonetically.

By the time I had finished it was time for the mid-day prayer so I went to the bathroom to perform wuhdu, (ablutions) and returned to my room where I laid the sheets of paper on the floor and stood to say my prayers by reading them as I made the normal prayer movements.

For ten days I was being moved to say my prayer far more than five times a day. It could be ten or fifteen times. Through this process I learned the prayers off by heart and found myself actually feeling a bit sad when it came time to break my fast in the evening.

One evening, towards the end of the fasting month, I was doing my latihan in the hall when I began to experience a sensation as though I was holding a large, heavy bowl of water in front of my stomach. I was swaying gently left to right and I could feel that the momentum of the 'water' was moving back and forth just slightly behind the timing of my body, just like a real bowl half-filled with water would.

As this progressed it seemed that this bowl was made of metal and was more like a barrel surrounding my body and extending from my chest to my legs. The water felt heavy and created a kind of force that now moved my body rather than my body moving the water, swaying from side to side.

At the next latihan later that week, I experienced almost the same thing, so I went to see Pak Sudarto, the translator of Bapak's letters. I explained the experience and he listened quietly with his eyes closed. Suddenly he let out a loud "Oh!" and he looked at me with a big smile and said, "God has given you a big blessing."

That was nice to know, but didn't really explain much. I would discover the meaning and purpose of that experience a few weeks later in Bandung.

From the Elite Jakarta Glitz to the Bandung Scene

The leader of the pop group I voted for at the festival had invited me to stay at his home in Bandung, and in early 1974 I went to visit him. His father had passed away a number of years earlier and, as the eldest son, he took responsibility for his mother and younger siblings, three of whom still lived at home.

They were Sundanese, (West Java Province), who have quite a different character to the Javanese (Central and East Java provinces). The family were more serious about following their religion than most of the people I met in Jakarta, and they had very clear principles that they followed in life. Not your normal pop group. But again, they were not fanatical Muslims, just disciplined.

I spent many nights discussing Subud and Islam with the eldest son who was several years older than me, and we formed a bond of friendship that has lasted to today.

I visited Bandung regularly during the seventies and always stayed at their house. Bandung is a town in the mountains and in those days it was much cooler than Jakarta. It was known as the Paris of the East during the Dutch era, and they lived in a very nice Dutch colonial house near the centre of town.

One day I took a visiting Subud brother and friend from England, Top Topham, to stay with them in Bandung for a couple of days. He was a professional musician, so they were more than happy to meet him.

A Spiritual Test

I knew that the three brothers had a religious 'guru' who was teaching them some sort of mystical techniques, apparently based on Islam.

The second night my friend and I were there, we were talking with the eldest brother after dinner, when I suddenly felt very uneasy. This feeling increased gradually and I knew this was my inner warning and preparing me for something.

At some point I felt a sudden spike of this feeling of an impending threat and spontaneously I told Top to go into the bedroom. He looked a little perplexed but went off to his bedroom without any questions.

Minutes later I heard the two younger brothers coming in the front door with two guests. They came into the family room at the back of the house and I was introduced to their friends. The eldest one was about 30 years old and the younger looked like he was in his mid-twenties

I immediately sensed that these were not ordinary friends and I was sure the older one was their guru. What I first noticed was that his face and his voice were very 'sweet,' but it was not the sweetness of natural honey. It was a kind of intense, refined sugar sweetness. Too sweet. Something wasn't quite right about him.

In the family room I was sitting in an armchair. Across the coffee table the younger friend of the guru sat in the other armchair opposite me. My friend, the eldest brother, and one of his younger brothers sat on the sofa to my left and at the far end of the sofa sat their 'guru'. The youngest brother had disappeared into his room.

The friend of the guru, I quickly realised, was more of an 'assistant guru' than just a friend, as he peppered me with the normal kind of questions Indonesians like to ask about my family, life in England etc. However, I soon understood that this was not a normal conversation. This was a technique of distraction, to keep me focussed on him and not the guru. The guru remained silent the entire time.

As this Q & A continued, I started to feel a strange kind of pressure moving around my body, like someone gently blowing, first on my ears and then on my nose. It continued in a way I can only describe as probing every opening in my body. As this was happening, I heard Topham in the bedroom being violently sick into the small sink.

As the probing force continued, I began to feel that 'metal barrel' that I had experienced in latihan was forming and surrounding my torso and abdomen, keeping that force from entering me. But the pressure then increased, somehow more insistent, more forceful, trying to enter my body, and I felt my inner rising up in a similar way to what I had experienced in the forest in America.

The assistant guru was still asking me questions trying to keep my mind occupied while the guru kept doing whatever he was doing. I was doing my best to answer him, pretending I didn't know what was going on. The 'stiff upper lip' expected of all Englishmen.

After about fifteen minutes my inner started to emerge and took over. It was growing larger and I could sense it had raised a feeling of great anger.

Suddenly I heard the sound of an explosion, I think in my head, and immediately the guru jumped up and said to his assistant, "Kita pulang dulu!" (Let's go home now!) His voice was no longer smooth and sweet.

My Indonesian friend and his brother looked somewhat startled seeing their guru depart so abruptly. I was shaken too from this experience, not being too sure what exactly had happened. After a few minutes Top came out of the bedroom looking decidedly ill. He had no idea before that, that these kind of mystic powers were real and could be felt physically. It was something he would still remember many years later.

I learned a month later, on my next trip to Bandung, that the 'guru' had been interested to know what kind of 'power' a person could get from Subud, and so had arranged to put me to the test. My Indonesian friend, with a wry smile, informed me that their guru had been sick for three weeks after that evening.

So, it seems I had survived my first 'spiritual attack', defended by the spontaneous actions of my inner alone. That was very reassuring, even if I had no idea how it all worked. The important thing was that God knows how these things work and had protected me by preparing me through my latihan.

For Top, it was a pretty intense confirmation that the strange world of mystical forces was indeed real and certainly not something to play around with.

In Indonesia it is a common thing, I discovered, for people to follow these kinds of religious gurus in order to acquire special powers and abilities they can use against others to get an advantage, and achieve what their heart desires. Usually things like wealth, fame, a promotion, revenge or respect.

Things they feel God hasn't given them enough of. They also use this way to influence a person they want as a husband or wife.

Many Indonesians I have met mistakenly believe that followers of Subud have the same objective, to gain some special powers. They have a hard time understanding that in Subud we have the complete opposite objective.

In Subud we surrender ourselves to the power of God, that we may be guided to what God has prepared for us in what we call our destiny. We seek guidance of how to worship and serve God, not how to serve the desires of our hearts.

Catch A Glimpse
Right Before My Eyes

Top Topham came to Cilandak another time with his girlfriend and had the intention of getting engaged in Wisma Subud. I was helping with the preparations that were being made for an engagement celebration to be held in the spacious latihan hall.

The backdrop for the ceremony was a huge bamboo trellis in which were hundreds of cut red roses. The trellis was at least three meters long and two meters high.

At the end of the ceremony Top asked me to invite Bapak to come and take a rose, to be followed by everyone else attending. I was the master of ceremonies and was standing by the microphone at the end of the wall of roses as Bapak approached.

Suddenly, about two meters away from where I stood, I noticed some movement amongst the roses and watched as one rose literally wiggled its way out to protrude several centimetres from the other roses as Bapak got closer.

Bapak took that rose, thanked the newly engaged couple and waited as his entourage came up and took their roses before leaving the hall.

I have no explanation for the rose suddenly 'coming to life', literally asking to be chosen by Bapak, but that is exactly what I witnessed. Such a small and inconsequential thing to happen, but it has remained very clearly in my memory all this time.

Perhaps one day I shall receive the answer of how and why that happened. It certainly said something to me about who Bapak was, that such a thing could happen.

A Stormy Farewell

One afternoon in Wisma Subud the residents gathered in Bapak's house to say farewell, as Bapak was leaving on an overseas tour. There was a very heavy tropical thunderstorm and some of those who were going to accompany Bapak on his trip were looking rather nervous about flying in this weather.

Bapak on the other hand sat relaxed and smiling in his large armchair as he chatted with various members until it was time to leave. There were a number of cars lined up outside under the covered entrance to Bapak's house, and when the time came to depart to the airport, the entourage, led by Bapak, bid farewell and moved out to the cars.

I went to the rear entrance of the house and joined some other members in their car to see Bapak off at the airport. Thunder and lightning were crashing all around Cilandak as we set off.

Halfway to the airport the storm had moved further south and by the time we arrived the sun was shining. Bapak and his entourage had already entered the airport, so quickly we made our way straight to the open-air waving gallery on the second floor.

In those days, passengers had to walk from the terminal lounge, across the tarmac, to the aircraft and climb the stairs to enter the plane. There were some twenty Subud members out on the waving gallery, waiting for Bapak and his group to exit the VIP lounge.

From the waving gallery we could see the aircraft parked

about one hundred meters from the terminal. Behind the aircraft we could see the mountains of Punjak, and between the plane and the mountains there were the very dark clouds of the storm. The sun was shining from the west.

Finally, Bapak emerged from the VIP lounge leading his entourage and started to walk across the tarmac. They turned and waved at us and we all waved back. As Bapak came close to the stairs leading up to the entrance door of the plane a rainbow suddenly appeared some distance behind the plane, perfectly framing the aircraft in a semi-circle of coloured bands.

We all saw it and we all thought this was an amazing coincidence, until Bapak started to make his way up the stairs. We all watched as slowly the top of the rainbow parted, as though being pulled back like curtains to the left and right.

Bapak got to the top of the stairs, turned and waved one last time and entered the aircraft. As he entered the aircraft the top of the rainbow rapidly came together as though closing again over the aircraft, and then slowly faded away.

Now we were all wondering, had we witnessed something more than a coincidence? But there was certainly no question that we had all witnessed this event.

I should say that on many occasions Bapak had mentioned that when a human being with a high soul leaves or arrives at a place, or is born or dies, the forces of nature give a sign. I believe I am one of many who can confirm the truth of that and not just because of this one incident.

As an update to this story I can report that on the death of Queen Elizabeth II, a rainbow appeared over Westminster, and a second rainbow appeared over the Queen's favourite residence at Windsor Castle. There is photographic proof of that occurrence. Several years before Bapak passed away he had mentioned that Queen Elizabeth II had a very high soul.

Partial Sighting

One evening in the early seventies, I was walking back to my room from the guest house verandah on my own. It was a clear, moonless night as I looked across towards the latihan hall.

I was feeling very quiet and peaceful and not thinking about anything, when suddenly I saw what looked like the extended wings of a huge bird glide from behind the latihan hall, over the dome and pass right over me. There was no head, body or tail. Only the wings spanning perhaps fifteen meters.

But this was not a real bird of this world. It was jet black against a black sky. In fact, it was as though this shape had been cut out of the black sky to reveal an even deeper blackness behind the sky, if that is not too confusing. There was no one there to corroborate my story, but it was no optical illusion.

The next night I was walking once again from the guest house and I wondered if the gliding bird wings would appear again. They didn't. But what did appear was another blacker than black bird shape that sped much more quickly over the latihan hall roof and across my path over my head.

But this was a very different shape, almost like an arrow head or sharp beak and broad head. It was gone within three seconds, but the visual impression was very clear in my mind.

Curiosity about these sightings got the better of me and I decided to visited Pak Sudarto the next evening.

He was sitting on his own small veranda. He smiled broadly when I came to his gate and he welcomed me in. I sat with him and told him about my experience and described what I saw.

He smiled, as he always did, and said, "That is good; later you will be able to see the colours!" That was it. Ever enigmatic.

Sadly, I never saw those birds again. But I did see other colours.

David and Goliath
Throw No Stones

One night I was in my small room in Wisma Subud listening to a recording of Jasper Carrot live at the London Palladium on a small cassette player, when a Subud brother from England banged on my door. I said, "Come in," and he opened the door. He looked harrowed and out of breath. Apparently an American Subud member was running amok on the guest house porch.

We quickly ran up to the guest house and I could hear the man shouting loudly. As the large porch area came into view, I saw him pick up a steel 'stacking chair' and throw it through the glass doors leading to the dining room, shattering glass all over the floor.

There were a dozen or so Subud members on the porch who were understandably standing well back and looking pretty nervous. The man was obviously in a rage about something, and he now had a deep cut above one ankle that was bleeding badly.

He was in his early sixties and stood 6' 4" inches tall. He was built like a heavyweight boxer, perhaps because he was a retired heavyweight boxer. It was his years as a boxer which had resulted in some serious brain damage, and I was surprised that he was ever opened.

The brain damage he suffered meant he had difficulty speaking and finding the words to make his sentences. It also meant he had difficulty with controlling his emotions, as was evident this evening.

But I had spent quite a bit of time talking to him in the month or so since he arrived, and when he was having a 'bad' time he would come to my room to talk and often fell asleep on a spare mattress on my floor until morning. So that is why my English friend had brought me to the guest house porch to try and deal with him.

I walked across the porch and tried to avoid the shards of glass. I put my hand on his massive shoulder and could feel the power of his anger, which he was attempting to restrain.

I called his name three times before he heard and turned to look at me. He then stopped ranting and quickly calmed down. Moments later there were tears in his eyes and, as I lead him back to my room, he explained what had set him off.

In fact, he was very diligent and sincere in doing the latihan and through that process had also received an ability to sense other people's hidden thoughts and feelings; but because his brain did not function properly, he would often over-react to those insights.

On this particular day a Subud lady from Europe was on the porch and he sensed how, when she smiled at him, she actually despised his presence and looked down on him. He was not very tolerant of those kind of feelings of superiority. Something we all knew that, sadly, this lady still had a way to go in her process of purification of that particular nafsu.

For him, to follow the latihan and the aims of Susila Budhi Dharma and still have feelings of superiority was the height of hypocrisy, for which he had little tolerance. The lady concerned certainly felt chastised by his very violent outburst. I should add that no one was injured, except himself.

He was in fact a very gentle soul, a gentle giant, who saw the kind of 'ugliness' that we humans try so hard to hide, when we are aware of it. After dressing his wounded ankle, he slept that night on the mattress on the floor until morning.

He passed away in America about four years after that incident.

Another Peeping Tom
Friends Without Boundaries

I had a few people over one evening for coffee and we were sitting out on the terrace smoking kretek cigarettes, which spluttered tiny sparks of clove that burned little holes in our clothes. We were discussing some things Bapak had said in a recent talk about the need to work in order to take care of our life in this world. This was in accordance with God's will for mankind. Everyone must struggle to get on in this life.

I was just sitting quietly, listening to their various opinions about this need to work and struggle, when suddenly Rusti Lane, an actor and performer from Los Angeles, pointed at me and in a loud voice said, "Except David! He only needs to ask, and he gets what he wants!"

Rusti barely knew me or anything about my life, but he kind of got something right. He had 'seen' something about me, but what he saw was not quite complete. I really wished he hadn't said anything, and I remember I felt pretty embarrassed as I tried to laugh it off.

He had touched on something that I thought I had kept well hidden, because I didn't understand it and I never considered it something to discuss. I only include it here because this writing project seems to have become a kind of 'tell all' book.

Today I have a much better understanding of what he was talking about and how it relates to the changes I went through in America and in the UK. It's back to having an obedient heart, which basically means that the nafsu, the desires, are being obedient.

What was actually happening was not that 'I only had to ask' and I would get what I want like Aladdin with his lamp, but quite the opposite in fact.

What Rusti had noticed was something I became aware of after I returned from America. As I already mentioned, once back in England I had lost all interest in 'branded' goods. I was pretty indifferent to material possessions, if they were not useful or needed for my life.

Then, over time, I found that something much deeper than my desires for fashionwear and Harley Davidsons had changed in me, which resulted in me only asking for things that I 'knew' I was going to get, things that were there, on my path in life, ready for me to pick up. Conversely, I didn't ask for, or want things that were not to be mine or not for me.

I guess to someone looking at my life might think I could get anything I wanted, just by asking. But the trick that created this illusion was very simple. I only wanted the things I was going to get.

This might sound like semantics, but it is a reality in my life since following the latihan of Subud that I have been spared the annoyance of pining and hankering after material possessions, while still appreciating their intrinsic value or beauty.

I can only explain it in this way that when I look at something I either get a feeling of detached appreciation of the human ingenuity and skill that has been invested in the item, like a watch or car, or, more rarely, I get a confident feeling of "that is for you', although not necessarily in the immediate future.

I don't know why I am like that, so I cannot offer any explanation. It just happens. But I am very grateful to God because life is so much easier when you are satisfied with what you have and not concerned with what you don't have. A lot of time and effort is wasted when we strive for things which are not meant for us. And if we succeed in getting them, they often end up possessing us rather than becoming our possessions; and if we don't get them, we have a constant feeling of disappointment or dissatisfaction in our life.

So, I am not saying that I don't believe in hard work and effort, I'm just saying it is nice to be guided in the right direction and not put a lot of time and hard work into something you will never get, or, if you do, doesn't really benefit your life in a meaningful way.

But that's just my personal quirk, not a suggestion for how everybody else should live, because each person has a unique nature. And at the same time I can also see how important those feelings of pining and hankering are to man's progress in this world, because they come from the desires and are very effective at motivating a person to work hard and struggle to improve their life. Without those nafsu we would all still be living in caves.

But I can give you an example of seeing one's destiny, which others witnessed, just in case you are interested.

Know What Is Yours and Be Patient

In 1998, Indonesia was hit by the Asian financial crisis and the US dollar exchange rate went from around Rupiah 2,500 per dollar to Rp 22,200 in the space of a couple of months. So, the cost of all imported goods, office rents and house rents shot through the roof.

As usual, advertising was one of the first industries to get really hit by this crisis and our advertising agency saw our clients cutting their budgets by over 70%, which meant with our overheads, we were running at about minus 55% on our monthly cashflow. In order to pay our employees' salaries, my wife and I went several months with little or no income.

This situation also resulted in me not being able to pay the annual rent on our house that year. It was hard times all round.

A year into the economic crisis we had a visit from our landlord, who did not live in Jakarta, to discuss how and when we could pay the arrears and the following year's rent that was now due. Our landlord and his wife, both in Subud, were exceedingly generous and patient and had no intention of adding to our stress; however, they too depended on our rent as they were retired and not that well off.

It didn't take long for us come to an arrangement, with a lot of built in flexibility. It was then that the landlord mentioned that they actually wanted to sell the house the following year. But they were concerned about our circumstances.

Now, from the day we moved into the house, nine years earlier, I had experienced that unique 'feeling' that this house was for my family, albeit in the future. So when the landlord mentioned selling the house, that feeling rose up again and I found myself telling my landlord quite emphatically "Don't worry, we are going to buy the house next year!"

The reaction of everyone was a mix of polite confusion and facial expressions that said, "You are joking, of course".

Understandable since we still owed the past year's rent and the current year's rent was due, while our little agency was barely surviving. But they saw I was serious, and the landlord's wife managed to say, "That would be wonderful!"

He and his wife left soon after, and I then had to try and explain to my wife why I had said such a ridiculous thing, because on paper it was clearly impossible. But I double checked with that unique inner feeling and it did not waiver. All I could say to my wife was, "That was my feeling and God willing, it is a true feeling from the inner"

A year later we bought the house, in cash, and have lived there ever since.

Only Want What Is Yours

It may look like I desired the house and was determined to own it and then, just by asking, I got it, but in fact it went the opposite way. I was shown, inwardly, "This will be your house in the future," and simply had to wait patiently for nine years until I was guided to act. Only then did I want it.

And what was that unique feeling? It's hard to describe. It is a feeling that lacks any of the normal feelings. No feeling of excitement, happiness, confidence or feeling lucky. No feelings or emotion that one would expect. In fact it is what I might describe as an 'old man's feeling'. Very detached, like someone who's seen it all before a hundred times and knows the outcome. There is a sense of certainty that even surprises my own heart and mind. That's the best I can do to explain it in writing. Obviously I am no literary genius.

Perhaps I can add one other characteristic, which is, there is no desire or ambition attached to that feeling. Just 'matter of fact'. That is why I call it unique amongst all my worldly feelings. But a very useful arrow to have in your quiver.

When it comes to my personal life, it stops me wasting time and energy running off chasing things that are not meant for me or staying up half the night imagining how great it would be to have it, or worse, staying up all night trying to figure out how to get it.

This was yet another benefit from my early period of crisis that took a few years to fully reveal itself to me. I never discussed it before, because it might sound like I'm boasting. In fact, this is the first time I have ever mentioned it, and in a book no less!

But my brother Rusty Lane caught a glimpse of it that night. That was a little unnerving to say the least.

Street Artist
The Skill Is What Lasts

On a visit to London with my family, we were visiting Trafalgar Square and passed in front of the National Gallery, where some very talented pavement artists were creating some impressive works of art using chalk and pastels. My daughter asked what happened to these beautiful 'paintings' at night, or if it rains, and

I said they get washed away every night whether it rains or not, and the next day the artists return and make new ones.

She found that hard to understand. "Why would they go to all this trouble only to have their work washed away? That's sad."

I found it hard to give her any kind of answer because, seen from a logical point of view, it was sad. However, as we continued to walk over to Trafalgar Square to feed the pigeons by the fountains, her question continued to float around in my head and eventually brought a different kind of answer, which, as you see, I have never forgotten.

What came to mind was that the life of these pavement artists was like the life of all human beings in this world. Our work is never done. Each night, while we sleep the past day is washed away, and then we must start again the next day, perhaps repeating almost exactly the same thing each day.

As I pondered this, I saw further how this could be an analogy for life and death also. This would answer another question my eldest son had asked some years before. He wanted to know if we could do the same things in the next life as we do in this life, like painting. I did not know the answer to that. I still don't have an answer.

But something in the pavement artist's life analogy did ring true to me. That we create many things in this life, but what we take into the next world is not what we create, but the skill, not the painting.

Through our work in this life, our soul grows and develops, too, in preparation for our work in the next life. However, I am sure it won't be making paintings on pavements. But with the skill and the training of our inner hands, eyes etc. our soul will be able to work in the next life.

I recall in one of Bapak's talks that he mentioned that we, our souls, will have to work in the next life, but in a different way to how we work in this world. That made sense to me.

So, this I believe is the spiritual purpose of our work in this life, and the importance of finding the right kind of work that fits with our talent and inner nature, if we are lucky.

Now I come to think of it, my daughter, now in her twenties, is probably still waiting for an answer. I guess she will just have to buy a copy of this book. You see, there is a solution for everything!

Return to Bandung
Worldly Enterprise and Opportunity

On my frequent visits to Bandung, I met many students from the prestigious University, Institute Technology Bandung (ITB), including the head of their ceramics department. From our discussions I became intrigued by the poor development of ceramics in Indonesia. There really was not any ceramic industry, except a lot of small factories producing tens of thousands of simple porcelain insulators for transmission wires for the government Electricity Company (PLN).

The traditional ceramic works that did exist in some villages were small cottage industries that would make items like huge storage jars for rice, water jugs and flower pots, out of low temperature fired terracotta. These items sold for a pittance and the families that worked in these cottage industries barely made a living.

Villagers would dig out the red clay from their fields, mould it on rudimentary hand powered potter's wheels, fire their products in simple wood burning kilns and sell their wares in front of their houses.

There were no potteries or factories in Indonesia producing any porcelain products, which meant every ceramic cup, mug and plate in Indonesia had to be imported. Even as a non-businessman artist, I could see that there must be a huge business opportunity here.

The problem stopping them producing good ceramics, I was told, was that there was no investment available to purchase the expensive electric or gas kilns and machines for preparing, pressing and moulding clays. Even using the best local kerosene fuelled brick kilns in the insulator factories, it was still too difficult to produce porcelain products.

I didn't have the heart to mention the fine porcelain produced in the Ming Dynasty, long before electric and gas kilns or mechanised ball mills and presses had existed.

I asked why no factories made stoneware, which is far easier to produce than porcelain, and I was told that Indonesians would never buy stoneware because it often has speckles of iron and other minerals in the finished product. Something that in the west was considered 'rustic' and desirable.

It all seemed very defeatist, as though a huge financial investment was the only answer. What also struck me was that no one could imagine that Indonesians might ever change their habits or taste in design. There was an overwhelming belief that Indonesians would reject anything new or different, like stoneware products. That kind of thinking, to me, was a real impediment to progress!

Anecdotally, I remember having lunch with a very successful entrepreneur in Jakarta. He was laughing as he told me the story of how he had just been offered the first western fast food franchise in Indonesia. His response was to deride the idea because, "Indonesians will never eat hamburgers and chips. Indonesians only want rice and chili."

I thought then he might live to regret the day he let the McDonald's franchise slip through his fingers.

It seemed to me that the people I met working with ceramics

all had a very negative attitude about their options for development without huge investments, and I was no longer surprised that the ceramics industry was virtually non-existent in Indonesia. To be fair, in the 1970s things truly were very difficult when it came to raising capital, and I could empathize with their fatalism, but I could not share it.

The Inner Gets Involved
Better Do Something

I sensed another stepping stone on my journey was emerging and I felt compelled from within to follow up on this stoneware idea. I never did any testing about this. It was enough for me that I felt a happiness with this idea and my heart and mind were energized by the thought of an adventure. I felt blessed to be on a new journey.

I knew that Indonesia had many kinds of clays and feldspar deposits, and I could see no reason why Indonesia could not have a modern ceramic industry, at least on the level of medium sized potteries.

So I pursued this idea and at one point I spent three weeks living with villagers, while surveying two areas in West Java known for high grade clay deposits since Dutch colonial times.

Over the next two months, I made a simple study and proposal to establish a pottery producing stoneware. It took a while, but eventually a small group of Subud members agreed to form a company and invest in my enterprise.

This was a huge adventure and an amazing opportunity for me at 24 years old, and I felt like a pioneer as I jumped blindly into the work with a very happy heart. I can summarise the first three months as follows

I arranged for the purchase of a piece of land about sixteen kilometres outside of Jakarta, just inside the industrial zoning.

That was as close to Jakarta as I could get. It was an eleven kilometre drive down a mud road to get to the site, which was really fun in the rainy season. Luckily I had also bought a beaten up 1952 Willys Army Jeep with four-wheel drive.

I had the opportunity to design a 16 metre diameter, 8 metre high half dome, made wholly from locally available materials of bamboo and 'ijuk' fibre thatched roofing.

The owner of an insulator factory in Bandung, who I had become friends with, came to the site to build a four cubic meter capacity kiln that would use kerosene for fuel.

I travelled to an area famous for terracotta ware and recruited eight experienced potters to come to Jakarta. I built eight decent 'village' quality houses for them and four houses for the other supporting workers. Once the pottery was running they were all joined by their families.

After the first 12-hour test firing of a complete mix of stoneware items, as expected, only about half the wares came out without any deformity or blemishes. But that was considered a success for a first firing.

Opportunity Knocks

At this time another Subud member, an American, who designed and made jewellery, and had a shop near Wisma Subud, invited me to join him in a handicraft exhibition in that same 5-star hotel in Jakarta.

During the exhibition, a Frenchman was looking over the pottery items and came over to talk with me. He was the Food & Beverage manager for a Hotel being constructed across the road, and he asked me if I could make custom pieces. I said I saw no problem.

He arranged a meeting for me with his head chef and we put together a number of custom designs made to fit several specialized dishes. At home that night I produced working drawings and I returned to the pottery the next day to brief the potters. Six days later I was presenting the first prototypes to the F&B manager who was over joyed and immediately placed a large order for our stoneware products.

I should mention that there was a 250% tax on imported ceramic ware at that time, so my pricing could deliver huge margins and still be far cheaper for the hotel than imports. Also, we could make short runs of custom designed pieces, which was a big help for the hotel's cash-flow.

Within four months the pottery was supplying three newly opened 5-star hotels in Jakarta, and two months later a 5-star hotel in Bali. After one year we were also supplying custom made pieces to two more 5-star hotels, one in Singapore and one in Hong kong.

Other things that brought me satisfaction and gratitude to God for this opportunity to follow my inner guidance, and bring an idea into reality include:

For three consecutive years the pottery was awarded first prize by the Ministry of Industry as the best example of a Village Industry in West Java.

The workers were paid over ten times what they earned selling their terracotta wares back home, simply by changing from low value terracotta to high value stoneware clay.

I had never run a business before and had no business experience, so this was a unique opportunity to learn from the bottom up, and test whether my inner could really guide me in my work.

I had forgotten almost everything I ever learned about ceramics at school. All I had was my passion and faith following my receiving.

The blue print for the enterprise simply popped into my head, and I simply followed with action.

I experienced how it is to have the heart and mind guided by the inner in my work.

I seemed to know things that I had never studied. I had no fear because I felt I was just following instructions arising in me, and it was a joy.

The most rewarding thing for me was to see how this small enterprise could lift some thirty-five workers and their families out of poverty so that all their children could go to school, all their medical needs were covered and they gained a lot of self-respect using exactly the same skills that had been passed down to them from their forefathers.

I was shown a great honour when I was asked to name two babies that were born to employees.

In the second year we had an exhibition at The Hyatt Aryaduta in Jakarta. I asked the Food & Beverage manager if my potters could see the exhibition the night before we opened. He said "Why at night? Bring them to the opening and we will give them lunch!"

This was the first time any of them had ever stepped inside any hotel, let alone a five-star hotel. In their best Sunday clothes, they walked through the lobby and entered the Ballroom beaming with awe and pride. This I felt was my best achievement, and I felt enormous gratitude to God for this great privilege.

Importantly, I was able to demonstrate that a successful ceramic business could be created using 100% local materials and equipment without any huge investment. The initial capital for land purchase, buildings and equipment was less than US$ 12,000. Working capital during the first year was around US$5,000. This included my salary and house rental.

About that Inner Protection I Spoke of Earlier

While I was running the pottery the factory manager came to me to tell me that my assistant was involved in corruption. He was responsible for buying between six to eight large oil drums of kerosene a week, but in fact each week the pottery was using one drum less than he was claiming and he was pocketing the money for the extra phantom drum.

Once I had concrete proof that he was involved in this scam, I brought the matter up with my silent Indonesian partner and the shareholders and they all agreed he would have to be fired, which I did. He did not take it well.

The Master Takes Control

At this time I was renting a house on a road just behind Wisma Subud, and one night, after a long day at the pottery, I was about to leave to go to latihan, but as I got to the front door I stopped. I then turned round and looked back at my living room. Without thinking, I walked straight to the sofa and lifted up the end cushion.

I was somewhat surprised to see a large dagger in its sheath. The handle was carved in the shape of a dragon with ivory eyes and the straight blade was about forty centimetres long.

I picked it up and went out on the terrace to call my night guard. I asked if this dagger was his and his eyes opened wide with fear and he said, "No!", and then he added, "That kind of dagger means that someone is out to kill you."

I took the knife into my bedroom and put it on top of the wardrobe, and then went off to latihan.

I returned quite late to find the young man I had fired the week before sitting on my front terrace. My night guard was nowhere to be seen.

I invited the young man in and he made a bee-line for the sofa. I sat in an armchair opposite him. He started to complain about being fired, even though he knew what he had done was wrong. He babbled on about second chances and the injustice of it all, while I watched his left hand slowly slip under the end cushion.

I could see his hand was searching around under the cushion as an expression of frustration and confusion grew on his face. Suddenly he jumped up and in an angry voice said he had to go home, and he left.

Second Try

A week later to the day, I returned from latihan and my night guard said all the lights to the separate upstairs spare bedroom and balcony above the kitchen had fused. The iron spiral staircase to this room was outside and he brought a torch to see our way up. At the top of the stairs was a balcony and I walked across it to the locked bedroom door.

Obedient Hands

The door key was always left on the wooden frame of the air vent that formed part of the door frame above the door. I reached up in the darkness instinctively to retrieve the key, without looking, but my hand suddenly stopped. I immediately sensed something was wrong, and I looked up into the dark, but could see nothing, until my guard shone his flashlight on to the air vent.

On the ledge I could just see something was on top of the key. We pulled a chair over and I stood on it to discover that a small, 30cm long, highly poisonous snake was coiled up on top of the key.

Using a long bamboo stick my night guard was able to hook the snake off the key and fling it into the trees.

One thing for sure, the snake could not possibly have climbed the smooth wall or the overhanging ceiling to get to the air vent. I had to assume someone had physically put it there, but my night guard was sure that this was some kind of 'black magic' attack as no-one had been to the house... I preferred my explanation.

I only know for sure that if I had been bitten by that snake it could have been fatal. We also discovered that the lights had not fused, all three bulbs had been unscrewed.

These two experiences, where my life was being threatened, were another example of what I had experienced in Paris when my legs brought me to the Subud hall. This showed me how the inner can take over, and direct our body and actions, when circumstances required special help.

The guidance is there, if we are mindful and do not resist, because I know, when I stopped at my door and walked to the sofa my mind was asking, "What on earth are you doing?!" and when my hand faltered reaching for the key over the door, my mind could have over-ridden my inner and continued to do what 'I' wanted, with potentially fatal consequences.

I literally thank God for all that obedience training and purification in England and America five years earlier, because, without it, I may not be here now to tell this story.

I continued to run the pottery for three years until I felt I had finished this phase of my training and it was time to move on. It was a sad parting with the thirty odd employees who had become like family.

I was very grateful to the four Subud brothers who gave me the chance to test my receiving by putting up the original capital. This was a major stepping stone in my life, and there are too many stories from this period for me to include here.

Uneducated Expert

Some months after leaving the pottery I was invited to participate in a very important workshop that was being held by the government. The purpose of the workshop was to discuss and share experiences related to the development of small businesses and cottage industries in Indonesia and identify the problems and opportunities. The results of the workshop were to be used by the government to form their future policies.

There must have been well over one hundred participants, and to the best of my knowledge I was the only westerner attending. I have no way of telling what impact that workshop had on government policies, but it was a memorable experience for me to meet many NGOs and businessmen from all over Indonesia.

It also provided me with the opportunity to shake President Suharto's hand at the Palace, and get a measure of the man in that instant. Judging by his smile, he must have thought I had wandered into the wrong room.

Where to Now?

It was soon after leaving the pottery that I met with Wilbert Verheyen, an ex-Catholic priest who had served as a missionary in Irian Jaya for over forty years. He had joined Subud and was running a fledgling Subud Charity called Yayasan Usaha Mulia (YUM).

His focus was on helping as many homeless, destitute teenagers and young men and women in Jakarta as he could. His plan was to establish a vocational training centre on the outskirts of Jakarta, and when he heard about my experience with the pottery he invited me to join the YUM project.

This felt like my next stepping stone, so I agreed.

At the time, Subud owned several hectares of land at Pamulang and about 1 ½ hectares was allotted to YUM for a vocational training centre, and a clinic for the local village community.

Once again I got a unique opportunity to design a building and oversee the construction of the clinic that would also provide accommodation for the nurses and the Dutch administrator, a nun, Sister Rina. It would also include a YUM office and very large meeting room, which would serve as the doctors' examination area behind curtains, and a spacious waiting area, twice a week.

This would not be a bamboo structure, but a permanent 'brick, mortar and reinforced concrete building.

After the clinic became operational, Sister Rina came to me and said she had never felt happier than living in that building. That was very heart-warming for me and reinforced my gratitude to God that I had been given this opportunity to expand my knowledge and construct a building that the YUM staff were happy to occupy.

Twenty-five years later, the last time I enquired, I heard that the building was still standing and still providing services to the local village community.

Vocational Training

Wilbert had asked me if I would be interested in running the vocational training centre for the teenagers and men. Another adventure. Naturally I agreed.

The big plan was to introduce the mature homeless men to the homeless women, some of whom had children, and try to get them to find a partner to marry. There was an incentive if they did get married in the form of a piece of land and a simple house in a YUM village being built about one hours bus ride from Jakarta.

The men were also taught a skill to make hand pressed con-blocks that they could sell to the growing number of construction projects going on in the area they would be living. They would each be given the simple equipment and enough sand and cement to make 1,000 con-blocks. This would be their initial source of income to start their own business.

It Takes All Sorts

Among the participants in this program was quite an assortment of characters. Most noticeable was a man called Alfons. He was an alcoholic and had been living on the streets for many years, basically as a small time thug. He was famous for threatening people with a large machete to extort money and generally everyone tried to avoid him. No one could stop him, or dared to try stopping him, from participating in the YUM project.

The first real encounter I had with him was when he turned up drunk at my house early one Sunday morning, with his machete. He woke me up with his shouting and banging on the door, which did not stop until I came and joined him on the terrace.

To his surprise, I invited him to take a seat. He sat down and immediately started demanding that I give him money, as he demonstrated his firm grip on the machete. I sat there quietly and was aware that my feeling was very calm and I had no fear at all.

He ranted on for about ten minutes making threatening gestures. I just stared at him until, finally I made real eye contact and then he went silent and stared back at me for a minute. Slowly a smile unexpectedly formed on his face until he burst into laughter. He then said, "You are my brother, you know who I am," in a slurred speech. He then put his machete down and started crying, asking my forgiveness.

For the next hour or more he described his life. He came from a wealthy family, but because of his drunkenness they wanted nothing to do with him. He had spent years on the streets hustling to survive. Years of drinking rough, cheap, home brewed alcohol that had damaged his brain, and affected his communication skills and impulse control. It was a sad story.

He kept in contact with me for more than twenty years. He

got married and had a son. He joined a government transmigration programme, but eventually returned with his family to Jakarta, He never really managed to stop drinking, but he was no longer a drunkard. In fact he became a very loyal and responsible husband trying to do the best for his wife and son.

I had not seen him for several months when, one night he turned up at my house in a rented minivan without seats in the back. He knocked on my door and he was crying as he motioned me to come close to the van. He slid the side door open and there, lying sprawled on an old mattress, was his deceased wife, dressed in her best dress, now badly soiled. She had died that afternoon after a long struggle with cancer.

He was taking her back to the original YUM village in Jongol to bury her. He said I was the only 'family' he had, and he wanted me to say a prayer for his wife, because he wasn't sure God would listen to his prayers.

I told him that God hears all prayers, and I promised I would say a prayer that night. Beyond that I could only help him with money for some kind of funeral.

A few years later Alfons also passed away and his son moved to Semarang to live with an uncle.

From Vocational Training to Employment

At the vocational training centre we had a lot of younger men who were not part of the YUM Village program. I had a concern that for these young men, just giving them training was not enough. I spoke to Wilbert about an effort to involve prospective employers in the training scheme.

Wilbert agreed and gave me permission to explore possible partners. I didn't have to look far. The Subud real estate company, S. Widjojo, had decided to go ahead and start developing the remainder of their land in Pamulang.

I went to their office and met Rashad Pollard, who had employed me in the advertising agency many years earlier. He was now handling marketing at S. Widjojo and was involved in the project management for Pamulang.

I explained my proposal to him, that in the vocational training centre we could teach the young men several basic skills in the construction business and I would like to offer them to the contractor engaged in the development of Pamulang, as apprentices. The contractor could use their labour at a very low cost because they would get their food and accommodation from the training centre for a period of six months.

Rashad thought this was a great idea and threw his support right behind it. In fact, he even offered the vocational training centre the job of clearing the way through an old rubber plantation to build the entrance road. This meant uprooting over three hundred trees between the main road and the construction site. In this way, some additional revenue could be generated for YUM projects.

But we hit a snag. Charitable organizations were forbidden to engage in any kind of business. We overcame this by setting up a non-profit company 'owned' by the Yayasan managers.

I had no idea about uprooting old rubber trees, but I did have a good contractor who built the clinic. He arranged for a huge, very old, ex-army bull dozer and one large dump truck to clear the trees. I had calculated one week to clear the trees and remove 40cm of topsoil along the road way in preparation for the road construction, as per the specifications from S. Widjojo.

As it turned out the job of clearing the trees was completed in one day. That was some bulldozer!

Rashad was quite impressed, so he invited the new Subud company to bid for the road construction contract, which we did and easily won. We successfully completed the roads, all built to spec, and to my delight many of the young men who went through the vocational training were employed by the contractors as full time construction workers and carpenters to build houses.

This was a very rewarding experience and an excellent example of what can be done when people and companies cooperate for a good purpose. Everyone won.

The Real World Doesn't Like Good Works

About three quarters of the way through the contract my visa ran out, and following Indonesian regulations I had to go to Singapore to receive my renewal at the Indonesian Embassy. When I went to pick up my passport I was invited to meet the head of the Embassy's immigration department.

He was very polite and asked me if I had upset anyone in Indonesia. I said I didn't think so. He then explained that he was very confused because he had received the telex authorizing my working visa that morning and an hour later he had received a telex saying I was black listed, and so he could not issue my visa and work permit. He was very sympathetic and somewhat embarrassed as he told me, "It may be two years before you can return to Jakarta".

Some years later I discovered that through the tendering process to build the roads at Pamulang I had inadvertently exposed corruption by the company that had been building roads for the Subud Real Estate enterprise for several years.

Rashad was most concerned and had ordered a review of their past contracts and sent surveyors out to check the actual specs of the roads they had built at earlier projects. He discovered that every road they had built was way under the spec they were paid for. This meant they had been adding 40% to 50% to their margins from the savings on materials. Apparently, this was relatively normal practice forty years ago.

That company was not happy to lose, not just a lucrative contract, but worse, to be exposed for their past fraud and be black listed for further tenders.

Our honesty in the cost break-down was the fatal mistake and that made me the target for their revenge.

Making a false report to Immigration about me was all it took to get me black listed. And so now I was stuck in Singapore.

Some Stepping Stones Can Appear Like Land Mines

Not only was I stuck in Singapore, but I had a wife and 18-month old son with me. My son, being British, had to have the same working visa as me. That was the regulation at the time. However, at the embassy they found a loophole so that he could return to Jakarta with his mother.

Working for a charity, I certainly didn't have any financial savings to fall back on. YUM had provided funds for our airfare and one night in a hotel, which would normally have sufficed.

Fortunately, one of the Directors on the YUM board had recently bought an apartment in Jurong and was able to contact me and arrange for me to stay there.

I accompanied my wife and son to the airport on the east coast for their trip home, and then I had to get myself to the west coast. Jurong is a long way from the city centre, and I arrived late in the afternoon, by bus, at the area of the apartment block, with a small carry-all containing very few clothes and personal items.

On entering the apartment, I was struck by its emptiness. There was a sofa, one armchair, a small dining table with four chairs, a small, low, long cupboard with a TV standing on it, a single side-table with a phone on it and one single bed in the bedroom with a folded blanket. Everything was covered under thin plastic sheeting to protect from dust.

The kitchen had a two burner gas stove, a couple of saucepans, some knives, forks and spoons, a set of four plates, bowls and mugs. It was a brand new building, mostly empty, and I don't think anyone had ever spent a night in that apartment.

The Long Dark Night of the Soul

I put down my bag and felt absolutely desolate and alone. I only had S$22 left and no credit card. No banks in Indonesia were issuing credit cards back then.

I left the apartment to look for a mini market to buy some milk, sugar and coffee. I seemed to be walking on autopilot. My body had no strength. I just felt numb.

I returned to the apartment and it was already dark. The newly finished building was silent and empty. My heart felt totally isolated and abandoned and my mind struggled to make sense of what had happened.

I spent the night mostly on my knees praying for forgiveness. I have never felt so hopeless, so powerless and lost in my life, and there was no shortage of silent tears. I had been stripped of everything. No family, no money and no security, because in two weeks I would have to leave Singapore when my visa ran out.

The prospect of being deported back to England, penniless and without my family, was the most plausible outcome I could think of.

By dawn I was totally exhausted and finally I surrendered. I had nothing left to fight with. I could see no options and I accepted that somehow I had completely failed in my life and I had brought myself and my family to this abyss. I did not lose faith in God, or blame Him, because I felt my situation was entirely the result of my own mistakes, even though I had no idea why I had been blacklisted at that time. I just felt I needed forgiveness.

As I stood staring out of the window at the sea on the West

Coast in the early morning light, I felt like an incarcerated man, and at that moment the last dregs of despair rose up once again. I went back to the bedroom and knelt again in prayer and eventually that last gasp of despair escaped into the air.

Then the phone rang!

"With every difficulty, there comes relief...", from the Al Quran.

I recognized the voice on the phone. It was Murray Clapham, an Australian Subud member who was a successful businessman living in Jakarta and a strong supporter of YUM. In typical Ozzie style, he made a light hearted joke about my dire situation, followed by a reassurance that help would be coming. He was sure he could get me a job in Singapore. My heart soared.

He then said, "You are an architect, right?" My heart sank. "No, Murry, I'm not a qualified anything," I replied. "But you designed and built that big Polyclinic in Pamulang, didn't you?" he asked. "Yes, but I am not qualified," I repeated, as my heart slipped back down into the abyss.

"Oh well, never mind. You call my friend Jeremy at this number. He's English. Maybe he can find something for you to do. Call him today after breakfast," he said and he gave me the number and then added, "I told him you were an architect."

At nine o'clock I called Jeremy Caddy. Murray had indeed been in touch with him, because I had to repeat the whole story about the Polyclinic and my not being an architect. To my surprise Jeremy's response was something like, "It takes more to build a Polyclinic if you are not an architect than if you were," and then he said, "Why don't you come over and I'll see if you can be useful."

The address for his office was on the East coast, near the airport, right on the other side of Singapore. This left me with a practical problem. I apologized to Jeremy, and explained that I had enough money to get to his office, but I wouldn't have enough to get back to the apartment in Jurong. "Don't worry about that," he said. "We'll sort that out when you get here." He clearly was a good friend of Murray's.

I found out later that Murray worked for the parent company of a large group, and Jeremy managed one of the subsidiary companies in the group.

Later that day I returned to the apartment in Jurong with $500 in my pocket and a job as Assistant to the Managing Director of an alluvial dredge building company. Jeremy made it very clear that I would be his personal assistant, not an 'Assistant Managing Director.' A very important difference.

I arrived back at the apartment with a shopping bag full of food. I had not eaten for over twenty four hours.

That evening I prayed again, but this time there were tears of joy and gratitude to God for turning the black abyss into a shining stepping stone. I would spend the next two years learning so much by simply being involved in so many new areas of industry, management and business negotiations. A world I never dreamed I would ever be able to enter.

The next day I started my new job. Again, to my surprise, my desk was in Jeremy's large room. And after being introduced to the staff and managers we returned to his office to start work. He said that my first job was to go out and find myself a house to rent closer to the office.

Within a two weeks, my family had joined me, we had a nice house and a budget to furnish it, and all we needed for a settled suburban life.

I Did Pay My Way

Toward the end of my first year I uncovered some major corruption that had been going on in the shipyard where the dredges were fabricated, which saved the company over S$150,000 in the second year, and a similar amount on every dredge they built thereafter. It seems that rooting out corruption was becoming one of my things.

Drug Fuelled Fantasies

I was sitting in the large meeting room one day looking at geological maps of Indonesia, when I came to a map of Kalimantan (Borneo). I was drawn to take a closer look as Pak Subuh had said that in the future, the Subud Centre would move to central Kalimantan, in the area of Pelangka Raya, the provincial capital.

I noticed that the lower half of Kalimantan was primarily sandy soil and vast areas of peat. I believe this huge area had been lifted up out of the sea by the action of the tectonic plates in the geological past. The whole of the southern half of Kalimantan was relatively flat and sandy as a consequence.

The next thing I noticed was that all the main transport systems ran north-south, and primarily relied on three great rivers that flowed down from the mountains in the north. There were very few roads.

I was also aware of the enormous potential for large scale timber industries and mining of everything from coal, feldspar, glass sands and oil, to gold and diamonds.

I was also aware of the government program for large scale 'transmigration' from the overcrowded island of Java to other islands.

By this time, I was up at the whiteboard, writing down these bullet points. A grand scheme was forming in my mind, too boring to go into detail, but in short I saw an opportunity to pool all these facts together into a single plan that would also include the sale of a lot of our dredges.

Basically the plan was built on the opportunity to create a system of canals to provide east-west transportation. I had enough data to show that the cost of a 30 metre wide canal would be about twenty percent of the cost of a 6 metre wide asphalt road. A canal would also immediately open up trade and commerce for the local population, who already were using waterborne transportation on the rivers.

By using Cutter Suction Dredges, it was possible to not only dredge the canals, but also mine the peat areas and pump the peat slurry up to two miles from the mining area. Peat, mixed with the sandy soil could form arable soil required for farming and food production.

At this point it was clear that it would be feasible for transmigration of farmers from Java. The Provincial government would need to invest in education, health and power facilities.

I recalled reading an article about a floating saw mill in Brazil, which would fit perfectly into this mix. Also floating fuel storage barges would be an essential part of the plan.

There were many additional things I wrote, but this should be enough to give the big picture. Basically it was a proposal for a Development Fleet for Kalimantan.

Two days later Jeremy called me into the meeting room and pointed at the whiteboard. "What's all this?" he asked. I apologized for my written lunacy and said I would wipe the board clean. "No, don't wipe it out. There might be something worth looking at later," he said.

It was late in the afternoon the next day that I was once again called to the meeting room where I was confronted by a room full of Indonesian guests that included senior Indonesian government figures involved in the State Oil company, the mining industry and, by pure accident, someone from the department for transmigration. This group were actually in Singapore for another big meeting and had just 'popped in' to accompany the man from the mining ministry, who actually had some dredging business to discuss.

Apparently, during the meeting, they had been trying to figure out all my scribbling on the whiteboard and had asked Jeremy to explain what it was all about. That question was now redirected to me.

Our visitors grew increasingly excited as they began to see the potential impact of such a fleet, but their time was limited and they had to leave.

Clearly Jeremy was both incredulous and impressed at the same time, and said we should look into this concept further. The next day he returned from a meeting with the owner of the parent corporation, Peter Fong. Jeremy told me how he had tried to explain my grand scheme to Mr Fong and, after a moment of silence Mr Fong just said, "Tell David to stop taking LSD." And that was the end of that.

I relate this story only as an example of how, quite inexplicably, an idea arose that was way beyond my knowledge, and pay scale, which even I felt was on the borderline of megalomania, and yet, for the Indonesian government officials it caught their imagination. This was another valuable lesson for me.

Note: Murray Clapham was a Subud member who was well known for his generosity and his support for anyone in trouble. I cannot express enough my gratitude to Murray for the help and support he gave me and also to Jeremy Caddy, for putting his faith in me, enough to give me a chance. Murray passed away several years ago. A great loss to Subud and to the world.

Back into the Fray

I had now enjoyed two years of a normal, well ordered, sensible, nine to five life in a well-run country where things made sense. And so it was with some trepidation that I returned to Jakarta as a representative of the group of companies that included the Dredge building company.

My first assignment was given to me by Peter Fong, the owner of the parent company of the Singaporean group. I was to arrange a meeting for an Italian company with the government Minister who was the head of Indonesia's Ministry of Technology and Development. Later in 1998, he would become Indonesia's third President, Dr. Habibie.

For the purpose of arranging this meeting, I was 'representing' the CEO of Italy's largest corporation, ENI. My only credentials were a name card from the Singapore Dredge building company and a letter from the parent company confirming I represented them.

The Lucrative Business of Obstruction

Initially, I contacted a friend who I knew had a connection within that minister's department. After two days I was told that it would cost Rp 40 million to arrange a meeting! That was the equivalent of US$20,000 at the time. This was not a total surprise to me as I had heard many stories about paying middlemen, but I knew that in Singapore they would have been shocked and seriously insulted at the idea of paying for a meeting.

At that time Jakarta was full of unemployed middlemen, who had connections, often relatives, in positions of some authority, and it was quite standard in Indonesia to pay a middle man a fee to make the arrangements for meetings. That is how they made a living. The people at the very top were not involved in these schemes, but I'm sure they knew it went on.

In a developing country, people had to survive as best they can. But there was a heavy cost, in terms of the inefficiency of getting things done, that was enormous.

The system at that time was set up to operate that way and it was almost impossible to meet a high placed official any other way, unless through a diplomatic connection. This practice has largely been stamped out these days. But having connections is useful in any country.

I felt caught in a cultural vice or catch-22. There was no way that my big boss, Peter Fong, in Singapore would pay to arrange a meeting, and I was being told in Jakarta that without paying there could be no meeting.

Finally, one day after lunch, I decided I had to act, so I set off for the high-rise building that housed the Department of Technology and Development, armed with my business card.

I went to the receptionist in the foyer and explained I wished to arrange a meeting with the Minister, and then took a seat to wait and see what happened. I was expecting laughter. But within ten minutes a young man approached me, introduced himself and asked me to follow him to the lifts. Now I was fully prepared to get a polite brush off by some junior official upstairs.

We exited the lift, on the 4rd floor if my memory serves me well. Here I was asked to sit in a small, very unpretentious waiting area. After about another 20 minutes, a man approached me holding my name card. I recognized him as Dr Habibie's right hand man, whose name I will not mention for fear of exposing him as being a normal, decent human being. I was both shocked and honoured. I was also quite nervous.

He invited me into his very large room which was pretty cluttered with stacks of books, reports and papers, like you would expect of an absent-minded professor. But I soon found out he certainly was not absent-minded. He was exceedingly intelligent, highly educated and very sharp.

He apologized for keeping me waiting, but he was in the middle of writing a report in English for the Minister to present in the coming days, which he had to finish. Something to do with coal and energy. I soon realized he had no idea why I was there, because he had to ask me.

At the mention of ENI he sat up straight and said, "Really; that's a coincidence. They are on a short list of candidate joint venture partners for this power project we are working on." Then, to my surprise, he asked me if I would mind reviewing his paper to check the English. Something I was more than happy to do. It barely needed any correction.

Whilst I was reading his report, I heard him make a phone call and speak to someone who I had to assume was the Minister. He then made a second call to who, I assume, was the Minister's secretary.

Some minutes later, as I finished reviewing the report, the phone rang and, after a very short conversation, he put the phone down and said to me, "OK, you can get 20 minutes with the Minister." He wrote down the date and time for me. He then returned to talking about the power project, the situation Indonesia faced to produce enough electricity to sustain development and a lot of other things that were way over my head.

He actually asked my opinion on a few things, as though I could say anything useful, but I felt completely at ease in this lopsided conversation. I left him still working in his office at 9.30 at night.

An extraordinary day, an extraordinary man. It was a true eye-opener for me to see how easy it can be to just walk in and follow normal protocol to arrange a meeting with a Minister without any need to pay Rp.40 million to a middle man.

There Was a Result

About two weeks later I was standing in Dr Habibie's large meeting room with the CEO of ENI and three other senior ENI managers. After a few minutes Dr Habibie entered with two assistants and immediately greeted the ENI visitors and myself.

He then launched into an enthusiastic rapid fire 'conversa-

237

tion' talking about the latest technologies that ENI were working on and what Indonesia needed, and how he saw an opportunity for ENI to become a good partner. He hardly stopped talking. I wondered if he knew more about ENI than the ENI CEO did.

Habibie was well known for being very disciplined, especially about time-keeping, but that day the meeting went for forty minutes. As for myself, I was fascinated by what I guessed was over a hundred plastic model aircraft of all types and sizes that literally covered the huge meeting table. I was wondering who got the job to assemble all these model kits. Aircraft manufacturing in Indonesia was an enduring aspiration for Dr Habibie, which he singlehandedly made into a reality.

Playing with the Big Boys

In the following months, I found myself attending quite a few meetings. One was with the owner of an American company, Radon Western Gear, which was the largest company in the world that designed and built hi-tech Tuna Fishing Boats.

After a series of meetings with the Minister of Fisheries no deal could be made at that time but, before leaving Jakarta, the CEO gave me his name card and told me that if I ever saw an opportunity for his company I should give him a call and he promised he would be in Jakarta within two days.

Another odd one was making arrangements for the British company Raytheon, that was tendering to supply several cutting edge simulators for training naval captains of the Indonesian Navy.

That deal also did not come about, but Raytheon did offer to bring me back to the UK for six months of training, after which I would be returned to Jakarta as their marketing rep. They asked if I would be OK with signing the British Official Secrets Act. It didn't sound quite like my kind of world and I passed it up. My life had been shaken and stirred more than enough!

My apparent USP, I believe, was my fluency in the Indonesian language, my understanding of the local business culture and the fact that I was British. But my heart was not really happy about any of these job opportunities.

In fact by this time I felt that this episode of my education in the ways of corporate deals and negotiations was drawing to a close, and now it was time to get a normal, middle of the road, nine to five job with a proper, regular salary.

I had no idea how to proceed. So I didn't. It wasn't as if there was any kind of 'Employment Exchange' I could pop into.

Finally, a Job I Was Qualified for

It was a Saturday afternoon and I was having a coffee with some Subud friends on the Guest House porch in Wisma Subud, when a car entered the compound and stopped in the parking bay next to us. A young man jumped out of the car and walked towards us. He was actually asking for me and I stood up to greet him.

Ten minutes later I was sitting in his car on my way to a recording studio. His boss had sent him to look for me in Wisma Subud, but he had no idea how his boss got my name.

At the studio I met the young boss, who explained to me that he was desperate for a native English speaker to record a voice over for a multi-media presentation he had produced. His government client had asked for an English version at the last minute the night before.

This was 1983, before digital technology was available in Indonesia. His company was the first and only one to have this cutting edge system that consisted of up to 24 Kodak slide projectors that could cover a huge 24 meter long 'rear projection screen', all controlled by a single computer.

So, I thought, he needs a native English speakers voice. I was pretty sure I had one of those, and so I agreed to record my first voice over. It took two hours and I received a very decent fee. I asked how he got my name and he mentioned someone I had no recollection of.

After finishing the recording, I sat with the boss chatting about his fledgling business and my current situation. Later I was driven home and I was wondering in the car what exactly I was going to do now, having just been appointed General Manager of Indonesia's first Multi-Media Production House. But my heart was happy.

Thrust Out of The Spotlight

The company grew and we moved to bigger premises after just six months. One day, not long after we had moved, the boss came into my room. "You know about lighting, don't you," he said. I wasn't sure if it was a question or a statement. Either way the answer was no.

I asked why and he said that his friend, a manager at the Mandarin hotel, had called him, desperately looking for someone to do the staging for a live show and it needed good sound and lighting operators. "I told them I had a good sound man and an English guy that could handle the lights," my boss said with a wry smile.

And so, three days later, I turned up at the Mandarin Hotel Ballroom to inspect the installation of the staging and lights and do a check of the large operator's control panel with over sixty switches and dimmers. I spent an hour marking on surgical tape what switches and dimmers were for which lights.

After lunch I went back for the one and only rehearsal, and that night I managed to get through the first show of more than fifteen songs with Sister Sledge. After the show their manager, who happened to be their mother, invited me to join them for a late night dinner in the coffee shop.

Two of the sisters wanted to see a bit of Jakarta's night life, so I took them to a pub owned by my old friends, the film actress Rima Melati and her husband Frans. I got the sisters back to the hotel by 1am, as I had promised to their mum.

The next night was the second and last show, and again I was invited for supper afterwards. It was like sitting at a family meal at Christmas, with everyone talking at the same time, but things quietened down after about an hour, when they started to discuss the rest of their Asian tour. It was during this discussion that their mum turned to me and asked if I would like to join them for the rest of their tour to handle the lighting. I was flattered.

If I had still been single with nothing to tie me down, I may have taken them up on their offer, just for the adventure and opportunity to see more of Asia, but sadly I had to decline. Still, it was a lot of fun for three days and my heart was happy, Sister Sledge were happy and my boss was happy! More importantly, I had learned something new that I could do.

I continued to work on multi-media programs, mostly for big marketing events, for several more months. I was learning a lot and expanding my 'network' of contacts.

Nothing Personal

It was coming up to the month of fasting when I saw an attractive woman turn up in the office. She walked around as though she owned the place and later I was to learn why, because she did! She was the wife of the boss and they were in the middle of a divorce. Something he never mentioned to me.

To cut a long story short, the company's finances were frozen by his wife, and no salaries could be paid. My boss reluctantly explained a very complicated situation and it was clear my employment was terminated unless I was willing to work for free. I left being owed one month's salary. I met his wife before I left and she apologised as she explained it was nothing personal, which I knew was true.

A Lesson About Money

And so I returned home to ponder my future and how I was going to put food on the family table and pay the bills. A few days later, the Ramadan fast started. I felt that this year, apart from food, drink and cigarettes, it was very important for me to 'fast' from my fears and doubts. For the month of Ramadan I would not look for work or worry about money. I had enough to scrape through for a month. Fortunately, my wife had no objections.

About a week into the fast a friend from England, Harvey, brought a visitor from Australia, who was part of a Subud contingent who had come to Wisma Subud for the fast, but also to make a presentation to Bapak and the members about a proposed project for the development of Darling Harbour in Sydney.

Harvey had brought him because their presentation was a multi-media format using 12 projectors, and my friend knew I had some experience in that field. The project team needed to hire the equipment and operators to run their presentation, and asked if I could arrange that.

I was happy to help and I contacted my ex-boss who immediately said yes. I asked him how much would he charge for equipment and operators and he gave me a highly discounted price.

Later, at home in Wisma Subud, I met the Sydney team to confirm that I could arrange everything as per their requirement. As a 'good' Subud brother, I wanted to support their enterprise and so I gave them the cost without including anything for myself. I felt that was right and, as I was fasting, I did not want to get involved with all those nasty material forces, like money.

I noticed that the three team members seemed stunned and I was worried that it was too expensive. In fact they were shocked by how cheap is was. "That's not enough!" one of them exclaimed. "Yes, but this is for Subud," I responded.

They then explained that this was an enterprise and a business. They had a budget for this presentation that was way more than I was charging. Harvey, who had joined the meeting, berated me. "You have to make money from this, that's how the world works!"

The Sydney team insisted that I doubled the price and gave me, in cash, the equivalent of one month's salary as a down payment. Harvey gave me a pat on the back and said, "Don't feel guilty about getting paid. This is a Subud business, not a Subud charity. You solved a huge problem for them and you deserve to get paid."

That night I sat and pondered what had happened. I could still feel that uncomfortable feeling of making a profit from a Subud enterprise, but now there was a glimmer of some new feeling that told me this was a lesson I needed to learn about my attitude towards money. I had to value myself a lot more than I ever had done.

After a very successful presentation and all the equipment had been packed and returned, I visited my ex-boss to pay for the rental. He was very happy to see me and he insisted that I keep the money because he owed me a month's salary.

So, being unemployed during a month of fasting, and with the intention of not thinking about work or money, I had 'earned' almost three months' salary! There were some very important changes occurring in my understanding about the material forces.

I remain very grateful to the Darling Harbour project team

and my good brother, Harvey from England, for moving me onto a very different path in dealing with the material forces when it comes to self-worth and making a profit.

A Voice in the Wilderness

About a week before the end of Ramadan, I received a call from an old friend, Glenn, who had been in Jakarta as long as I had. He was not in Subud, but was of kindred spirit. He came from North London and had that familiar accent and sense of humour of a Londoner.

We had worked together briefly in 1972 in the agency managed by Rashad Pollard, and would bump into each other every now and again, always picking up where we had left off as though we met weekly. But this time I hadn't seen him for more than a couple of years.

He asked me what I was doing and I said, 'Fasting.' He burst into laughter. "Yes, but I heard you were not working." I repeated that I was fasting and didn't want to think about work or unemployment. Another laugh and then he began to explain that he was working for a multi-national advertising agency as an Account Director with the primary responsibility of looking after their main client, Richardson Vicks.

In fact, the agency had to have an expatriate account person as a condition for winning and keeping the Richardson Vicks account. And that was his dilemma, because he had been offered a much better job at another agency, but he felt bad about leaving his current boss in the lurch and possibly losing him the Vicks account. His new job required him to start a soon as possible.

So now he wanted to ask me a favour that may benefit me too, which was to take his place for one or two months to give his current boss time to find a permanent replacement. He knew that when I left the old agency back in 1973, I had more or less vowed never to go into advertising again, so he worked hard to persuade me, based on our personal relationship.

Two days later I was being interviewed by his boss and it was agreed that I would start a week after Lebaran, the end of the fast. My friend would remain for one month for a kind of handover period on the Vicks business.

Thus began one of the most fun times I had known in Indonesia. It reminded me of my time working in the hotels in Swanage.

Two events stand out in my mind and illustrate how that month went.

On my first day, we left for a meeting at Richardson Vicks and we went in his car. A very large and powerful, second hand, blue Holden, known in the office as 'The Tank'. I sat in the front passenger seat and we slowly moved out of the car park onto the main Highway.

Suddenly Glenn hit the gas and I rolled back almost onto the rear seat. He burst out in laughter. He had failed to inform me that the passenger seat was not actually attached to the floor of the car.

On another occasion, we left to meet the Oil of Ulay brand manager and I noticed as we walked out to the car that he was wearing tennis shoes, the left one of which had a hole cut in it where his big toe stuck out. This was not standard attire for client meetings. I mentioned this possible oversight and he explained that his gout was playing up again. I told him it might be time to buy some new feet.

But that was not the end of it. We were sitting in front of the brand manager's desk when Glenn crossed his leg, reached down and took off his tennis shoe and started massaging his toe in front of the young brand manager. She was clearly very perplexed. Perhaps she put it down to our eccentric London culture. She was right.

It was a month of hard work and laughter that went by all too fast!

After he left the agency I took over his duties and a month later the boss asked me if I could extend one more month, as he still hadn't found another ex-pat for the position. I agreed, and he agreed to provide a car for my personal use.

A month later the boss offered me the position of general manager with a substantial increase in salary. A position I held for one year in which the agency was profitable every month. Previously the agency had never managed to make a profit for more than two months in a row.

Unfortunately, the agency was part of a group of companies that was run more as a family business, and profits were not being reinvested in the agency. Further growth was impossible. I met the boss who owned the agency and we decided to part ways. I received a good bonus and it was an amicable separation.

Hop, Skip and Jump

For some weeks before I left that agency, I was getting calls from an Australian friend in another multi-national agency, JWT. He was the creative director and was having a hard time working with the American Account Director handling Kodak.

Worse than that was that Kodak were also unhappy with the American account director and were threatening to move to another agency. He was almost begging me to move and wanted me to meet his boss for an interview.

Now seemed a good time to make an appointment.

A month later I was the account director for Kodak, Unilever and Citi Bank. My salary was considerably more and I was given a much nicer car. I was now with J. Walter Thompson, the world's oldest and largest advertising agency. JWT had joined with a small, but successful local agency a year earlier.

This was a huge stepping stone in my life.

But before I get into that, let me return to the matters of the inner, because all this time, since working at the multi-media company and ad agency, my life in Subud continued and the latihan was still the mainstay of my life.

Meantime: Back to the Mystical World
A Royal Visit of the Ethereal Kind

After one year at JWT, I took my annual leave and spent a week visiting Solo in central Java. The day before we were to return to Jakarta, I was taken on a day trip to a small town on the edge of Jogjakarta called 'Kota Gede'. This was the site of the first Palace of the Kingdom of Mataram, established by Panembahan Senopati in 1575.

In the area of the original palace, behind a high wall, is a building which covers the tombs of some twenty kings and princes of Mataram descending from, and including Panembahan Senopati.

To enter this area one must first don a special sash around the waist. At the single entrance to a fairly large courtyard, visitors must crouch down and listen to an Islamic prayer sung by two very old Javanese men, dressed in their official traditional Javanese 'uniforms' who are known as the 'Keepers of The Tombs'. Once inside the courtyard, visitors must continue to crouch down and attempt to walk, or rather 'waddle' approximately 30 meters to the large building that houses the tombs.

Before entering the building, the two 'Keepers of the Tombs' sang another Islamic prayer, which was fine, but then they started to sing a prayer in ancient 'high Javanese'. The effect of this prayer was very heavy and oppressive, and seemed to make everyone crouch even lower, more from fear than reverence, I think. When the prayer finished, things felt a little lighter and we entered the building.

Inside, the tombs were set out in rows with enough space between the rows for two people to walk side by side. Most of the tombs had a wooden frame built over them and heavy white linen 'curtains' hung from them. Some of the curtains were closed others were pulled back.

As I looked about me, I noticed several of the earlier visitors were still in the building and were kneeling or crouching at various different tombs, apparently in deep silent prayer or meditation. I was told later that these people came to these graves to ask for help from the power of these long dead kings.

They may ask for a relative to be cured of an illness, or to get a promotion at work, or some power that would make them respected and weaken their rivals. All clearly desires from their earthly hearts.

As I slowly passed by the tombs I felt very strongly that around some of the tombs there certainly was a force present. Other tombs felt light and I would say 'empty' of any presence. I found this interesting.

From Kota Gede I returned to Solo where I was staying with a family who were descended from the royal family of the Sultan of Solo.

That night I went to my room quite late and went straight to bed. Within minutes of closing my eyes I sensed a strong presence in the room and I sat up in bed. In the dark room I saw there was a man standing next to my bed. He was dressed in a long, black cassock and was wearing a dark red turban. I could see his face quite clearly and his expression was very stern. My heart was pounding.

This 'being' exuded an enormous power and in my mind I heard him say sternly, "Mau apa!!?" which in English would be something like "What do you want!!?" Inwardly I spoke the words, "I do not want anything except what God intends for me to have."

This seemed to make him annoyed. I would say he was not happy to be there in the first place, and then for me not to ask him for anything was further wasting his time. His anger was palpable. Feeling his anger sent my heart into overdrive, and I got out of bed and went to the kitchen to calm my heart down.

About an hour later, after some tea and a couple of cigarettes, I ventured back to bed, only to have this figure return again asking me what it was I wanted. Again I respectfully declined to ask for anything and again I felt his annoyance. And again I left the room to escape this dark, oppressive force that seemed to have attached itself to me.

I stayed awake until morning and when the owner of the house came out for breakfast he was surprised to see me up already. I explained to him what I had experienced and he asked me, "What colour was his turban?" I said it was a dark maroon. He said he was very surprised that this dark figure would appear to a westerner.

I asked him who this man was and he laughed. "A dark maroon turban, that was Panembahan Senopati!" He then added with a laugh, "You should have asked him to make you rich!"

So now I had two experiences that made it clear that there are other dimensions to life in this world. I liked the giant birds back in Wisma Subud, but the man in the maroon turban was very unpleasant. That oppressive feeling he brought felt like it was trying to pull me into that different dimension, and it stayed with me the next day as we drove from Solo back through Jogya. It only 'evaporated' as we left the boundary of Jogya on the southern road back to Jakarta.

Another Midnight Stroll

On another occasion my best friend Ramzi from England was visiting, the one I met in Swanage and who later joined Subud about the same time as I did. It was to his house that I took a taxi from Heathrow on my return from America.

It was the late eighties when we took a sightseeing trip around central Java with me doing the driving. In Solo we stayed with the same family as my previous visit.

At about 11pm one night we decided to go for a walk and we came to the Alun-Alun of the Kesunanan Palace. The Alun-Alun is a large, open field about the size of two football pitches, surrounded by a high wall and one large arch way opening from the public road to a driveway, cutting across the Alun-Alun, that leads to two huge doors that are the entrance to the inner road that encircles the main palace.

These great wooden doors must be at least six or more metres high and at night they are closed and locked. In front of the doors is a relatively small, rectangular fenced off area encircled by the entrance roa. This was where a military guard would be deployed day and night in the past.

My friend and I entered through the archway into the Alun-Alun and continued along the driveway straight towards the entrance leading to the inner palace compound. We followed the road around the fenced off area and approached the huge wooden doors. As we got close to the doors Ramzi started to feel a strong presence, which I felt too. I told him that, according to my relative, the palace is still guarded at night, not by soldiers, but by two enormous Jinns.

As we came close to the doors, I looked up to the top of the arch and sensed that this was the height of the two Jinns.

Ramzi said, "Lets walk around one more time to test whether the feeling comes again." It did.

For those who believe, I can say that there are many Jinns who work in the palace, which is a key part of ancient Javanese mysticism. Life within the Kraton (Palace) continues following all the ancient rituals and it really is like stepping into 'living history', although it is slowly fading away as the modern materialistic world creeps in.

My experiences tell me that there is much more truth to the ancient stories of mystical beings and powers than most westerners realize. I believe these stories, if not allegorical, are far more real than merely mythical.

But Subud takes us away from these ancient mystical worlds and focuses us on the worship of God and God alone. It is true that sometimes, through our latihan experiences, we are shown just enough to know that those other worlds or dimensions do exist, as do the Secret Arts of Mysticism, and they are very heavy for the soul, because it leads to darkness, where the soul gets trapped in this world, or worse, after death.

Back To The Real World

Part 1: The Original Built-in Smartphone and Inner Internet

In 1986 I had been working in the Jakarta office of the J. Walter Thompson advertising agency as the senior Account Director for one year. I had, at that time, a total of four years' experience in advertising, but like almost everyone else in the Jakarta advertising industry, I had never received any training. We all had to learn by doing.

In 1988 George Clements, a vice-president, and International Director of Strategic Planning & Research at JWT, arrived from Toronto. He was, at that time, the person responsible for conducting training and workshops worldwide. He had come to run a three-day workshop called 'The Thompson Way' to be held at a hotel in the mountain resort known as Punjak, one hour from Jakarta.

The agency had invited several brand managers from our key clients to attend and join our creative and account servicing teams, one of which I was leading.

After two days of going through the 'Thompson Way' each team was given an actual case study in the form of a real, original client brief and brand history including research reports and a summary of the market conditions and trends.

The assignment for my team was in the form of a book that was about 5 cm thick. This included what the agency team in Toronto had received from their client as the brief to come up with a strategic recommendation and creative advertising campaign proposal.

All the teams started working on their projects after dinner on Saturday night and had to prepare a strategic and creative presentation for Sunday, after lunch.

My team had six copies of the brief and, as team leader, I passed out five of them. Immediately my team started studiously reading away. I could see that it was going to take several hours for them to read and digest so much information before we could even begin any analysis and brainstorming on strategy.

Then they would need several more hours to write the strategy and a creative brief before they could produce the actual creative materials ready for presentation. It was clear that my team would get no sleep at this rate. This really was too much like the real world of advertising.

Guidance When Needed

I picked up my copy of the brief and started to flip through it. Every so often my fingers would stop and I would read a few sentences, seemingly randomly. I was actually picking out certain issues about the brand. Some key historical points and current threats they were facing. I decided to start writing these down in bullet points on the large white board.

My team were soon torn between looking at what I was writing and getting through the case study book. After about ten minutes I was done so, I began to discuss with them the strategy for the brand, based on the issues I had identified. We were soon into brainstorming to prepare the strategic recommendation.

At 11pm George and my boss did their rounds of the teams to check on our progress. They entered our room and George stood and looked at the white board. He then checked with some of my team members and answered some of their questions.

As he left, he called me over and, in a low voice. said, "Have you seen this case study before?" to which I said no. He then said, "What you have figured out there on the whiteboard in two hours, took us three weeks to figure out in Toronto."

I didn't know what to say. I could hardly discuss the advantage of having the inner guide your fingers, and your brain being given the answers before the mind got to work thinking about a problem.

Suffice to say that a year later I was offered the position of Regional Strategic Planner for JWT South East Asia.

So now I had proof of what Bapak had spoken about, that, when needed, through the latihan, I had more than just GPS legs. I also had remote controlled fingers and a brain that could access some invisible inner internet for information and answers.

I didn't need to ask Google, which was a big relief, because Google didn't exist back then.

So, I could not explain to George how I had done it, because how it was done was beyond explanation, yet it was the most important thing I learned at the workshop about myself. I could not tell him that I just flicked through the book and followed an inner indication of where to stop and what to read, jumping over masses of information that was of little relevance to finding the solution. This meant my team and I avoided wasting hours wading through a mountain of unhelpful data and were able to get some sleep before we presented.

I tell this story to demonstrate and confirm that our inner really does know things, which logically for the heart and mind would seem impossible to know. This was, for me, another very practical, worldly benefit of doing the latihan and going through my rather painful process of purification.

However, this is not a reason to become a Subud member and do latihan, because we cannot know what gift may come to us, or when.

Not that I am saying that the process of purification is over. I have no illusions of being pure and holy, and I believe the process of inner refinement never stops for as long as we live, because we all continually make mistakes and fail every day, often without realizing it.

Reading this last chapter, I can see how I must sound pretty full of myself, as though I am somehow special. I can't explain how uncomfortable that makes me feel, because that is not the purpose of this book at all.

I can only repeat again, that my intention in telling this story is simply to demonstrate that through the working of the latihan, over many years in my case, ordinary people from all walks of life can receive real guidance, that truly fits with their nature and needs. You do not have to be special in any way, just patient and sincere in your worship.

Back to The Real World Part 2

What do we mean when we say 'the real world'? For the heart and mind that can be quite an unsettling question. I would describe it as the material world we currently grow and develop in. It is the world we work in. And work is mandatory for all human beings in this world.

That is part of the reason I am writing this book. Although I am retired now, I know I still have to work, and writing is one of the jobs that I can still do and it is what is in front of me. Writing also makes my heart feel happy. I'm not so sure about the readers though. Still, one lives in hope. I digress.

We work because we must earn what we need to live in this world, but that is not the only reason. Work is an experience that teaches us about our talents and skills and how to use them. That is why, when I was a young man, I was so concerned about not having a proper job and not knowing what kind of work would fit my nature and talents best.

You may remember the letter that I received from Bapak advising me not to study and that the correct work for me is whatever made my heart happy. A somewhat confusing answer, because it gave no real direction and did not specify anything about what talents I may have.

Rectifying an Error

It was in the early eighties that I was talking with Bapak's English translator, Sharif Horthy, about my continued mild confusion regarding Bapak's advice, "Do what makes your heart happy." He also agreed that it was unusually vague and, without telling me, he brought it up with Bapak a few days later.

Some weeks passed before I bumped into him again and that was when he suddenly remembered his conversation with Bapak. He informed me that the letter I had received in the UK. was not an accurate translation of Bapak's answer.

What Bapak had actually said was, "When your heart is happy you can do anything." Sharif then added that he didn't think Bapak meant that I could go off and 'happily' start doing brain surgery the next day.

"When your heart is happy, you can do anything." Wow, that was a very different interpretation.

Looking back at the great variety of the work I had done in Indonesia, I began to understand what Bapak meant. For me it certainly explained my experience with the pottery.

During my first ten years in Indonesia I had worked designing and building catwalks and sets for fashion shows, setting up and managing a pottery for three years, designing and building a large polyclinic for the local Subud charity YUM, been the assistant to the Managing Director of a dredge building company in Singapore, worked in a multi-media company, writing and producing Indonesian advertising jingles amongst many other things. The only common denominator between all these different jobs was that my heart was happy doing all of them.

In all of these jobs I had received no prior training, nor did I have any experience in any of these fields. Every time a new job offer, or project presented itself, if I felt good about it I simply dived in as though starting on an adventure. If I felt a job was on my path, like a stepping stone, then I had no fear and my heart would be happy. Money and immediate rewards was never the deciding factor at that time.

Further, just as I had experienced in America and England, the knowledge and insights about people I met, who I knew nothing about, could simply manifest in my mind, not as a result of thinking. Today, looking back, I realize how the knowledge and ideas that I needed to do my work, could also just 'be there' and pop into my mind as I worked.

It didn't seem to matter what type of work I did, so long as I felt I was on the right path, because that is what made my heart happy. No wonder the Kingston helpers had problems testing about my talents and the right work for me to follow. How I made them suffer!

Work and Happiness

There are many successful people I know who are very lucky to be doing the work that fits perfectly with their talents and most say that when they are working it does not feel like work. Naturally this means they are very happy in their work, and usually in their life too. Generally, it is true to say that they also achieve material success.

My understanding of the importance of work, beyond the obvious need to earn money, is that the inner is also educated and acquires skills through the action of our body and faculties. It is therefore important that our work should match our inner nature and utilize the talents we have been given.

I can't say that my understanding is complete or even true, but this is what I believe. Through our work we can actually develop spiritually by bringing our inner inspiration into this world. Through the proper use of our intellect and imagination, we can receive all the ideas and guidance for making our life more comfortable and secure in this world.

I am not talking about those rare earth-shattering ideas, but the more mundane ideas that can still have a huge impact on our life, and perhaps society too.

Someone in the distant past 'imagined' a chair and then proceeded to make one. The first chair. It was very useful and soon became very popular (that's just my guess). Then more people imagined how to improve on this initial chair. And clearly chairs are a great benefit for mankind.

Sometimes we allow ourselves to work without a clear picture of the end result, but we can still be guided to a positive conclusion. This we call experimentation. Many artists and scientists work in this way, and look at what wondrous things have been brought into this world by artists and scientists. From paintings to great cathedrals to medical cures.

So the source of ideas is inspiration from our inner that we then work physically, using our heart and mind, to bring what has inspired us into this world, in a process that allows our inner to develop by participating, through our physical body and mind.

This, I recall Bapak saying, is knowledge that the soul will carry beyond our life in this world, because we have made it an inner and outer reality.

For practical reasons, even if we have not found work that we feel resonates with our inner nature, I believe we should still continue to happily work at whatever work is there before us. Through being active we can pray to be brought to our correct work in life. If we sit in our bedroom waiting for opportunities to arrive, our prayers are likely to remain unanswered. In the material world we must always make an effort. Fasting is an effort.

As I have described earlier, I had a lot of problems as a teenager wrestling with this whole 'work ethic' issue. Perhaps my artistic leanings added to my difficulty as, in my early years, I just wanted to paint or make music. I saw myself as an artist, not a businessperson or traditional worker.

I fell into that common trap of pigeonholing myself. As a result, I would turn away from jobs based on a false idea of who I was and what I should be doing. I did not understand that many of the right stepping stones in life may require us to go in directions our heart and mind, logically are uncomfortable with. As a case in point, I can look to that time I did odd jobs, including washing up for my neighbours which, in a very short time, led me to a job restoring old masters.

But as I previously mentioned, the testing about "look for a job, but don't take one" left me feeling happy, and all the time I was doing odd jobs and washing-up, I was content in my faith that this was what was right for me and what I had to do at that time. Not to complain, not to feel despondent at doing such menial work, and not to lose my confidence, because I also knew it would not be for ever.

Over time I realised that there is something valuable we can learn from doing any job, and that a job you don't like isn't going to be your life-long career. So, my advice to my own children is, just do whatever job is available and learn as much as possible while you do it, even though you may not like the job. This is something usually referred to as 'paying your dues'. I prefer the term 'University of Life'.

I firmly believe that with every effort we will reap a reward, sooner or later. Over the years I have had many jobs and I learned that it was possible for me to be happy even in a terrible, often underpaid job, because I saw my effort was putting credits into my future, rather than just focus on the present job and feel miserable.

Optimism, in the face of adversity, is a measure of faith.

But please note that this was my attitude when I was single, which allowed me the luxury of staying positive, and freely experiment with my life, because I was only responsible for myself.

I have a deep empathy for those many struggling families who are living on minimum wage, with parents working at more than one job, and still not able to provide a secure life for their children. The risks of experimenting with changing jobs can be daunting when you have a family to consider.

Learning About Myself by Doing

Returning to the JWT workshop, George's comments became the first clear indication of what my talent is. Not music and not painting, but something to do with 'thinking' and an ability to 'intuitively' cut through to the core of a problem. I hope that is true, and I trusted George's opinion.

I can say this now. Never was this 'talent' clearer to me than when I was presented with volumes of data, particularly research reports, by my clients.

By observing my clients, peers and colleagues over many years, I had seen how easily we can become dependent on mountains of data and research, hoping that somehow research reports and charts will tell us what we should do, and then make the decisions for us. Certainly, one of the original objectives of research was to minimise risk and identify opportunities.

Indeed, it seems clear that market research and data originally must have been a simple tool to gain an advantage by providing a clearer picture of the market, consumers, and competitors, for a company to identify opportunities and navigate their brand's expansion. That much I believe is very useful especially for people new to the brand.

My concern comes when research starts creating multiple segments and tries to identify minute differences between a 14 year old girl from the 'C' socio-economic class living in semi-urban areas with a single parent, who likes sport and K-Pop and spends 3 hours a day on social media, compared to 14 year girls from the 'B' socio-economic class living in urban centres with a single parent, who like going to the cinema and listening to rap music and spend 4 1/2 hours a day on social media.

By the time you repeat that research, with three hundred 17-year olds, then three hundred 20-year olds and three hundred 25-year olds, you will end up with well over five hundred pages of bullet point facts and charts. Information overload that all too often leaves people unable to see the wood for trees.

What I am sure happened was, someone saw a business opportunity to sell market research services. The research report was their end product and over time they needed to keep finding ways to 'add value' by making the research more comprehensive, and that means more complicated. In the same way many electronic products provide a host of functions that will never be used.

With computerization, the raw data from the field researchers could be used to produce endless combinations and groupings of consumer segments, their habits, media usage, food preferences, favourite shampoo brands, educational levels, age, disposable income etc.

So research companies created an industry and competed with each other, with the result that their products became increasingly expensive, increasingly detailed and increasingly irrelevant.

By the time I became involved in modern marketing it seemed clear to me that both clients and the researchers had forgotten that consumers are not aliens, they are human beings, and that they, the clients and researchers, are human too, and outside of the office they also become consumers like everyone else.

After thirty years as a strategic planner I can honestly say that about 90% of all the information clients provided us in their briefs and quantitative research reports, was mostly irrelevant to finding the right strategy for a brand's future success, and would tend to lead clients to a safe, 'me-too' brand positioning.

I was gratified to hear at a meeting with Unilever, when the CEO explain that she always followed research... but only if it confirmed her gut feeling. How could I not respect that kind of courage? Her career at Unilever Indonesia spanned thirty years, so I guess we can say she was successful.

She was the one who told my boss that she would not be happy if I was sent to Toronto for six months training with George. She wanted me on her business. That was a very welcome boost to my self-esteem.

I understand that this will sound like boasting, but I only ever flicked through all those reports and briefs until something jumped out, or my finger stopped at a page. But to tell the clients that would sound like extreme arrogance on my part, or anybody's part. It probably sounds like arrogance to you too. But hang on, it gets worse...

It would also be like a huge insult that, after all their years studying to get a marketing degree, followed by years of hard work gaining experience and knowledge, they were relying on a complete amateur (me) who just happened to do latihan and had attended a three-day workshop on the Thompson Way.

So, I kept very quiet about my lack of formal education and past job experience.

I honestly wished I could share my inner experience with these well-educated, hardworking, smart professionals. I often felt that the mountains of data that these companies relied upon actually created problems for brand managers and marketing managers. It was really a case of 'not being able to see the wood for the trees'. I am sure the same applies to many other non-scientific fields, not just marketing.

Without the inner guidance, which most people, I would say, experience as 'intuition', a person must work incredibly hard to read and review the masses of information that are produced these days, just to find a few useful nuggets hidden in all that data. I should note that the CEO of Unilever knew her stuff as a professional, yet never lost her trust in her human intuition.

I Wasn't a Great Boss

I also had a problem back at the agency because there was no way for me to teach my team how to do what I was doing. Each person has to find their own inner teacher and then have the courage and confidence to trust their inner teacher's guidance. Call it 'inner tuition'.

Unfortunately for my team, all too often they would become too dependent on me. They would give up too easily and wait for me to give them the answer or point them in a direction. This was very counterproductive to their own development. This was a problem I felt very bad about and never solved.

Sourcing Our Inner Guidance

This ability to work intuitively is a further demonstration and lesson for me that hard work and studying alone cannot open a reliable connection to that inner source of knowledge. The exception, I believe, is those who are naturally talented in their field, who are lucky to fall into the right kind of work, which they will find easy, even ordinary, and enjoy a source of ideas and guidance from their inner, often without even realizing it.

When an exceptionally talented person with a sharp intellect is opened to their inner guide, great things are brought into the world. People like that we usually call geniuses.

No, I have no illusions of being a genius! I don't think advertising and marketing ranks on that level anyway. But that is exactly my point. My latihan helped me in my work, even on such a lowly level as marketing toothpaste, shampoo and motorcycles. Work is work.

Newton, Einstein, Mozart, Rembrandt, are just a few historical examples of ordinary men who received exceptional ideas and insights that fuelled their talents to the full, for the benefit of all mankind. These are the geniuses.

The prophets too, from Abraham to Muhammad, were able to know the secrets of the spiritual world, and bring that knowledge into this world, to lead men to an understanding of how each individual person, and societies as a whole, should act in ways that are pleasing to God.

They knew these hidden mysteries without any worldly teachers or training. The source of their knowledge was not from books or studying, but simply through the grace of God, opening their connection to their inner library.

Just in passing, I wonder why no Prophets are called geniuses?

Many atheists will consider this to be complete nonsense, but if you ask them, "Where do new ideas come from?" they cannot answer. Original ideas just appear, they are not the result of thinking, they come when the thinking is done, when it stops, even if it stops for just a second, often accompanied with a sigh of giving up.

My experience in advertising has also shown me that no one can really study 'how to be creative'. After more than thirty years in advertising, I can attest that from observing so many young men and women who desired to be creative, and worked very hard at it, most never came up with a new, true 'advertising' or 'campaign' idea. Many of them would put the blame on a lack of training. I felt very bad for them and empathized with their frustrations.

The few who did come up with original ideas often had no training, but would go on to become legends in the industry. They are the ones who earned the big bucks!

My experience taught me that often the more we actively think and analyse, the less new ideas we have. Our overthinking gets in the way of, and even blocks, inspiration.

Actually, that is very logical because we can only think about and analyse things that already exist. Whereas creative ideas are what pop into our mind and show us something that doesn't exist yet.

What we can work at and study is 'craft'. A craftsman, say in a furniture factory, can make excellent copies, as good as the original, but few of them can ever come up with their own original designs.

Tourists to Bali will know this when they visit souvenir shops where they will see rows of almost identical, beautiful wooden carvings produced by groups of highly talented and trained craftsmen who are copying the original piece that a truly creative artist produced for them to reproduce en masse.

It is a common experience that ideas and solutions pop into our mind when we give up or just stop thinking and searching with our will. I have heard that there is a popular belief that this happens most frequently when we are sitting in the bathroom. … Eureka!

Here I would like to clarify again how one of the most important benefits of the latihan for me, and I believe potentially for every Subud member, has been the synergy between my worldly efforts in my work and the guidance from within.

What I learned from the Thompson Way was how to organize my thoughts, knowledge and experience and put it down in an easily understood format on paper, to create an unbroken argument to support a strategic recommendation. This was like a template. But what it could not do is fill in the sections for you. It could not give you the answers or the content, only a format for thinking.

What I experienced was that the inner guidance or inspiration would provide an almost instant understanding of the content that I should put in the template. It would bypass the mountains of endless diversions listed in the research data and client's laundry list of suggestions and would home in on what would turn out to be crucial.

This inner source, or intuition, would also offer some very radical and unique insights which, in my experience, would regularly go against conventional wisdom and conclusions suggested by formal research. And it is worth stating that the kind of strategies and creative recommendations that go against research require a lot of courage to present to a client, and even more courage by the client to approve them.

On more than one occasion a client became upset with me, because my risky, (no risk, no glory) strategic recommendations would be based on insights into consumers and competitors that were completely untested, and unsupported with research. However, I am happy to report that a year later they were very happy they took the risk.

Over the years there were three occasions that I can recall, with different clients, where the clients became very suspicious, almost paranoid, because they had just spent tens of thousands of dollars conducting quantitative and qualitative research that had exposed the very same insights as I had just presented to them for free. I think I may have missed a good business opportunity there, but then I'm not that smart.

They had kept those research reports to themselves and not shared them with the agency, because they were considered too valuable strategically, and were highly confidential.

I was frequently challenged by both clients and even my own team members, with the question, "How do you know that!?" I could hardly explain what was going on, because I would have to tell them almost everything I have written so far in this book. All I could do was shrug my shoulders. Much the same as with George Clements in the workshop.

This I can describe now, but at the time I was far too busy to think very much about 'how' I did my job. However, I was aware that each time I sat down to write a strategic recommendation, my heart was always happy, which I later realized matched with Bapak's advice to me about the right kind of work for me.

For the most part, like with this book, in my work I simply sat in front of my computer and started typing, with little or no idea what the recommendation and strategy would be. I would type a few paragraphs and then read my own words, or sometimes read as I typed them. I often surprised myself by what I was typing – things I had never thought of.

I could have asked myself, "How do I know that?" But I didn't feel the need to ask. I just felt a great deal of gratitude that this was happening to me and grateful for the rewards that came on all levels, inner and outer, from the result. This continued from 1986 until 2014, when I retired from advertising.

No Free Lunches

I need to point out here that I also learned another very important lesson from my work. While it is fine to have all these insights and inspiration from the inner, without the training and knowledge that I got from the JWT workshop, I would not have been able to use my inner guide effectively.

Without that education and training, using any gift of inner guidance would be like trying to carry water from the pump without a bucket. Or giving the inner Formula 1 driver a 1952 Willys Jeep to compete in a Grand Prix.

So I finally learned the real value of education, training and experience.

Prior to that workshop, my presentations were all over the place and filled with all the normal charts and references that sent people off thinking in several directions, none of which, when I got to the conclusion, were relevant to my final recommendation. The mountains of information I would present was more to satisfy everyone that I had done a lot of work and I was a credible professional, so you can trust my recommendation.

Fortunately, everyone else's presentations in all the other

267

agencies were the same, so I wasn't too worried about job security. Ignorance is bliss, especially when everyone around is equally ignorant.

I am very grateful to the J. Walter Thompson company, and I owe a lot to George Clements for that three-day workshop and follow-up chats. They turned me from an enthusiastic amateur into a 'highly effective professional'. (Not my words).

The workshop provided me with a Formula 1 racing car. My inner guidance then showed me how to drive it!

So, joining the dots, in Paris I was shown that legs can be guided from the inner. When leafing through a hefty case study in a workshop, even the fingers can be guided to what is important. And through my daily work I was shown the proof that even the mind and imagination can be guided to add value to my work.

I could begin to taste what Bapak had so often talked about, how our work can become part of our worship when our inner participates. Something so many Subud members have experienced.

Forty Years and Still Learning

I hope that these stories are not going to be overkill. The reason I have spent so much time on this subject is to confirm that through the latihan and the process of purification, any human being, even me, can experience the manifestation of their inner guidance in their day-to-day life.

This manifestation is not just a feeling of happiness or just a reduction in stress levels, which are good things in themselves, but there are many ways and methods to achieve that kind of peace in our heart and mind using our will and desires, like meditation and yoga.

But the latihan goes much deeper than our hearts. It goes

beyond what our heart and mind can comprehend or imagine. It is beyond our will and desires, yet we can experience the results of our latihan, the proof.

You do not need to be a saint or special person to receive this gift from God. Every human being is encompassed by the power of Almighty God. According to my humble experience, a sincere wish to worship almighty God is enough to get started.

In The Midst of the Hubbub
Distance Is No Obstacle

It was just another day, and I was sitting at my desk in my room in JWT, when I started feeling a kind of vibration which grew to the point of being like severe shivering. My hands were shaking so much I could not write. But I had no sense that this shaking was actually to do with me. I knew it wasn't a symptom of sickness and I did not feel at all worried, but I was curious.

A few minutes later my boss came into my room and immediately noticed I was shaking. He looked very worried, but I told him I was fine, so he gave me some report to look at and left, clearly still feeling concerned.

I knew that this was a latihan experience, and now there was a deep feeling of sadness rising within my chest and forming a lump in my throat. I decided to go into our large, swanky Directors bathroom, where I locked the door and did a latihan for about ten minutes. Slowly the shaking subsided, but the feeling of sadness lingered for two more days.

And it was on the second day that I was in a recording studio when I got a call from my mother in England. She was crying as she told me my brother had passed away from a heart attack two days earlier. She had only found out the next day and it took her another day to get through to me.

Now that my heart knew what that experience was, it felt the deep grief as I tried to console my mother from the other side of the world.

There were another two occasions when I experienced shaking like that, but more subdued. They were on the days my father passed away and several years later when my mother passed away.

Now, many years later I wonder, if I had progressed more in the latihan, I might have been able to see them at that moment when they passed. It was clear that an inner connection existed that traversed the world, but only manifested in my feelings and body, but not yet in my mind.

It was like the night time sighting of the two birds I had, where I could only see the black, silhouette shapes but not yet the colours. I still have a long way to go in the latihan to reach that level.

The British Agency

Around the time J. Walter Thompson offered me the position of Director of Strategic Planning for Southeast Asia, I found myself in a dilemma. A regional position would mean having to move to Hong Kong, and for family reasons, that just wasn't feasible at that time. J.W.T. then very kindly offered me the alternative of Sydney, Australia, but that would not solve my problem.

I was also thinking about the future for my family because there was no prospect of a pension for an ex-pat in Indonesia. The only route for securing financial security after retirement was by owning a company and building a nest-egg. But with no financial capital, that option was not practical. To start my own agency would require at least half a million dollars. Imagine me, with my background, asking a bank for half a million dollars. Well I couldn't take a loan even if I was silly enough to try, because banks were not allowed to make those kind of loans to foreigners.

So I was in a bit of a quandary. The old "leave it up to God, things will work out" attitude was all well and good for many things in life, but not when facing questions of banking laws, ownership laws and so on. I really needed a more practical solution. I had to do something, or at least that is what I thought.

While J.W.T. were waiting for my response to their offer, I received a phone call from my old friend Glen, of Blue Holden, Richardson Vicks days. He had a proposal that he thought may interest me. And so it was that a week later I was sitting in a hotel coffee shop in Singapore for a breakfast meeting with the regional CEO and regional CFO of Britain's largest advertising agency.

They were interviewing me as a candidate for their Local Partner in Indonesia. (Yes, partner, not representative!) In the offer I would have the majority shareholding. Basically, I would be the owner. They would provide all the finance to set up and run the business for two years, by which time the agency should be able to pay its own way. They had several multinational clients already waiting for them in Indonesia, so cash flow and the two-year target should not be a problem.

There was no negotiating, the thick contract was there on the table to sign. To tell the truth I was rather stunned.

I had just been offered my own agency without having to invest anything except my time and effort. So, what on earth would I negotiate?

Fond Farewell

On returning to Jakarta the next day I went to my boss to explain that I would not be taking up their offer of a regional position. I actually felt sad. I had learned a lot in the five years I was with

J.W.T. and really felt I owed them. I had also made some very good friends who I would miss in a new, fledgling agency.

I feel very grateful for those five years with JWT, and to George Clements for that three-day workshop in Punjak, and Lee Perchel, VP International, for all their support.

Seven years later the Asian financial crisis hit, and the British Agency decided to pull out of Indonesia, thus leaving me with 100% ownership of the agency.

Incidental Anomalies

During my thirty years in advertising, when my focus was much more on my family and career, there were nonetheless odd experiences that popped up that reminded me that I was still walking down my spiritual path. These were one-off experiences that, you will be glad to know, do not require a long background explanation or time-line to fit in the general narrative of this book.

Courage to Surrender

As any Subud member will tell you, when standing before God in the latihan, what you will receive is entirely dependent on God, and your depth of sincerity to surrender. God will not force you or beat you into submission. God gave man the incredibly powerful 'double-edged sword' called 'choice'.

Our choice to surrender to God's will is what determines our direction in this life and for our future life. But I know all too well how the heart or ego often wants to hold back from fully surrendering, perhaps out of fear of the unknown, or losing the sense of being in control. And I know very well that it does take courage to let go of our safe, familiar understanding of our self and of life!

During the last few years of Bapak's life, he began adding the word 'courage' to the basic requirements for spiritual progress in receiving the latihan, beyond the well-established advice of sincere surrender, patience and faith.

Over the years I have talked with many Subud members and amongst them have been a few who feel that their latihan is somehow 'stuck'. That they seem to be repeating the same things in latihan for months, even years, with little change, even though they feel they have faith, sincerely believe in the power of Almighty God and truly pray that they can surrender to His will. And yet still they feel that they have made little progress.

In recent years an understanding emerged in my thinking about part of this problem of being 'stuck' spiritually, and how it related to Bapak's addition of the word 'courage' in his advice.

The small understanding that presented itself to my mind was in the form of an analogy. I saw a group of people standing at the top of a cliff who were waiting to learn how to fly.

They had already been given wings in the latihan, but now they were waiting, surrendering patiently, with sincerity and faith, to receive the instruction book on 'How to Fly', so that they could then 'jump' off the cliff and safely experience the mysteries of flying in the spiritual realms.

The reason, I believe, that Bapak said 'courage' is required is because the flying lessons and training they are waiting for only come after we jump!

That adds a whole new meaning to the phrase 'a leap of faith'. That can be a scary thought and it really does take courage. Without that courage the latihan will feel stuck, until we jump and let go of that fear and truly surrender.

Trust the Instructor

You cannot know ahead of time what experiences will manifest within you. That is decided by God and we are all unique so our purification and spiritual progress will always be tailored to our individual needs and capacity. For God, that is easy.

To expand the 'flying' analogy, some of us have a real fear of heights. So for some, the first cliff they stand on may only be a few meters high. For others, with more courage, their first cliff may be tens of meters high or even a thousand meters high.

I am very sure that the depth of our sincerity to worship God and the amount of courage to surrender our fear of the unknown to receive whatever God deems best for us also determines the 'height of the cliff'. So the limiting factor for our progress is not God or the latihan, but rather our sincerity, faith and courage. Things we have very little say in.

There are two occasions I wrote about earlier, that when I look back on them illustrate this limitation. The first was when I was in the forest in Ohio, in the middle of the night and had an 'out-of-body' experience, and the second was in Solo, Central Java, when the spirit of Senopati appeared one night next to my bed.

Both of these experiences sent my heart into overdrive. My mind could not rationalize what was going on and I was terrified. In both cases I feel it was my fear, or lack of courage, that cut those experiences short.

I believe if I had a stronger faith, and had been truly surrendered, I would have been shown more, gone further. As it is, I feel those two experiences were incomplete. I wasn't ready to jump from that height at that time and, as Bapak often said, God will not force us to go beyond our individual capacity.

This addition of the element of courage is not about being gung-ho, impatient or trying to force our spiritual progress. Far from it. We must have patience, because if we try to force this process, say by doing ten latihans a day, we will certainly end up either biting off more than we can chew or becoming incapable of managing our worldly life.

So, as Bapak advised, sensible moderation and discipline to do latihan regularly, with patience and sincerity, is the healthiest approach. But, as every Subud member knows, Bapak also emphasised that when we come to do lahihan, it is the depth of our sincerity and willingness to accept change in our self and our life, that will determine how deep the latihan can penetrate, remembering always it is God who knows our true capacity to receive.

To surrender our ego, our familiar self, to whatever God decrees is best for our well-being, even if at times it might be unpleasant or scary, is not as easy as it sounds. That level of sincerity takes a great deal of courage for any of us.

The Tyranny of the Heart
When the Kids Steal the Car

The most fundamental desire of the persona that we call the ego, is to have full control of whatever we do, what we think, what we feel and the decisions we make.

The ego also desires to choose what we believe and don't believe, including in spiritual matters about which, ironically, our worldly heart and mind, filled by those desires, can know nothing about except hearsay.

The ego and desires that fill the heart and mind are the foundation that we build our material, outer life on to live and function in this world.

This persona that inhabits our coarse physical body is created and then develops on this earth through the influence of our worldly experiences – our parents, peers and education, which all interact with our heart and mind. As a society, many of these same influences and knowledge are shared between people and handed down over many generations to create what we call 'culture'.

The ego is usually very reluctant, and even afraid, to step out of this familiar culture that it has grown up in, and even more afraid to relinquish its absolute control of our heart and mind. From this fear will often arise internal arguments to resist any suggestion that there is a real, tangible, spiritual force within human beings that can override the desires of the ego.

Spiritual realities are instead converted into worldly doctrines, rituals, methods, parables and stories that are easily accessible to our intellect, and which allow us to incorporate 'spiritual' teaching into our everyday, worldly culture by bringing it all down to the material level, where our hearts and minds can feel they are still in control.

So instead of the spiritual light lifting human awareness to a higher level, the heart and mind bring spiritual knowledge down to the material level where, unfortunately, the ego, lacking true guidance, can interpret and manipulate this knowledge for its own benefit.

Once the spiritual truth is available in the worldly form of words, then for many people those words become carved in stone. Unfortunately, different societies will make their own interpretations and their varying interpretations become law, which becomes power and authority in each society. History also shows us how these teachings can become extreme and devoid of inner content, far from the true, original meaning.

This can be a danger for the Subud Association too. If members begin to 'imagine' they are spiritually high and think they must introduce new things like doctrines and methods based on their own experiences during purification.

Then they may be able to convince some others to join them as their pupils and the pure simplicity and truth of the Subud latihan will be polluted by the desires of their heart influencing their imagination, with the result of turning Subud into a kind of religion or cult. History teaches us that the nafsu are relentless in their quest to control our individual experience of life in this world for their own satisfaction.

The Corruption of Truth

Once this worldly manipulation of spiritual knowledge by the human ego is established in law it becomes part of national pride and patriotism. By using these corrupted tools, misguided teachings by leaders, we can see throughout history, that people will not only fight and die for their land, for resources, for wealth and material possessions, but will even be willing to die for man-made religious doctrines.

That is how clever the nafsu are at influencing man's mind in order to maintain the illusion of control over everything, including, incredibly, God's guidance, Angels, Heaven and Hell. Things that they personally know nothing about.

Religions and spiritual beliefs, once given a label, can become the same as a possession, like a car or a football team. If someone scratches your car you might erupt in anger, as though your own body had been injured. If someone criticises your home town football team you may be willing to fight them physically, as though defending your home and family.

You might even resort to throwing rocks and bottles that can cause serious injury and even death. That is the nature of the human heart that is filled with lower forces. An analogy would be the kids that steal the car and go for a joyride and have several accidents. Because the undisciplined heart, influenced by the nafsu, is like a kid with unrestrained desires that will happily risk abusing and damaging their own body. This may be with drugs, alcohol, gambling, promiscuity, and all the other vices.

The same can happen with religion, if a person's religion is criticised, or simply confronted with a different religion, a fight can break out, even a war!

Men will gather on the streets, ready to fight and even die in a war about their religious beliefs. Willing to commit suicide for something that cannot be touched, cannot be possessed, cannot be measured, bought or sold and belongs to no-one.

That is the folly of man's heart under the control of the ego and the lower forces! Unfortunately, many leaders are aware of this and use it to achieve their own political ambitions for power and wealth. They use intangible, fiery words to harness the power of the mob to gain material riches for themselves. Add to that the illusion of status, power and prestige and you can see what an overwhelming force exists in this cocktail of desires that can turn them away from the right path.

The Emperor's Clothes

For something so ethereal, with no intrinsic material value, it is ironic that so many people still desire to be seen as 'spiritual' and 'noble'.

For some people this is a form of ambition, for others it is a sincere desire, but still, just a desire of the heart and ego nonetheless.

So people who have this desire, this ambition, will often make great efforts to follow one of the paths of the many spiritual leaders, gurus and teachers available in this world, by studying their teachings, following their rituals, rules and methods, believing blindly in their advice and explanations.

In this way, it is possible for anybody to become a spiritual or religious leader simply through studying books, the same way as they would to become a doctor or lawyer.

But we know that not all doctors are good people. There are some who sell prescriptions to drug addicts. There have even been cases of doctors and nurses who have murdered their patients. There are Lawyers who have cheated their clients. Judges in wigs and robes who accept bribes to subvert justice.

So studying and passing exams, then wearing a uniform, a doctor's white coat, a suit and tie, wigs and robes or carrying a *sadjadah* (prayer mat) is not a guarantee that a person's true character and inner nature is that of a good human being. They may just be a good actor who has learned his lines.

Such a person might well be attracted to Subud for reasons of their own; that could do a lot of harm to the brotherhood.

It should be clear that this approach of studying and performing rituals to attain knowledge from the higher spiritual world, even for a sincere and humble believer, can only achieve results limited to experiences of this world, because the tools being used (the heart and mind) are the tools for our life in this world. That is simple logic.

The fountain of spiritual knowledge can only be given, or withheld by God Almighty, and we cannot assume or predict God's decision. This is something I have believed since I was quite young and noticed how in all the stories of the prophets and servants of God they were always shocked and fearful when they were first called to their mission.

So, the prophets had not been expecting to receive a revelation from beyond this material world. You can say it was a surprise or shock for them. This shows that it is entirely up to God who shall receive revelation and when it will be sent.

But a person who 'desires' to be a prophet would not be shocked, if they had been studying and working hard to 'achieve' some revelation from God in the same way they work to achieve normal goals in life using their will, ambition and desires. If that was the way the prophets received their first revelation, they would not have been surprised at all.

But man will receive nothing unless God wills it.

279

Needless to say, there are much deeper things related to this subject which are well beyond my experience and understanding, so I can say no more.

There Are Consequences

For newly opened Subud members, Bapak explained this idea of seeking God and seeking special abilities in many talks. He gave many intriguing insights into the mysteries of what human beings can achieve by using just their will and worldly tools on this material level, and why that can be a huge temptation and diversion from following the true path of only worshipping God, with some pretty dire consequences for the soul, if we venture off into the mystical secret arts.

Once again, I would recommend all new Subud members to read Bapak's talks for a much deeper understanding of this side of life on the material level, just to satisfy your curiosity, and hopefully to guide you away from the very real dangers that dabbling in the 'secret arts' will have for your inner life, both in this world and the afterlife.

With Bapak's guidance and the very limited experiences of a novice, I can offer the following on this subject. But I repeat again, it is far better to read the talks of Bapak than anything I can write. But I hope this may encourage you to do that

According to Bapak, some people who pursue asceticism, semi-religious methods, spiritualism and mysticism, really are able to acquire some astonishing abilities, like, being able to see into the future, healing, communicating with Jinns and many other activities that generally come under the umbrella of 'magic and mysticism'.

But as wonderful as these powers may sound, none of them can bring a person closer to God. In fact, seeking these kind of 'abilities' with their will, even with 'good' intentions, can be a great hindrance to finding their path to the true human level in the next life.

It is different however, if we receive these abilities spontaneously through the latihan, which I have seen happen, because in such a case we have no desire, and have made no effort to look for any 'powers', therefore it is a gift from God in accordance with His will.

I have seen several Subud members receive, without asking, a special ability for a particular purpose, and when that purpose is completed, the gift is withdrawn. Other times a new ability will be received unexpectedly and become permanently one with that person.

When an ability manifests itself spontaneously through the latihan, contained within that ability is the knowledge of when and how to use it according to God's will, free of the influence of our desires. In this way we are protected from any bad consequences.

Be Careful what You Wish for!

When a person asks God for some special power or ability and makes great sacrifices and efforts by years of fasting, praying and meditating, it is quite possible that God will grant their wish. Who can restrict God's grace?

But when, and how to use that power becomes the responsibility of that person, because receiving that power or ability is the result of their will, of their ego, driven by the desire of the heart. And a heart that is still filled with material forces and worldly desires does not know the way back to heaven. So following this path of the ego will just lead the soul deeper into the darkness of the material world.

This is why Bapak always said that the only one who can guide us back to the true human realm is God. Therefore, we should not try to use our will and desires to seek God, because to do so will actually obstructs us in our purpose, which is to receive guidance from God.

That advice used to confuse me, but now I understand what is actually so obvious. Our desires that reside in our heart, and our intelligence that resides in our mind, were created as tools purely for our life in this world, and therefor they are limited to what exists on this material level.

But, at the same time, it is right to make an effort towards God, and for that we should use our religion as a guide for our heart and mind. Religion shows all mankind how we should live and how we should treat others with the intention and hope of becoming a human being who is pleasing in God's sight; and when we are pleasing to God we can hope for God's blessing to raise up and guide our soul , both in this world and in the next.

I hope I am not boring you, but this understanding is a core belief in my life.

From this understanding came my belief that I can only find the right way in my life in this world, and in the hereafter, by sur-rendering my will, my desires and ego, to Almighty God, as much as I am able to.

Further, my belief, based on my experiences, is that in the spiritual realm the only effort we can make is to prepare our-selves, as best we can, to receive the guidance we seek. We can-not hurry it and we cannot choose what we receive. It is all in the hands of Almighty God.

Once we are opened, our spiritual progress is entirely deter-mined by Almighty God, and what we receive is exactly what truly fits our individual needs. Our efforts should be directed towards living a good life, avoid wrong doing and resisting the urges of the lower forces that arise from our heart.

Beyond that my friend, we can only surrender to Almighty God.

Wrong Doing and Forgiveness

Here is a fun subject most of us prefer not to think about. The reason it is fun is because most of the things we do that are wrong just feel so nice, so satisfying to our heart and minds... and usually they don't feel in the least bit wrong ... until the next day.

We know when we insult someone or get angry or physically abuse someone, that we are acting wrongly. Pretty much everything covered by the Ten Commandments we can all feel are wrong, if we violate them.

But I would place the Ten Commandments at the bottom of the pyramid, being the most basic set of laws required to allow human societies to form and develop in relative harmony.

If we are able to follow the ten commandments then we can say that we live a good life and probably feel pretty confident that we will go to heaven when our time on earth is up.

One could just stop there and go about life without any further thought about sinning, heaven and hell.

In my early teens I pretty much saw life, right, wrong and religion like that. I didn't have any problems believing in only one God, I didn't blaspheme, I wasn't too good with keeping the Sabbath, I tried to honour my parents as best I could, I managed not to murder anybody and, being single, I wasn't concerned about adultery. I did not steal and very rarely told a lie and I certainly never coveted my neighbour's cattle or any of my neighbour's goods.

In other words, for the most part, I was about the same as ninety percent of the population. However, as I got further into my teens and spent most of my free time with older people in their early twenties, I saw things were much more complicated for young adults than I had thought.

While the Ten Commandments were pretty clear on fornication, murder and stealing they didn't seem to cover things like alcohol and drugs. Stealing was wrong but what about borrowing without asking? Lying was wrong, but what about gossip and bending the truth? It seems there were a multitude of things which felt wrong to me, but were both common, and generally accepted by most of society.

Fortunately, as I described in the early chapters, because of my young age, these older people around me protected me from the excesses of the sixties. I could be a witness but could not participate. This allowed me time to observe and consider what they were doing with their lives. It also allowed me to see the consequences of their actions and their lifestyles.

This is where I was in my life when I came into Subud. I often found myself pondering what it was in human nature that led some to die of a drug overdose, girls to become single mothers, guys to be caught up in a cycle of unemployment and alcohol abuse, and others to be sent to prison for stealing.

And why so many others went through the same high risk lifestyle but emerged in their late twenties relatively unscathed and went on to have good jobs, get married and settle down with little more than a lot of crazy, exciting memories of their youth –, and perhaps a few regrets.

I was not into the idea of 'karma' in the sense that when bad things happen it is some kind of payback for mistakes made in a previous life, or earlier in our life. I have seen many people who all made virtually the same mistakes growing up, but they did not all suffer the same consequences.

This always intrigued me as it relates to our sense of justice and fairness in this world. It was like an anomaly hiding in plain sight. There must be some important piece of knowledge missing that could explain this.

Even as a young child I was confused by the injustices that I saw around me or, more accurately, why God allowed these injustices to continue.

This was one subject that I regularly raised on my walks in the forest. Why did God allow people to get away with so many bad things? Where was the punishment? Why was punishment left to the next life when the hurt and suffering was happening in this life?

It has taken many years for me to just begin to get a sense of what the explanation is for me, according to my understanding.

It was a few statements from Bapak that opened a whole new vista of knowledge for me on this subject. Although, at the time, it quite dumbfounded me.

Bapak's explanations seemed to fly in the face of every tradition of justice and fairness I had been brought up to believe. It took a number of years for me to pierce through my rigid belief system of 'right and wrong' that was pretty much set in stone during my formative years. But as I learned to question everything I had been taught I began to perceive a bigger picture that put into context the depth of Bapak's words.

I have to paraphrase Bapak's words as I have not yet identified the talks that Bapak spoke on this subject, but basically Bapak explained that when a person has the 'inner nature' of a thief and gets caught stealing, seen from the spiritual world, it is actually wrong to punish them or send them to prison.

Wow! That sounded so radical, so controversial to me. It would lead to a lawless society, pure anarchy. That can't be right, I thought. It goes against the Ten Commandments!

Well, first let me say that Bapak was not promoting a lawless society and was not being radical. Bapak was offering an insight into this whole issue from the inner point of view, not from our normal, worldly view of established, stable societies.

The key was in the words 'inner nature'.

The understanding is that a person's actions are determined by their inner nature and character, and that is true for all of us. From the inner perspective we cannot blame (punish) someone for following their inner nature over which they have no control.

Let me use this analogy. It would be like blaming a fox for killing a hen. The fox is simply following its nature.

But there are consequences for the fox, because the hen belonged to a farmer and the farmer values his hens more than a fox. In fact he sees the fox as a threat to the stability of his farm.

From there my understanding took another small step forward. But please remember, this is only my understanding, for me, that I am sharing. If you continue reading this I thank you for humouring me.

Living with 'Jelly Brains'

Before I can continue with the fate of the Fox I need to take you on a slight detour.

Bapak often talked about the various forces that influence mankind in this world, starting with the lowest material force that originates from the earth and exists in trace amounts within our bodies. Then there are the vegetable and animal forces that exist within man because we consume vegetables and meat. Bapak explains about these forces in great detail in his book *Susila Budhi Dharma*.

Unfortunately for me, I had a hard time understanding the reality of what Bapak wrote, and spoke about, during my early years in Subud. It all sounded very esoteric and barely relevant to my life. Trying to think about all these forces and levels would give me jelly brains, so I knew I would have to be patient until, hopefully, my thinking had been sufficiently purified and trained to understand Bapak's words.

Now here I am, somewhat reluctantly, simply sharing what I

understand today, after almost 50 years of doing latihan. But it is still just my understanding of Bapak's words.

So, in this world human beings can own things, including animals, and they make up their own rules to protect their possessions, like chickens, which may result in the death of the fox. But still, from the inner perspective, the fox did not commit a crime. Man just made up that crime because it suits man's desire to own hens and eat fried egg sandwiches. So, it's justice for man, injustice for foxes.

I realized that the same applies to human societies. We have, and we need to have laws and rules to maintain peace and harmony between human beings. But why, I asked. If we are all human beings, surely we all know how to act towards each other!?

Here is where a big part of the puzzle of what Bapak had described about forces and animal natures fell in place for me. Quite simply man needs laws and rules because some of us have the inner nature of a fox, and some of us have the animal nature of chickens, rabbits, tigers etc. Literally.

This is not new, except the true meaning has been forgotten. We still refer to these animal natures as they influence human beings in our daily language.

He acts like a bull in a china shop.

She's as timid as a mouse.

They act like sheep; they just follow the leader.

He's as crafty, (sly, wily), as a fox.

He's like a wild boar.

Like a snake in the grass,

He's a naughty monkey,

Stubborn as a mule,

So what's the connection? I asked myself. How does that happen? This became the next question to peel this onion.

Every human being is influenced by these animal forces because our bodies are created in the same way as the bodies of animals. God even created various animals for us to consume.

Our mothers consume meat as our bodies are forming during pregnancy. So the force or inner nature of animals are already present within us, even before we are born. We cannot escape them.

So the nature of these forces enters our bodies through the food we eat. That sounds a bit Zen, and it probably is. But things were beginning to become a bit clearer for me.

I Am Intrigued... You Might Be Bored

Allow me to digress a little here because I want to mention how, when science talks about DNA and stem cells, I see parallels with what Bapak speaks about regarding the influence of these forces, as seen from the inner reality, including how the mistakes and shortcomings of our ancestors can be passed down to us to resolve.

I find myself sensing that there are some dots here that I need to connect. You may prefer to skip this chapter because it is purely my speculation.

Science tells us that every single cell contains DNA, the genetic blue print for the entire human body. It also contains a huge amount of DNA code that is dormant, that exists in all other forms of life in this world.

The same is true for every cell of an animal and every cell of a plant. So it begins to become reasonable and rational to consider the influence that all 'living' things have on human beings because the essence of all living things exists within the human body at the cellular level.

I have decided to take mercy on you now, and not write about my thoughts on quantum physics, quarks and neutrinos. Let me just say that I see many more dots to be connected between science and Bapak's explanations that he received over 90 years ago, long before DNA, genomes and quantum physics were ever exposed to the public in Europe, let alone in a developing country in South East Asia.

If you do spend time thinking about this, let me assure you that it will not help at all to get you to heaven or make you a better person.

Back to the Farm

Returning to the fox and chicken, I believe that we all have a dominant nature from all the various vegetable forces and a dominant nature from all the animal forces and the same for the human force.

In some people I believe it is quite clear which dominant forces are working in them, if you can feel it. For others they seem able to keep these forces well hidden. Hence we have the saying "A wolf in sheep's clothing".

Through the latihan I know we can experience, or perhaps it would be better to say we can meet, many of these different forces and recognize their different natures within our own being. Then we can recognize them in others. Over time we will be shown how these forces influence us, and everyone else too, in our daily life.

This will help us understand why we do the things we do and why others do what they do. When we recognise the fox in someone we will not judge them so harshly if they are always chasing chickens. When we understand, rather than judge, we can experience a deeper level of patience and empathy.

Hopefully, for the most part, we will also be able to choose friends who have a good nature which will help us to avoid the sin of sitting around judging others. Did I just unwittingly make a judgement?

For a more complete and deeper understanding of this subject, once again I recommend reading Bapak's book, and for those in Subud, read the relevant talks that Bapak gave. Whatever insights I may have, they are just the tip of the iceberg, because I know I have only scratched the surface.

My last comment on this subject is to say that whatever forces are dominant in us, and they may not be very nice ones, we should be thankful for the gift of the latihan because through the process of purification these forces can be changed.

Yes, a chicken can become a mighty eagle and a fox can become an obedient border collie. These are not changes that we choose or can will for ourselves. They are real changes to our nature that only God can bring about and they will happen gradually and spontaneously.

Meantime, perhaps we can learn to be more forgiving, more understanding and more patient with people who are struggling to deal with difficult forces that have great influence on their actions and thinking. But of course, in this world there are a farmers and so there will be consequences for the foxes, because the hens must be protected. Society cannot thrive based on anarchy.

Annoying Teenagers

Fear not, I am not going to explain where babies come from, but one thing I noticed, as a teenager, was that there were quite a few things that parents and religions forbid, but never really explain why. As parents we also tell our children they shouldn't do this and can't do that, but too often we also cannot explain why.

Few kids today are willing to accept answers like, "Because I say so" or "Those are the rules", or "Because it's wrong" as sufficient reason to change their activities or attitudes to many issues in today's world.

One obvious subject, not just for teenagers, is, "Why is promiscuity forbidden in religion?" When my son asked this question, I had no stock answer on file that made sense in the twenty-first century. "Because God says so!" just wasn't good enough.

So, I quietened my mind and, like on my walks in the forest as a child, asked, "What is wrong with being promiscuous?"

As I quietened myself what came to me was an analogy, an image, of dozens of large wine glasses filled with crystal clear water.

Then I saw two glasses move towards each other and, as they touched, a small drop of uniquely coloured ink (yellow) entered their water. The result was, as they exchanged water, the content of both glasses took on the same yellow tint.

Each pairing of the other glasses received a uniquely different colour of ink which, as they exchanged water, gave their content the same unique colour tint. Blue, green, red, orange, violet etc.

Then some of the glasses moved off and approached a different glass and as they touched, they received another drop of different coloured ink. That resulted in the mixing of two colours. If the first pairing resulted in yellow and with the second pairing was blue, then the result would be the two glasses would take on a denser green tint.

If then one of those glasses moves off to another glass and repeats this process it will receive yet another different coloured drop of ink from that third pairing.

If a glass continues to pair with ten, twenty or more different glasses, we can imagine what the colour of their content will become. Now, imagine if each colour had its own flavour. Some sweet, some savoury others fruity. After pairing with multiple partners and mixing ten or twenty flavoured colours, the content of that glass is going to be a foul tasting, opaque, dark brown sludge.

And then, say one day that person, who outwardly may be very handsome, well dressed and well educated, meets a beautiful woman, who has restrained her lustful desires, and he falls in love with her and she with him. It doesn't take long for him to propose marriage and the wedding day is set.

After their wedding they will consummate their marriage, and at that moment she will surrender to her husband her glass of pure, crystal clear water that she has carefully guarded all her life, for him to drink. In return he offers her his glass of foul tasting, thick brown liquid.

If a woman is able to be inwardly aware, she will feel her inner descend toward darkness and heaviness, but usually humans are completely consumed by the physical and emotional pleasure they experience, and are unable to feel the deeper, inner consequence of this exchange. The man also will probably not be aware that his content will actually become a little lighter, a little clearer, through this exchange.

Over time the inner content of the woman will be brought down closer to the level of her husband. A level they both will share. A level where she will not be able to feel her inner light or to develop her soul in the right direction.

The reverse is also true, if a woman has not restrained her desires and mixed with many men and she marries a man who has not indulged his lusts, he will be brought down into darkness too. Recall the story of Samson and Delilah.

So the reason promiscuity is so forcefully forbidden by religion is because of the consequences and risks for the soul. The potential health risks and other unintended consequences can also bring much misery and suffering in this life, but the inner damage is far more consequential.

Are They Doomed to Eternal Darkness?

Even if we have indulged in wrong behaviour, for as long as we are alive in this world, we are not doomed, because for as long as we are alive, there is always the Grace of God and we have the opportunity to change. But there are conditions. First there must be a sincere intention to change our behaviour. Second is an awareness of the consequences of past mistakes and to sincerely seek God's forgiveness.

If the man or woman is really blessed, they can still receive God's mercy, which is what we receive in the latihan.

Through the latihan, if God wills, slowly the couple will receive new, pure water, that will flow into their inner. Over time this will dilute the impurities they have accumulated and eventually it will purify and flush the glasses clean.

Failing this, if either one simply continues with the bad behaviour, when their life comes to an end their soul will be in darkness, and it will be too late then to change their condition.

That is why, I believe, promiscuity is treated so seriously by all religions. The sin is the damage it does to the soul and the consequences in the next life.

Of course, there is also the pain and suffering that may come during their life from living this kind of lifestyle. Broken hearts, unwanted pregnancies, health issues, not to mention that anger and violence can all result from a life of promiscuity.

An analogy of a 'soul in darkness' was what I experienced on the Notting Hill Gate underground station. A soul encased in tons of wet clay.

So that was one question I finally felt I had answered for myself, and hopefully for my son. At least for now.

Annoying Kids
Are UFOs real?

I believe it was in 1975, during Ramadan, that the under-thirties living in Wisma Subud gathered in front of the Latihan Hall at 4.30pm, to play Volleyball while we waited to break our fast at

6pm. This was a daily event during Ramadan that year. I was always curious where we all got the energy from because it seemed counter intuitive for people who had been fasting since dawn to be playing volleyball.

I was on the team facing north, away from the latihan hall. During one of the many times the ball had gone out of play, I was simply standing, staring over towards the cottages when, suddenly, a long silver object shot into view in the sky, coming in from the west. It stopped momentarily and then shot off to the east. It was all over in three or four seconds.

In shape, it resembled a pencil or silver flute. A long, thin, silver tube. Even though the sky was still bright I could clearly see four, very bright, thin bands of light. Two red, one green and one blue, that were fairly evenly spaced along the tube.

I did a double take and then looked to my team mates. One young teenager was staring back at me. "Did you see that?" I asked. "Iya," he answered to affirm he witnessed it too. We looked around and it was obvious only we had been looking at the sky above the cottages at that moment. So we just shrugged our shoulders and got ready to receive the serve coming from the opposite team.

For the curious I cannot add much more. It was impossible to gauge the object's size or distance. There were no trees or buildings close enough to use for size comparison. It was silent and incredibly fast. I doubt any human could withstand the G-forces when it stopped and then sped away.

I know Bapak was once asked about the existence of UFOs and I remember him saying that they are real, they come from this earth, but from the future and, you definitely don't want to meet the occupants!

I believe Bapak has made a few other comments over the years about UFOs and aliens, but because this is a subject that I am not particularly interested in, I have not attempted to search through Bapak's talks looking for more information.

I saw what I saw, that is all, but it was enough for me to believe what Bapak had said about UFOs. Bapak's explanation feels more right than the claim that 'Queen Elizabeth II was a reptilian alien who shape-shifted at night, that I have read on the internet.

Annoying Kids: Where Does Fear Come from?
We Don't Scare Easy!

This is one of those weird questions that kids tend to ask parents. But I enjoy getting questions like this from my children, because they prompt me to ask myself the question too. So, I share my thoughts with my children and try to discover some new things for myself at the same time.

Nothing I say here should be taken as true because, unlike Bapak, I cannot guarantee where these thoughts and explanations come from. I share these thoughts more as an offering of some food for thought.

So, as my son asked this question, I closed my eyes and tried to empty myself of thoughts to let his question become like a prayer inside me. A prayer which I hoped my inner would respond to, God willing.

I have had quite a lot of experience with 'fear', especially in the first three years after I was opened, which means some of my understanding comes from those experiences, almost fifty years ago.

With my children, I tried to 'peel the onion' when answering these types of questions so that they may begin to approach problems in a focussed way.

I began by explaining that it seems that fear has several purposes in our lives. You could say there are many kinds of fear.

Worldly Fears

This is what we all are familiar with, and it clearly is a valuable tool for our survival. I do not have to say very much about that. But I observe these worldly fears have two sides, one positive and one negative.

Some positives

Fear that restrains dangerous impulses that could result in pain, injury and even death (speeding, trying drugs, stealing etc). There is the "Fight or Flight" response to fear in the face of physical danger that is critical for survival.

Fear of consequences that restrains the impulse to anger and other negative actions like stealing or lying.

Fear increases adrenalin which raises our physical and mental abilities, commonly called 'an adrenalin rush' when faced with danger.

Some Negatives

That adrenalin 'rush' can become addictive and make risky activities attractive.

Fear can undermine confidence, which will hold us back from trying new things or standing up for ourselves when we are abused. It can also undermine a person's confidence and become an obstacle to realizing our full capabilities.

Bigger Negatives

When fear dominates reason, it can ruin lives. Generally, these fears are called phobias.

Irrational fears are very pernicious because they usually have a tiny element of rational logic to feed the pessimistic thoughts. Fear of flying is a good example.

These examples are more than enough to describe the common experiences of fear in our day to day life to kids.

The Ultimate Fear

I think we can all agree that the ultimate fear in this life is the fear of death, and that fear, I believe, is nearly always at the root of all those other fears. It took me almost forty years to understand this and further, to understand that it is only the nafsu in our heart that experience fear.

The inner does not share that fear, if it can separate itself from the heart. In fact, I have reason to believe from a few experiences in latihan that the inner, far from being afraid of death, may actually welcome leaving this harsh world and going home, like a soldier returning from the wars. But we have to complete our duties in this life first.

So why are we afraid of death?

The Brochure Lied

From the point of view of the heart and mind, especially when we are young children still being taken care of by our parents, this world looks like a brochure for the greatest theme park ever. Full of fun, toys, games, and excitement.

This childhood brochure grows and by the time we are teenagers we already have a catalogue of fabulous shiny objects and things to be experienced and possessed. Things our nafsu want, and that desire motivates us to work and study.

Through the imagination our desires grow. It starts with cookies, then comes the X-Box and iPhone, and ends up with luxury cars, mansions, yachts, private jets, parties, private islands.

These are what our nafsu need and want to satisfy their desires. But they are never satisfied because things are always being added to the catalogue.

The power of this catalogue is felt acutely when we imagine driving that car, living in that house, wearing those clothes etc.

For the nafsu this world is heaven.

But the reality is, compared with the afterlife, life in this world is hard and harsh. Everything requires effort. Our soul is aware of these many hardships because it experiences them through our heart, mind, and body as part of our education and development.

The heat and the cold, hunger and thirst and search for shelter from the elements were experienced by the very first human beings until today.

We must study, do homework, and sit exams. We must find a job and work for money to buy all the things we need, like food and clothing, to keep our physical body alive and operational. And that's in what we call this modern world of convenience!

All this hard work and effort is done by our heart, mind and physical body using the will and desires they contain. And yet, ironically, even with all this hardship and even severe suffering, it is the heart and mind that fear death.

This is because, as I understand it, this is their world, and they can only experience this current life when they occupy a physical human body, which they enter after conception during the growth of the foetus.

Conversely, when the coarse body dies all the forces that operate our heart and mind, our will, and desires, must return to their realm. For these entities the death of the human body, is like being fired from a high paid, senior position in a prestigious company doing the best job you ever had and sent back out on the street.

I can perhaps use the analogy of a chauffeur. He is hired by a rich aristocrat and is provided with very comfortable accommodation, excellent food, and a smart uniform. But best of all, he gets to drive a Rolls Royce every day. He enjoys the comfort and pleasure of living on a fine estate, eating wonderful food and experiencing the luxury of a Rolls Royce.

Then, one day the master decides to sell his estate and move overseas. The Chauffeur goes into a panic. What will become of him? He, together with all the other servants beg the master not to leave. But the master has no choice and can do nothing. Finally, the day comes when the master thanks all his servants, including his chauffeur, for their service and gives them all a golden handshake before bidding them farewell.

The Rolls Royce is sold back to the showroom and the chauffeur must now take the bus back to his small, cold, terraced house in the village and return to his simple life, simple food and to having to walk everywhere.

Well, this is just an analogy to give an idea of my understanding of how it is for all the forces that work like servants to keep the physical body alive until the soul moves on and leaves this world.

The fear of death is only the servants' fear. The soul will be free of the harshness and burdens of this world, provided the soul has not become corrupted by this material world and possessed by the servants.

What I explained to my kids came mostly from my early experiences when in America. Over the years I began to understand what that fear was about. Of course, this is not a guarantee that my understanding is right. For me it is absolutely real, but I can only present these explanations as an hypothesis.

I do have some confidence in my understanding, because it seems to be in line with explanations Bapak gave about this very complicated aspect of life and death. So, to some very small extent, I can say, for myself, that I have witnessed the truth of what Bapak spoke of.

I thought this was important because I am aware of how much fear robs us of our potential in this life. I had to experience all kinds of fear, most of which made no sense at the time, but eventually I discovered the part of me that wasn't affected by the fear that my heart and mind experienced. Through the latihan, my inner emerged as a separate entity that could remain firm even when my heart was full of fear and doubt. This process took many years for me.

As I wrote earlier, my heart and mind are none too bright, or courageous!

How Come Life's Not Fair?
Facing Disappointment

Don't count your chickens before they hatch, and even then... This was another apparent conundrum my kids grappled with. But an interesting question that I would like to have some understanding of too. So, once again it's quieten the mind and surrender the question and see what emerges in the silence.

We all experience disappointments in life and everyone has their own way of dealing with them. But I was always curious as to why I did not seem to suffer as much as many people around me did when I faced similar disappointments. This was particularly true if it involved material things.

Over the years, as the proverbial observer, I began to see more of what was going on in many people, that caused them to suffer so much disappointment when things didn't work out. But like most people, I always sympathize and try to empathize with every person I meet who was suffering some form of disappointment. This is especially true when it comes to my own family.

When my children or friends have experienced a big disappointment, I first offer my sympathies and then usually wait a day or two to see if they can get over it, or if they need to talk about it. As general advice I have spoken to my children on ways to avoid or reduce much of the pain of disappointment, based on what I had observed going on within myself.

You can probably imagine that my little lectures were generally considered more of a test of patience by my children, or an inducement for them to go to bed.

Inviting Disappointment

The most important piece of advice I gave my children to avoid disappointment was, "Don't let your imagination start enjoying something before it is in your hand or your bank account." I tried to explain why this was so important, based on my observations growing up.

So often I have seen friends and colleagues launch into a fantasy world when they get some news that 'promises' to bring them good fortune. It maybe a new job, a promised promotion, a pay rise or even an inheritance.

When we do this, it means we are already under the influence of the material forces (that is, money), before we have even received anything, because, in our imagination and feelings, we are already enjoying the money, and it can feel so good, so right!

To illustrate the point, imagine someone quitting their job because they found a lottery ticket on the way to work, and they really believe it is fate and this must be their lucky ticket. That's extreme, but illustrates the power these forces can have, and how easily they can get into our hearts and imagination.

How about a wife, who in October is gathering brochures and planning a kitchen renovation, because her husband heard he will be getting a large year-end bonus in December?

Or the new 'small business' owner, who, when his company gets its first big order, is so elated that he immediately goes out and buys himself a new luxury car and signs a lease on a bigger office based on the projected profits?

It's hardly surprising that the inner voice has an up-hill

battle to even be heard, let alone give guidance in these situations. The thoughts and feelings created by the imagination are so wonderful, so exciting, so satisfying for the heart that there is almost no possibility of our being inwardly quiet enough to hear or feel any inner guidance. They are swept up by the influence of the nafsu fuelled by the lower forces.

And Why Is that Important?

Well, we are talking about avoiding disappointment. So, the point here is, the inner knows, if the lottery ticket is a winner or not! Your inner knows if a large windfall of money is on your path of destiny, or not.

The inner knows if the company the man works for will fall foul of a supply chain problem and end up losing money, which means the company must cancel all the bonuses.

The inner knows if the business owner's factory is going to be hit by a hurricane and flooding in two months and will lose that big contract, leaving the boss on the verge of bankruptcy, having to sell his car and new office building at a loss.

This, I have observed, is the fate of those people who cannot resist the temptation of the material force of money, or the things money can buy, resulting in their hearts and minds being swept up in a euphoric fantasy created in their imagination. This belief in self-made fantasies, is what blocks the guidance of the inner feeling that tries to warn us not to proceed in a wrong direction.

For these people, the most common result is huge disappointment. In the worse cases this euphoria can trick people into making terrible decisions, as illustrated above, and they can end up losing everything, even be left with enormous debts.

"Beware of the whisperer of evil, who whispers into the hearts of men and then withdraws." *From the Al Quran.*

I must emphasise here that there is no suggestion that

through the latihan we will be able to receive the numbers of a winning lottery ticket, or the name of a winning horse or weather warnings about future floods. So please don't get all excited, because it will only be your heart and imagination overwhelming your rational mind.

The experiences I have had, and many others in Subud have spoken about, is more akin to a firm indication from within that is little more than a 'yes' or 'no', 'Do it' or 'Don't do it'. It takes time to both recognize this kind of guidance and even longer to trust it. It is usually quite subtle, but it can save us from some pretty bad decisions and stop us wandering off into the jungle of disappointments and missed opportunities. Our hearts may not always agree. Some disappointments are required in life for our own progress.

After the Euphoria

People who are left with debt can attest to the heavy burden the lack of the material force (no winnings, no bonus, no big order, no money) can cause. The enormous negative pressure on the heart and mind. The exact opposite to the euphoria that those same forces used to influence and take over our decision making.

So, again, my own experience, and observations of others, confirms and points to the deeper meaning of the power of the material forces over man's life in this world. Therefore, the latihan is so important, because in the latihan we experience the separation of our inner self from that material influence, so that we can learn, over time, to recognise these lower forces and eventually manage and control them, so that we do not get swept up by the euphoria of our nafsu driving our emotions and our imagination.

I heard Bapak talk about something like this, and I recall his advice was that, "We should be happy when we get good news, but not too happy, and we can be unhappy when we get bad news, but not too unhappy."

Bapak was always so succinct in his advice. In a nutshell Bapak's advice is pointing to the result of having an obedient heart that doesn't indulged in 'feel good' fantasies created by the imagination. A heart that does not get overwhelmed and buffeted by the influence of the material forces when circumstances change for better or for worse.

However, I have also observed that some people actually seem to enjoy living a roller coaster life of ups and downs. Being calm, and not overly affected by good and bad events, appears to be too boring for them. It's as though they need the drama in order to motivate their enthusiasm. But that is an observation, not a judgement, because that may be how their true inner nature is.

For me, I think that having a lot of drama may be great when you are single and you wish to fill your life with adventure and excitement, but it may cause some difficulties when trying to raise a happy, stable family. But I could be wrong. There are always exceptions.

Worse than Money

When it comes to disappointment, there are forces much stronger than money even, that can cause a different kind of pain and anguish together with the disappointment.

These involve those wonderfully intangible things called love and trust. This is a subject for at least two books that can be added to the millions of books, poems, sonnets, plays and films that have already been written. I happily leave the next book on this subject for someone else to write.

My only contribution is that I see the same mechanics working on this 'human' level as with material things if we are not careful. This is a problem many teenagers and young adults encounter in life.

Having strong feelings of love towards someone who we cannot have a romantic relationship with, is simply a more intense version of what we experience with material objects. Take a part-time salesclerk who desires to own a Rolls Royce. Not impossible, but extremely unlikely. The most probable outcome, however, will be a lifetime of disappointment.

Now let us take a beautiful young woman who starts working in your office and who you feel a strong attraction for. This powerful force of attraction arises in your heart, and you soon start imagining how wonderful it would be if she was your girlfriend. The euphoria builds day after day for a month.

She in return is always warm and friendly and clearly likes you, but completely unaware that you can't sleep, you've lost your appetite and don't want to do the things you normally enjoy. She is constantly in your thoughts, and you feel convinced she is the one for you.

Then one day you discover she is engaged to a wonderful, handsome, wealthy young man (or he might be a dishevelled, poor, struggling artist whom she adores.)

Either way, you have spent a month enjoying a fabulous imaginary relationship with this wonderful woman, which now has been destroyed in one second. Like a balloon popping, your euphoria turns to bitter disappointment in an instant!

So once again, enjoying something that you don't yet have is inviting disappointment. It is also very difficult to avoid doing this until the heart learns to be obedient, patient and cautious when the nafsu get excited.

Trust You, Trust Me?

I think it is pretty clear that our heart and imagination can be our worse enemy when it comes to things that we desire and wish for. But the same culprits come into play in questions of trust. This is especially true when we begin a relationship, either romantic, friendship or in business.

We need to know; are we right to trust this person or are we simply 'imagining' how good it would feel if I trusted this person?

The fact is, our heart and mind alone cannot answer that question, but our inner knows the truth. Just like our inner knows if that lottery ticket is a winning number or not.

This then is another way the latihan can benefit us by teaching us not to be swept away in euphoria or drown in depression and disappointment, by training our hearts to be obedient and patient, especially when the lower forces try to influence us.

But we cannot completely remove disappointment and suffering from our lives because we are not perfect. As human beings we inevitably sin and make mistakes every day. Many times, we are not even aware of our mistakes. So sometimes we need to experience difficult times in order to break down obstacles to our progress, like arrogance and stubbornness, in our personality .

Our inner guide may let us make decisions that lead to disappointment, but in that failure, we may reap a hugely valuable benefit for our future progress.

Sometimes we need to learn some painful lessons to teach our heart to be obedient. The inner knows that too. Not all disappointments are accidents. They may be hard lessons we need to teach the heart not to misuse the power of the imagination.

Well, that's the result of my ponderings over the years. I'm sure that there are shorter ways to explain it and much deeper truths still to be revealed.

Selling You Your Dream!

When, as a teenager, I first became aware of an industry that produced a variety of 'How-To' self-help books, I had great difficulty in understanding exactly how they could work. I am not talking about the kind of books that, say, offer valuable advice to parents with autistic children, or books that educate and offer practical solutions for everyday problems.

It is books with titles like "How to become a millionaire in ten easy steps", or "How to become successful without really trying" that I continued to have a problem with for many years.

Surely, I thought, if these methods really worked, there would only be successful millionaires in the world. So my conclusion was that the only successful millionaires were the people who wrote and sold those books. But then I thought, the bigger mystery is "Why do people buy these books!?"

After joining Subud and doing latihan for several years this question came back to me, and by then I began to see what was going on. Something that became crystal clear when I found myself working in advertising. It all comes back to the influence of the material forces and how the nafsu manipulate our hearts and minds. I could see another recipe for disappointment.

But this was deliberate, planned disappointment, and the motivation was money.

Marketing: Using the Material Forces

I need to step back to 1970 to illustrate what became the basis for my conclusions.

The key to understanding the influence of the material forces, for me, was in the change I experienced after returning from America, when I became aware that I no longer had the desire to possess those specific objects we call brands.

My desires at that time had become very closely aligned with my 'true needs' and that meant I sought, and was satisfied with just the basic, generic benefit of the products I needed.

I no longer hankered after a Harley Davidson as I had done in my teenage years. A pair of jeans was just a pair of jeans, the brand did not matter. Function, price, and appearance were my criteria for choice. I had become a marketer's nightmare!

It was clear, although I didn't understand it at the time, that my inner had to some degree separated from, and started to identify my individual nafsu with the result that my heart was no longer so dominated by the influence of some of the most common material forces used to influence us.

I have seen that, even in my lifetime, this influence of the material forces has continually gained power as man has learned how to use the material force to manipulate people through the power of marketing.

Marketing and advertising is like playing with material forces on steroids! The entire objective is to turn a basic human need into an imaginary burning desire. In some cases, even the 'basic need' is purely imaginary, simply created by advertisers who then feed the consumer's carefully cultivated desire.

In fact, this has been the 'talent' of all good sales men ever since man started having things to sell. Headlines like "You can't afford NOT to own an XYZ." Is a common piece of advertising trickery to build the perception of an exaggerated need or problem that "only our product can solve".

Somehow wearing a particular brand of jeans will solve your problem with finding a fashion model to go on a date with. Sports cars promise the same. Even deodorants promise to make you irresistible to the opposite sex.

No, it won't. We all know that. So why does it work? It all goes back to that wonderful fantasy feeling our imagination creates for our heart, which in turn corrupts our mind that holds the purse strings.

So, getting back to the self-help books, it is clear that it starts with the premise that everyone desires to be a millionaire. Marketers know that people have many desires, including wanting to be rich. These desires remain dormant in the heart for as long as a person can see no possible way to achieve what they want.

But what happens when suddenly that person is presented with a way to make their dream of being a millionaire come true? Like seeing a book that claims to have the answer.

They will probably buy the book, and… make the author a millionaire.

But will they become millionaires themselves after reading the book? Perhaps one in a million, the ones who already have the nature and talents to become a millionaire with or without reading the book.

There is an even greater threat to cause a person to part with their money, which preys on that dormant desire of the material force to be rich. That threat is gambling. If the desire is particularly strong then gambling can become an addiction and ruin many lives.

The same use of these forces is true for OTC medicines, diet books, supplement ads, exercise equipment, to name just a few. They all hold out a (qualified) promise of something that is generically desirable by saying, "Now, with this product, it is absolutely attainable".

The advertiser only needs to wait for their target customers to start thinking and imagining about how wonderful it would be to 'lose 20 pounds a week', 'double their energy in 90 days', 'remove wrinkles in a month', 'women can't resist a real man who uses XYZ cologne', and they have made a sale, because the customer's own subconscious desires will rise into their imagination and will become the salesman. The most insidious thought the marketer hopes to create in our mind is 'it could be true, I'll give it a try!'.

There is a lot more in the marketing mix such as price, where it is advertised, where it is available, endorsements and vague research data, that all work to reinforce the idea to try the product. But this is not a book about advertising and marketing.

What's that Got to Do with Subud and the Latihan?

Well, I use this as another example of how my own experience in life has enabled me to appreciate the wisdom of Bapak's words about how, through the latihan, over time, all the different forces that reside in our hearts, will separate from our inner feeling, so that we can recognise when we are being influenced and manipulated by those forces.

Again, I must say that I have no illusions about understanding these things to anywhere near the depth and breadth that Bapak received, but I am grateful that I have received just enough to know, for sure, that Bapak's explanations are true, even when they go far beyond my experiences in the latihan.

I'm still learning even as I write this book.

And in case you are wondering, yes, I still buy Heinz Baked Beans because, for me, the generic brands don't even come close in quality and flavour. I wonder if Heinz will sponsor this book now, after such a convincing endorsement? That way of thinking is how the nafsu work!

Even though I have spent almost 30 years working in advertising and marketing, I can still be influenced by advertising and promotion, just like anyone else. But for the most part I am aware of it and can make the decision whether I give myself permission to go along with the game or not. It is part of living in this world after all, and I believe we should participate and have fun in life, so long as we do no harm to others or to ourselves.

Just a Note as a Subud Member

During almost thirty years working in advertising, I never took a client with a lousy product, and I would never agree to use lies or exaggerated claims in our ads. My job was to win customers away from my client's competitors, and grow market share, not to cheat consumers. I also turned down lucrative cigarette clients, much to the surprise of my peers in other agencies, because I felt that by encouraging people to smoke, I would be doing harm, albeit, I am a smoker.

A Convenient Segue

Working in advertising can be considered as working in The Devil's Den. That is a general perception of the industry, and often it can be the case. From working in three leading multinational agencies, I certainly felt that clients often expected agencies to do their bidding regardless of ethics, and even the agency's own finance directors would pressure the agency teams to compromise on ethics to win new clients.

I will give this actual example. A well-known, multinational pharmaceutical company requested us to come up with a packaging design and advertising campaign for a new brand of analgesic.

After the briefing I went to lunch with the marketing manager and, over dessert she explained how the new brand was actually the same product as their current failing brand, except now it would only have half the efficacy. The campaign she wanted was to encourage people to double up on the dose and take two tablets instead of just one. Which would be the same dose as a single tablet of the current product.

To top it off, she proudly announced that they would sell their 'new' brand at twice the price per pill of the current brand. Twice the price per pill and requiring two pills meant four times the price for the current product!

The rational for the high price would be that the product would be positioned for a specific kind of pain. The higher price would also create the 'perception' with consumers that the new product must have much higher efficacy than the old one. Price perception is a well-established tool in the brand management toolbox that sadly is proven to work in most cases. Consumers will assume a higher price means higher quality, or in this case, higher efficacy.

For coming up with this strategy to give consumers half as much efficacy for twice the price, and then encouraging them to take twice the dosage, she was expecting a promotion to marketing director.

This was clearly a plan to cheat consumers in order to quadruple revenues, so I refused to work for this client, which almost got me fired. Another team from the agency did take on the work and I am happy to announce that within a year the brand failed miserably. Strike up one for the consumers!

She still got the promotion though.

So, Again, What Has this Got to Do with Subud?

I see this as just one example of why Bapak was always encouraging Subud members to set up enterprises. Like most members who had been brought up as Christians, when Bapak first started talking about enterprises my initial response was not enthusiastic.

There was quite a bit of confusion because, traditionally, mixing spiritual matters with making money was considered incompatible with the teachings of Christ.

However, over time the idea of starting enterprises became better understood. What Bapak talked about was the fact that, if we worked for someone else, we will not be able to follow our own nature and inner guidance in our work. We will be forced to compromise. As Subud members, this can create difficulties and could slow our spiritual progress.

When, in 1997, together with my wife, we were able to establish our own advertising agency, we were finally free to determine all aspects of the business, from how we treated employees to which clients we would accept.

This was very much like my experience in setting up the pottery many years before.

I am happy to say that within a couple of years we had become the local agency that multinational agencies actually feared to compete with.

We were able to treat our staff better, were more dedicated as a team and produced many award-winning campaigns. We focussed on the work and the money simply followed. We never 'chased' the money. We never chased new clients.

When it comes to money and business, I recall Bapak saying that we should not worry about money coming in, we should only concern ourselves with how the money goes out.

This is contrary to modern business in terms of forecasting revenue to justify a budget to investors. The fact is that a forecast is just an educated guess and therefore very risky. Corporate finance management today is incredibly complicated, and these complications have been driven primarily by greed masked as increased efficiency.

Because we owned the agency, my wife and I had the opportunity to really discover our true strengths and weaknesses and to grow by following our own inner guidance while using our professional knowledge, talents, and experience. To put into practice what I experienced in the JWT workshop with what I had experienced in the latihan.

Even today, three years after we retired, many of our ex-employees who took jobs at other agencies still complain about the way they are treated in their new jobs. They feel undervalued and no longer learn anything. They just make the money for their bosses and reminisce about their years at our agency. I regret not being able to help them, but at the same time I feel this is further confirmation of what Bapak had talked about in terms of running our own enterprises in a different way to non-Subud businesses.

From the profits we made we were able to support and donate to several Subud entities and individuals, and non-Subud charities too, which was also part of Bapak's hope for Subud enterprises. But Bapak was always clear that, if circumstances do not allow us to establish an enterprise, then we must still work, and we should be prepared to do whatever work is available.

And while Subud enterprises must still follow the practical rules of doing business, the hope is we do it better than the normal, non-Subud companies. Subud should be able to demonstrate that there is a viable and desirable option to running a business from the modern capitalist approach that is eating up the planet and creating massive inequalities in societies all over the world.

Pioneers Don't Live Comfortable Lives
Bapak called for 'pioneers' to create a new future and show a new way based on an inner understanding of man's true duties in this world. But I am sure that Bapak would not wish us to claim this lofty aspiration as something that our hearts and minds understand, or even fully comprehend, because any such thoughts mean we are almost certainly sowing the seeds of failure. This is a tricky thing to explain, and I hope I don't bore you.

In essence, I believe that the owners of a successful business, like a Bank, can choose to be a powerful tool to do good, and demonstrate the true purpose of a Bank, for the benefit of society as well as being very profitable.

However, a new Bank that wishes to demonstrate the true purpose of a bank and be a benefit to society cannot 'choose' to be successful. Success must be earned.

So, while we may receive an understanding of the higher purpose for an enterprise, the first priority is to be successful in the material world and, with the help of our inner guidance, we should strive to be more successful than our competitors.

Only with that success can we fully demonstrate our own beliefs and principles towards employees, customers, and society in general, beyond the usual tax deductible schemes of supporting charities.

Without demonstrating the viability of our approach, with a new concept for running a business, we cannot have an impact in the world, and the existing system will continue.

I do not know how many Subud members have been able to set up enterprises that are based on an inner awareness of the purpose of an enterprise and are materially successful, to the envy of their competitors. I am sure there are many, including self-employed individuals, who are successful.

What I do know is that to run your own enterprise brings a multitude of rewards and benefits, and I am grateful for the privilege and opportunity to have had that experience for over twenty years.

It should be noted that there are some big companies and corporations in the world who are demonstrating a more enlightened approach to their purpose in society, but they work from worldly feelings and ideals. That is not to downplay their enormous contribution to the welfare of poor societies around the world. God's guidance is not exclusive to Subud members. Nothing can restrict God's power and grace which envelops the whole of creation.

Clouds Come from Heaven, Topography Belongs to the World

As a worldwide association, the activities of so many Subud members should have a real impact on the character of society. But the impact is limited if we only act as individuals and remain in our internal Subud interactions. Only through enterprises we can multiply the impact exponentially.

To illustrate that, I would say that without enterprises we are all like individual raindrops, however, together we can create a mighty river, but no individual drop can determine the course that the river takes to reach the ocean.

We can only pray to receive an idea for an enterprise and then we just do the work that needs to be done, which is before us, using all the normal professional tools that exist, but hopefully we use them in a better way.

If we can do that, and do it well, success and money will follow. Then how we use the money will also be guided to both build the business and do good works. Only with large successful enterprises can we affect the course of the river.

Being Good in the Wrong Way?

I have known several Subud brothers who wanted to set up an enterprise because they felt a very sincere wish to follow Bapak's advice; and while Bapak was still alive, I listened to many members explain how they wanted to make Bapak happy, and to make Subud bigger and stronger in the world.

While these are honourable goals, over time I noticed that rarely did any of these enterprises come into being, and many of those that did manage to start did not achieve the success that was hoped for.

I have pondered this apparent conundrum over the years and here I offer my humble understanding of what appeared to me as a common denominator.

As I said in the preface of this book, I have long believed that Bapak always hoped we could stand on our own feet and truly follow our own, individual path to a common destination. W,hen we do that, with God's blessing and the latihan, we shall each be able to return to our path of destiny in this life. That is, we return to the best and most noble path that God has already prepared for each of us. On that path, everything we need for life is already there, put in place.

The insight here, for me was, that to assist with Bapak's mission we need to look outward. We should not unwittingly treat Bapak like a cult leader as the focal point of our efforts.

Each member should use the special tools that Bapak was given and passed on to us, in addition to the talents we were each given at birth, to become good examples, and a benefit to society in general. If in the process we can establish successful enterprises and become a positive influence in the world, that is what will make Bapak very happy.

I am sure that my views may be considered controversial in some quarters, as it may appear that I am voicing my opinions as though I believe I have some special knowledge or authority to give advice. Rest assured, dear reader, I do not. I am simply sharing what I believe is true.

In fact, I review what I write with great trepidation, because I feel the very real responsibility to every reader to write my truth, without exaggeration or sugar coating. A very heavy responsibility and humbling experience, to say the least.

I can only go back to my original premise that, like all Subud members doing latihan, we should be able to discover an understanding of life that is out of the mainstream of the world. After decades of doing latihan, all the long-term members who I know, have gained many very useful insights into the human condition and the workings of life in this world that are both meaningful and valuable. The only difference between most of them and myself is I felt moved to put mine down in writing.

I sincerely wish more of my friends would write their own books to demonstrate that the latihan really has removed so many of the veils that cover man's eyes in this world. Each story I hear, including those that do not align perfectly with my own, I see as different facets of the same issues.

There is no conflict because, as I said earlier, I believe each one forms a tiny part of the kaleidoscope that makes an incomprehensibly beautiful pattern that God alone can see. I guess the old analogy of three blind men trying to describe an elephant would be most fitting. One holding the trunk, one embracing a leg and one clasping the tail. Each one's description is right, yet none see the whole picture. What you can say is, they can all confirm that elephants really do exist.

Here's another analogy. You might imagine a sumptuous 5-star hotel international buffet with a spread of a thousand different dishes, prepared for a hundred hungry people to help themselves. As they leave the restaurant two hours later, you ask each of them, "What's for lunch?" You will get a multitude of answers as each person describes what they chose from the buffet, which may leave you confused and seriously doubting what's on the buffet menu.

So while you can't know the entire menu, what you can be sure of and be happy about is that they all confirm that there is lunch. Every human being is unique and will have their own understanding about what is for 'lunch', and none of them are wrong.

So it is, I believe, that every Subud member has a unique destiny and path in life and what they receive through the latihan will fit with their needs for their journey. They may all differ, and be quite varied, but what is sure is they are all moving towards the same destination.

The Conundrum of Spreading the Latihan

From the very beginning, Bapak made it clear that although he had been given the task of spreading the latihan kejiwaan around the world to any and every person who wished to receive it, there should be no promotional activities, and even Subud members should refrain from seeking to convert or persuade anyone from joining Subud. That people should come to Subud of their own free will. If they ask questions, then Subud members can answer, but without any desire to 'sell' Subud or convince anyone to join.

Quite a daunting mission to be given to a young Indonesian man living in a small Indonesian town, earning a very modest income in the mid 1930s. In fact, at the time it would have seemed quite preposterous that Bapak would ever be able to afford to travel around Indonesia, let alone overseas.

Bapak also wrote his autobiography, which is a truly fascinating book. Far more fascinating than this book. So, I recommend that anyone interested in Subud should avail themselves of the great personal benefit from reading Bapak's life story.

The Silent Message

And so, how was Bapak to achieve his task of spreading the latihan around the world?

It's like a catch twenty-two. How to spread the latihan throughout the world without promotion, or advertising. There is no knocking on doors or standing in front of Supermarkets handing out leaflets extolling the fantastic benefits of becoming a Subud member. There can be no claims that "Subud is THE WAY". Subud members are not even supposed to raise the subject of Subud with a non-Subud member unless asked, or under very special circumstances like helping a friend or colleague facing some serious personal dilemma.

So how is Subud supposed to grow and increase membership? Perhaps the more intriguing question is, "How has Subud managed to spread to over eighty countries with thousands of people opened and active, without any advertising, promotion or recruitment campaigns?"

That question can best be answered by Subud members themselves, because I know that a book could be filled just with a selection of the incredible stories of how thousands of individual Subud members discovered Subud and were opened in the latihan. In such a book it would be impossible not to see the hand of God working in their lives, even before they finally found Subud.

But God gave this mission, to bring the latihan to all the people who wish to receive it, to Bapak, and he passed on that mission to every Subud member. That is not to say that God has withdrawn His grace and guidance and left the fate of Subud totally in the hands of Subud members, but I do believe that there is a test implicit in the gift that we have received to continue with Bapak's mission to whatever extent we are capable.

The only caution from Bapak was that we were not to become like worldly salesmen and saleswomen. We are not 'selling' Subud and should never look at ways to grow membership through common worldly marketing techniques employed by big organizations, including some niche religions. The Latihan is not Tupperware or Amway. It cannot be purchased or owned by anyone. It does not exist to make members rich or poor.

The Latihan is like a stream of pure fresh water, a gift from God for anyone who is aware that the 'water' most of us drink in this modern world is heavily polluted and, by comparison, foul tasting.

After years, indeed generations, of drinking polluted water, the toxic effects have penetrated deep into human beings while living in this world. These pollutants are so much part of our human experience that they are considered normal. If we can drink the pure fresh water then we can begin to dilute the toxins, and over time slowly flush the pollutants, the lower forces, out of our bodies, our thinking, and feelings.

Each time we do Latihan we are given a measure of this pure fresh water and we may experience some pretty strange, even unpleasant, things as they are flushed out. But we may also experience some incredibly blissful things when some ancient blockage is finally removed during latihan.

This process of purification is the work of the latihan. It cannot be controlled by our desires, and it is entirely up to God because only God knows the capacity and unique needs of every individual human being. That is God's work, according to Bapak. The job of Subud members is to recognise the process of purification and avoid repeating the mistakes, actions and behaviour that will return the pollution. There is little point in polishing your shoes in latihan if, after latihan, you immediately go back to looking for some muddy puddles to play in. That will become an endless cycle with no progress.

But I digress once again. When it comes to the growth of Subud without 'marketing', it occurred to me that one answer would be to write a book. But not a book about Subud specifically, because that you can find that on Wikipedia, and better still, in the many books written by Bapak and other Subud members.

What I felt might be helpful, would be to describe the ways the Subud latihan has actively changed my life and character. To demonstrate, to some small extent, that the latihan is truly a spiritual experience that works beyond the heart and mind to awaken the inner, the soul, and works to purify us from within until the heart and mind can be pacified and become aware of the guidance and knowledge that comes from the inner. Guidance that is usually lost in all the noise and hubbub our hearts and minds constantly make.

As I said earlier, I have met so many Subud members whose lives have been filled with quite amazing stories related to their experiences before and after being opened in Subud, that I wish they would all write their own book.

Indeed, there already exist many books about Subud or related to Subud, but so far I have not come across any that attempt to describe the inner and outer reality, working together, as experienced by members. However, in writing this book I have come to understand that is no easy task.

The very action of writing this book has shown me how hard, indeed impossible it is to remove one's self, one's ego from the process. To be mindful of every sentence I write to avoid any embellishments or exaggerations in describing events, and to remain aware that any explanations I offer to the meaning of those experiences is only 'my truth' because the only one who knows the truth of all things is Almighty God.

Every reader may have their own interpretation, their own experience that is their truth, which I very much respect. To me, these variations of experience and understanding are just pieces of the vast kaleidoscope of knowledge spread across humanity that still cannot encompass the greatness of God.

*

Entrance to Wisma Subud, Cilandak, Indonesia in 1971.

World Congress, Cilandak, Indonesia,1971.
Bamboo Long Houses built to house 1500 international guests, with the
newly completed Latihan Hall in the centre background.

Photo by kind permission of Sahlan Simón Cherpitel https://livingsubud.com

World Congress, Cilandak, Indonesia, 1971.
President Suharto and his wife with Bapak (right).

World Congress, Cilandak, Indonesia, 1971.
Participants relax between sessions.

World Congress, Cilandak, Indonesia,1971.
Photomontage of plenary sessions with Bapak
and entertainment for Bapak and family in
the new Latihan Hall.

David meeting with President Suharto after a Government Workshop on Transfer of Technology, 1979.

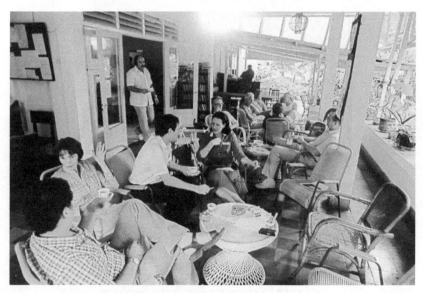

Wisma Subud, Cilandak Guest House porch in the 1980s.

1985, Wisma Subud: David, Ramdan Simpson, Harris Roberts, Mansur Geiger, Hannah, Mathew Mayberry.

David with his wife, Elektra, London 1992

David on a commercial shoot in 2009 with 7 times MOTOGP World Champion Valentino Rossi.

Alma, Aisjah, Ramzi, Maurice, David and Eta at the New Zealand Subud World Congress, 2010.

David (right) at home in Jakarta, jamming with Yardbirds guitarist Sanderson 'Top' Topham in 2014.
Sadly, while this book was in production, Sanderson passed away in London, January 2023.

Shed builders Ramzi and David at the Warrior's second home in New Zealand.

David's eldest son, Hassan, and his wife, Nikki.

David's two youngest children, Halley and Jonathan,
leaving to study in New Zealand in 2016.

An Arbitrary Ending

Just like a night of heavy rain quietly comes to a stop, so I feel the words for this book have stopped, as I stare at my computer screen.

Why now, why at this point? I do not ask. The journey of writing this book has been a joy and a great learning for me.

So much we lose in the rush of life that we forget the life we have been given. We forget the huge debt or gratitude we owe to God, our parents and siblings, teachers, friends, bosses, and strangers. All who participated in our lives as we participated in theirs. Thus is the fabric of humanity woven and the patterns formed, and the kaleidoscope of human experiences forever expands.

From early childhood walks in the forest, to summers in the sun and winters in the cold, parties in Notting Hill, esoteric neighbours, duck hunting in Watersmeet, Tibetan dances, donkeys and farewells to alcohol and pork. From busking in the street to National Committee meetings, to fine art and a hippy fest in Skymont. Amsterdam and Paris. Without money, security, or property other than a guitar.

From South London to South Jakarta with a small suitcase and a free ticket. To start again, from the bottom, with a US$75 farewell gift in hand, just following an inner compass. To live several years from hand to mouth with contentment and confidence. To spend time in villages and meet the President in the palace. To start a humble pottery, to meeting with government ministers. Lunch meetings with CEOs of multi-nationals to breaking fast in a dusty roadside kiosk.

Marriage, children, and some stability, and owning a successful Advertising Agency. To enjoy the comfort of a Jaguar and a BMW for the wife, and own our own house. To have maids and a driver. To be able to give some back to Subud charities and those in need. And still the journey continues…

It begs the question; How?

It is my belief that God was always there in my life, right from the beginning. That is true for every human being. But in my childhood I really sensed God's presence like an indulgent grandfather. Through times of pain and difficulty I was always comforted by that presence and therefore had some kind of confidence that 'all was for the best'.

But as I grew into my teens, I wanted to venture further into the world of shiny objects, where so many have gone before, and many not returned. I knew I did not want that fate and so, I believe, I was brought to Subud and the Latihan. And through the latihan I began the process of growing up, both inwardly and outwardly with some guidance to keep me from wandering too far as I explored life in this world.

An additional blessing for me was to be brought to Wisma Subud in 1971 and to have sixteen years living under the metaphoric roof of Bapak Muhammad Subuh, the founder of Subud. It was here that I had the opportunity to listen to so many of Bapak's talks, and feel the current, like a massive river that carried all of us doing latihan along on our individual journeys. And even after Bapak passed away in 1987, that current continues within every member doing latihan.

And then there have been all the individuals, so numerous I could fill this book with their names. The incredible generosity, kindness, and patience of so many people who could expect nothing in return from me. I sincerely pray they may all receive a goodly reward for their goodness to me and know I am forever grateful.

I feel so much gratitude to God, to Bapak, to friends and family, that it is impossible to raise any complaints, or even think about the difficulties and challenges in my life in a negative way. You cannot complain and feel gratitude at the same time. The two cannot exist in one's heart together without becoming a whirlpool of repressed confusion that will halt our journey to become, with God's grace, a complete and noble human being.

So, my last thanks are to you, the reader. You are now part of my journey, too.

I must ask your forgiveness if anything I have written has in any way offended or disturbed you. It is my prayer, my hope, that something in my story will resonate with you and the light we all have within will grow and be a benefit to others in a way that is pleasing to God. Thank you.

David,

Jakarta, 21 January, 2023

*

Acknowledgements

Clearly I must thank Bapak Muhammad Subuh Sumohadiwidjojo, who brought the latihan of Subud into my life, as he did for tens of thousands of others. That, I believe, was his mission and for me became my blessing.

I must also thank those who brought me into this world, my mother, Olive Joan Warrior, and my father, Robert George Warrior. I pray for their souls and hope they will receive me as their prodigal son in the next life.

I owe a big thank you to so many people that my mind boggles. With regards to finishing this book I must thank Laura Paterson for her effusive encouragement, and Marcus Bolt who handled all the nitty-gritty side of editing, proof reading and publishing.

Ramzi and Aisjah Addison have been the best of companions on my journey sustaining me in body and soul over the past fifty-five years. And Maurice Baker is another companion I value all this time.

Sachlan North, my go-to helper in my early years in Subud, ever patient, calm and wise.

Pak Sudarto, who lead me into a deeper understanding of my self.

And to the hundreds of people I have met on my journey, who have shown kindness and given me support, I apologize that I find it impossible to name you all, but my gratitude goes to each one of you.

And encompassing us all, I give thanks to Almighty God for everything that I have received.

*

OTHER BOOKS ABOUT SUBUD

A Special Assignment : Varindra Vittachi
Living Religion in Subud : Matthew Sullivan
Antidote : Salamah Pope
History of Subud Vol. 1 : Harlinah Longcroft
Aspirant! : Ronimund von Bissing
Autobiography : Muhammad Subuh Sumohadiwidjojo
Saving Grace – 50 Years in Subud : Marcus Bolt
An Angel on My Sofa : Maurice Baker
(available from www.amazon.co.uk)

To order any of the above books and/or for
a full catalogue, contact:
Subud Publications International Ltd
Loudwater Farm, Loudwater Lane
Rickmansworth, Herts WD3 4HG UK
email: spi@subudbooks.co.uk
or visit: www.subudbooks.com

CONTACTING SUBUD

Look in your local telephone directory under Subud,
or via the internet:
www.subud.org